Abalone Tales

Abalone Tales

Collaborative

Explorations of Sovereignty

and Identity in Native California

LES W. FIELD,

WITH CHERYL SEIDNER,

JULIAN LANG, ROSEMARY CAMBRA,

FLORENCE SILVA, VIVIEN HAILSTONE,

DARLENE MARSHALL, BRADLEY MARSHALL,

CALLIE LARA, MERV GEORGE SR., AND THE

CULTURAL COMMITTEE OF THE YUROK TRIBE

Duke University Press

Durham & London

2008

© 2008 Duke University Press
All rights reserved
Printed in the United States of America on acid-free paper ∞
Designed by C. H. Westmoreland
Typeset in Warnock Pro Light by Keystone Typesetting, Inc.

Library of Congress Cataloging-in-Publication Data
Field, Les W.
Abalone tales : collaborative explorations of sovereignty and
identity in native California / Les W. Field ; with Cheryl Seidner
. . . [et al.].
p. cm. — (Narrating native histories)
Includes bibliographical references and index.
ISBN 978-0-8223-4216-8 (cloth : alk. paper)
ISBN 978-0-8223-4233-5 (pbk. : alk. paper)
1. Indians of North America—Fishing—California. 2. Indians of
North America—Ethnozoology—California. 3. Indians of North
America—California—Social life and customs.
4. Abalone culture—California—History. 5. Abalones—
Social aspects—California. 6. Abalones—California—
Folklore. I. Title.
E78.C15F54 2008
639'.4832—dc22   2008013525

Contents

ABOUT THE SERIES   vii

ACKNOWLEDGMENTS   ix

INTRODUCTION Why Abalone?
The Making of a Collaborative Research Project   1

I Artifact, Narrative, Genocide

1 The Old Abalone Necklaces and the Possibility of a
  Muwekma Ohlone Cultural Patrimony   19

2 Abalone Woman Attends the Wiyot
  Reawakening   50

II The "Meaning" of Abalone
TWO DIFFERENT ABALONE PROJECTS

3 Florence Silva and the Legacy of John Boston:
  *Responsibility at the Intersection of Friendship and
  Ethnography*   62

4 Reflections on the Iridescent One   84

III Cultural Revivification and Species Extinction

5 Cultural Revivification in the Hoopa Valley   109

6 Extinction Narratives and Pristine Moments:
  Evaluating the Decline of Abalone   137

CONCLUSION Horizons of Collaborative Research   161

NOTES   173

REFERENCES   179

INDEX   193

About the Series

Narrating Native Histories aims to foster a rethinking of the ethical, methodological, and conceptual frameworks within which we locate our work on Native histories and cultures. We seek to create a space for effective and ongoing conversations between North and South, Natives and non-Natives, academics and activists, throughout the Americas and the Pacific region. We are committed to complicating and transgressing the disciplinary and epistemological boundaries of established academic discourses on Native peoples.

This series encourages symmetrical, horizontal, collaborative, and auto-ethnographies; work that recognizes Native intellectuals, cultural interpreters, and alternative knowledge producers within broader academic and intellectual worlds; projects that decolonize the relationship between orality and textuality; narratives that productively work the tensions between the norms of Native cultures and the requirements for evidence in academic circles; and analyses that contribute to an understanding of Native peoples' relationships with nation-states, including histories of expropriation and exclusion as well as projects for autonomy and sovereignty.

We are pleased to have *Abalone Tales* as one of our two inaugural volumes. It is an innovative attempt at collaborative, dialogical ethnography whose experiments with research and writing are relevant inside and outside academe. Volume contributor Julian Lang once wrote that ancient knowledge, as created by the ancestors, contains the essence of tribal sovereignty. Field, Lang, Silva, and a diversity of Native commentators illustrate this insight for today's world as they engage with the profound truths and mysteries embodied in abalone. They question the nature of voice in ethnography through a contrapuntal experiment with co-authorship. Field counterpoises his own interpretations of Ohlone encounters with anthropology to a range of Native narratives, refusing to reduce them to a single "Indian voice." In the process, Field and his collaborators guide us toward the lessons we can derive through our own intellectual engagement with the creative genius of our ancestors.

Acknowledgments

In a collaborative work such as this volume, there were many people who were completely essential to the making of the work. In light of the conditions shaping the production of this book, an acknowledgments section cannot simply make note of these essential contributions in a standard manner. Such contributions saturate the entire project. Nevertheless, I will use this section to thank all of the individuals, tribes, and institutions without whom this book would not have been possible.

Ongoing support for this project has been provided by the Wenner-Gren Foundation, the National Endowment for the Humanities' Extending the Reach Faculty Research Grant, and the University of New Mexico's Resource Allocation Committee.

In particular, I thank the following tribal organizations: the Muwekma Ohlone Tribe, the Federated Coast Miwok, the Yurok Tribe, the Table Bluff Wiyot Rancheria, and the Ohlone Costanoan Esselen Nation. While I did not establish a formal relationship with the Hupa Tribe, I worked with so many people in the Hoopa Valley, many of whom also work for the tribe, that thank the entire tribe, as well.

The following museums granted me access to their collections, and without that access I would never have come into contact with some of the most extraordinary objects in California Indian history. To figure out which objects would play a role in this book, I had to see many more than I actually discuss, but there was for me a very steep learning curve involved in undertaking this facet of the project. Sherrie Smith-Ferri, Director of the Grace Hudson Museum (Ukiah, California), played an absolutely essential role in this process, and Craig Bates, Chief Curator of Ethnographic Collections at the Yosemite Museum, has been a guiding inspiration for all of my work in Native California since the beginning of my involvement in that world. The Clarke Museum (Eureka, California) very kindly made its collections accessible, and Brad Marshall, board member of the museum, who also is a central contributor in chapter 5, certainly aided and abetted that access. Thanks to Leslie Freund, formerly of the Phoebe Hearst Museum of Anthropology at the University of California, Berkeley, for helping me get into those collections and to Lisa Deitz at the University of California, Davis, collection.

In Europe, I thank the curator anthropologists at the following museums: Sabine August of the Museum für Völkerkunde in Frankfurt; Dr. Jean-Loup Rousselot of the Staatliches Museum für Völkerkunde in Munich; Gisela Sigrist of the Museum für Völkerkunde in Freiburg; Staffan Brunius of the Folkens Museum Etnografiska in Stockholm; and Berete Due at the Nationalmuseet in Copenhagen.

The essential contributions of Florence Silva, Julian Lang, Cheryl Seidner, Merv George Sr., Bradley Marshall, Callie Lara, Darlene Marshall, Alan Leventhal, and Rosemary Cambra will become obvious to readers as they get into this volume. I thank these dear friends, each a brilliant and creative intellect, each a source of energy for his or her families and peoples.

I could not have completed this project without the following individuals, many of whom are also friends: Greg Sarris, Pete Haaker, Leona Wilkinson, George Blake, Bob McConnell, Rudy Rosales, Hank Alvarez, Lorraine Escobar, Tharon (Xew) Weighill, Philip Laverty, Sean Lee, Tom Gates, Bob McConnell, Walt Lara Sr., Buzz Owen, Norm Sloan, Frank Shaughnessy, and Gislí Palsson. Thanks to the California Department of Fish and Game for tasty abalones served at the Ohone Abalone Feast. In my department at the University of New Mexico, I also thank Carole Nagengast, Marta Weigle, Beverly Singer, Louise Lamphere, David Dinwoodie, Suzanne Oakdale, Mari Lyn Salvador, Sylvia Rodriguez, Keith Basso, Joe Powell, Kim Hill, and Magdalena Hurtado. All provided (variously) support, references, ideas, enthusiasm, critique, and patience for this project and the writing of this book. I am fortunate always to feel supported by other luminaries in anthropology who are also dear friends: Dick Fox, Carol Smith, Katherine Verdery, Virginia Dominguez, and Michael Kearney. Finally, I thank certain old friends who always play a key role in my ability to actually do anything: Frank

Henderson and Wendy Harrison, Adam Stern and Denise Harmon, Sonia Stern, Charlie Zechel and Mari Snow, Wes and Theonia Boyd, Rebecca Stith, Alison Seevak, Donna Blagdan, Dan Kozarsky, Jo Montgomery and Ruth Conn, Wendy Cadden and Barbara Nylund, Heidi McKinnon, and Bennett Johnston. Thanks to Bennett, we finally met Luke and Emily Frey and stayed on several occasions in the alternative reality of their fine vineyard north of Ukiah. Many thanks are also given to Nina Wallerstein and David Dunaway, superb friends who are such an important part of life.

My family played a major role in this project. Vee and Sam Dysart provided a stable home base, endless meals, and loving support in San Jose during the five years of ongoing research. Reinaldo Scarpetta, my father-in-law, early on signaled his approval of the research. Of course, the key players were my partner, Gia Scarpetta, and our three children, Lukas, Simon, and Maia, who spent sabbatical 2000 roller coastering around California and Europe and, during the following three summers, followed a slightly less daunting version of the same. Their willingness to go anywhere and do it all was boundless, but they also formed the glue that bound together friendships and experiences and made sense of it all. Gia Scarpetta, the love of my life, also took all of the photographs.

My mother, Frances Field, passed away before the completion of this work. My father had done the same during the research for my first book. I dedicate *Abalone Tales* to Fran, a beautiful, graceful, and uniquely inspired individual. Fran always wanted to study history, and she pursued that dream here in New Mexico in the last years of her life. She is still flying toward the sun, behind the Sandia Mountains. I am proud to be her son, and I think she would have liked this book very much.

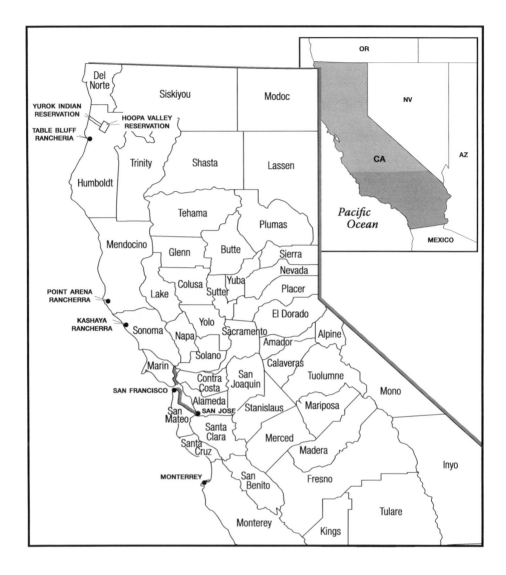

Map of Northern California, with relevant research locations indicated.

Introduction

Why Abalone? The Making of

a Collaborative Research Project

Like Native American peoples across the North American continent, the lives of individuals and communities in Native California are intertwined with struggles over both political sovereignty and cultural identity. Sovereignty, or "forms of autonomous control" (Field 2003) over territory and natural resources, is thus inextricably intertwined with the disposition of historical and contemporary material culture, the use of Native languages, and the enactment of customary practices and narrative traditions among Native peoples of this continent. In both Native and non-Native discourse, there are certain animal entities that, as complex and multilayered cultural symbols, historically have been considered to congeal the complex meanings and struggles about identity and sovereignty and continue to do so. Buffalo are frequently treated as this kind of entity for the Native peoples on the Plains, while salmon are similarly considered for many peoples in the Pacific Northwest. The gray whale is such a creature for the Makah Indians of northwestern Washington State. Among Native peoples of California, abalone is potentially also such an animal, and I conducted several years of research assuming that this was true. In this book, I will present multiple perspectives bearing on the material and symbolic relationships between California Indian peoples and abalone that both support and ultimately undermine such an assumption.

I came to think of abalone in this way because of the remarkably complex significance of the abalone mollusk—as resource, as food, as a material with which to make regalia and adornment, and as powerful narrative—to Native peoples of California. To document these significant relationships, I conducted fieldwork with a number of individuals from different tribes and communities, all of whom share a painful history of rupture, loss, and colonial occupation and among whom cultural revitalization and struggles for social justice and political sovereignty are occurring. Abalone's multifaceted symbolism and historical presence in both daily life and ceremonialism provided a substantive theme with which to explore common issues of concern and interest in contemporary Native California. Both the research agenda and the analysis of information collected were shaped by varied sorts of collaborative relationships that developed with different individuals and communities, which in several cases led some of these individuals to contribute their own written and oral texts to the body of the book. Therefore, this book consists of a number of very different kinds of texts that offer not only divergent content but also contrasting formats in which my own and others' analyses are presented.

Abalone and Native Nations in California

The abalone is a mollusk: a single large shell covering a soft-bodied creature. It is a gastropod: in reality, a very large snail. Classified as the genus Haliotis, the earliest fossilized abalone shells have been found in sediments approximately 100 million years old (Haaker, Henderson, and Parker 1986). About 130 abalone species and subspecies inhabit the marine waters off rocky shores of every continent. Mention of abalone can be found in Aristotle, in paintings by Brueghel, in Japanese records from the fifth century A.D., and in five hundred years of Europeans' observations of marine life from the Canary Islands to Australia, from New Zealand to the islands of Guernsey and Jersey, and from the coasts of Africa to California.

Eight abalone species live in California's coastal waters, and they are considered large among these animals. The California red abalone is indeed the largest abalone and can grow up to eleven inches in diameter. The interior shell of the red abalone and the other Californian species— especially the pink, green, black, and white abalones—display remarkably colorful iridescence, in many cases brilliant opalescence, in comparison with other abalone species, with the possible exception of the New Zealand abalone, known as paua. In any event, abalone shell has been used by Native peoples of California for a long period, exceeding eight millennia. During this time, abalone shell has been and continues to be used to make necklaces, pendants, rings, and other personal adornments, as well as fishhooks and other utilitarian tools. Pearls formed in the digestive tracts of the mollusk, as stunningly iridescent as the shell, have also been found in very old ornaments and are currently very highly valued. Sacred abalone regalia forms an essential component of the ritual materials deployed in the Dreamer, or Bole Maru, religion still practiced by Pomo-speaking and other Native peoples of California's Mendocino and Lake counties, as well as in the World Renewal religion shared by Yurok, Karuk, Hupa, Tolowa, and Wiyot peoples of Humboldt and Del Norte counties.

Archaeological, ethnohistoric, and ethnographic data show that abalone has also been an important food for Native peoples living along California's coast for an equally long period. Its harvest and consumption was particularly important in coastal areas from Los Angeles County to Mendocino County. Abalone meat was actively traded, particularly in a dried form, to inland regions and other coastal areas where the mollusk was less plentiful. Like that of all shellfish, abalone meat is a highly nutritious and concentrated food, and there is every reason to suppose that it not only provided an important source of sustenance but also was valued among the favorite foods of Native California peoples. It is quite delicious.

Since the first decade of the twentieth century (see, e.g., Goddard 1903), ethnographers have recorded numerous narratives about abalone told by Native peoples living in an area stretching from Santa Barbara to the Oregon border. Stories about abalone, the First Creature of the sea, are still told by Pomo-speaking people at the Kashaya and the Point Arena reservations (Oswalt 1964). The richest corpus of narratives that are still told about abalone is concentrated on the stretch of coastline along Humboldt and Del Norte counties. Among the Wiyot, Hupa, Yurok, Karuk, and Tolowa peoples, these stories focus on a spirit being named Abalone Woman. The many versions and interpretations of the Abalone Woman narrative, as told and discussed by different individuals from these tribes, reflect historical and contemporary concerns with value, violence, gender, coming of age, and intertribal relations, which are all central issues in contemporary Indian cultural identities.

Not all California Native peoples have maintained their relationship with abalone as food, sacred material, and narrative, because this relationship was profoundly affected by the manner in which Spanish, Mexican, and American colonial regimes transformed each particular Native people. Because California was admitted to the union in 1851, the Native peoples of this state entirely missed the era during which nation-to-nation relationships—formalized through treaties between "Indian nations" and, first, the English colonies and later the young federal republic —recognized Native peoples' curtailed yet still significant rights and territories. By the middle of the nineteenth century, the United States had redefined Native peoples as "domestic dependent nations" whose territories were engulfed by the expansive republic and subjected to ever more constricting redefinitions of their rights to resources and territory. In the late nineteenth century and through most of the twentieth century, the federal government on several occasions attempted to completely disarticulate Native peoples by terminating and revoking their sovereign status, relocating and forcibly resocializing Native communities, and harshly disrupting the transmission of Native languages and cultures. The fate of Native peoples in California has been affected by these later efforts more, perhaps, than has that of Native peoples in any other part of the country. The role of anthropologists in these processes was complex and sometimes complicit.

In and around the San Francisco Bay Area, the history of peoples speaking eight distinct but related Ohlonean-languages provide a case in point of such colonial processes. Ohlone-speaking communities were transformed by Spanish missionizing and early Anglo urbanization. Epidemics, forcible internment in the missions, the decline of plant and animal ecosystems that had sustained Native lifeways, and the displacement of Native communities by ever larger populations of immigrants all contributed to irrevocable changes for the Ohlonean peoples. Their persistence notwithstanding these immense challenges, however, was undermined by the research and writings of anthropologists and the criteria for legitimizing Native identity that anthropologists developed into the mid-twentieth century. Epitomized in the extinction sentence

Alfred Kroeber pronounced over the Ohlonean peoples in his authoritative tome *Handbook of the Indians of California* (1976 [1925]), anthropological work could be used to buttress the exclusion of certain Indian peoples from the severely constrained set of rights formal federal recognition entailed. The Ohlonean peoples did not secure federally acknowledged status and accompanying reservation lands as the Pomo-speakers and the tribes farther north did (see Lightfoot 2005). The damage caused by this outcome would be difficult to overestimate. In doing the work of re-legitimating the Ohlonean peoples (see Field and Muwekma Ohlone Tribe 2003; Field et al. 1992; Leventhal et al. 1994), archaeological and ethnohistoric information demonstrate the long-term significance of abalone as food and sacred material and suggest that in this region too, Native people told significant narratives about abalone.

Collaborative Fieldwork and Analysis

This book offers explorations of the continuing but profoundly divergent ways abalone remains important (or is once again becoming important) to Ohlone, Pomo, Karuk, Hupa, Yurok, and Wiyot peoples. These explorations highlight contemporary struggles over sovereignty and identity, specifically in the arenas of natural resources, material culture, and narrative and their transforming significance. Each chapter illustrates one or several facets of these complex historical and contemporary issues, elaborated through the relationship between particular California Indian peoples and abalone. Each chapter portrays the distinctive voices of individuals from these communities in combination with anthropological analyses.

James Clifford's critique of ethnographic authority and his call on anthropologists to produce "polyphonic ethnographies" (Clifford 1986) —ethnographies in which multiple voices are heard and multiple perspectives are expressed—helped to inspire such an approach. According to Clifford, polyphonic ethnographies would greatly reduce, perhaps even eliminate, the authoritative voice of the anthropologist in ethnographic texts, which, he argues, has dominated ethnographies at the expense of the people with whom anthropologists work. Polyphony would create opportunities for those with whom anthropologists work to not only provide data but also to analyze information, a task previously reserved for the anthropologist. The production of such ethnographies, as described by Clifford and more recently elucidated in a "handbook" format by Luke Eric Lassiter (2005) and as a case study in Colombia by Joanne Rappaport (2005), hinges on profound relations of collaboration between anthropologists and individuals who were called "informants" in the past, but who some now call "interlocutors" or "collaborators," among other terms.

It is worthwhile to ask what advantages accrue to producing such ethnographies and engaging in collaborative methods of research. In a recent symposium I organized with Richard Fox, about which an edited volume has been released (Field and Fox 2007), a dozen anthropologists considered the kinds of collaborative ethnographic and analytic work they are currently doing in terms of the changing conditions and relationships that shape anthropological research. The symposium participants took as a point of departure, rather than as a point of arrival, the fact that collaborative research and writing are important not because anthropologists have suddenly decided to make them so but, rather, because they are obliged to work and write in this way by new relationships with the world in which they work. I have found that to be the case in my ethnographic research in Nicaragua, Colombia, Ecuador, and Native California: I have not deployed collaborative methods and epistemologies out of my own intellectual ingenuity but because there really was no other way to "get to" the subject matter I wanted to research. Charles Hale (in Field and Fox 2007) describes experiences like my own as demonstrating the real advantages of collaborative research: Collaboration makes possible research that would not otherwise be so and, he writes, produces "better" data.

Doing fieldwork with Native peoples in California, I tried to extend what I learned in my first book (Field 1999a) about indigenous identities in Nicaragua. That book had grown out of a long series of extended conversations with individuals in which themes and ideas were collaboratively produced and revised, precisely because these themes and ideas were already important to these individuals. I did not consider the people with whom I had worked in Nicaragua informants as much as colleagues, and I regarded their ideas and analyses as the result of their role as intellectuals organic to their society at that point in history. From this Gramscian vantage point (see Crehan 2002 for an excellent discussion of anthropological uses of Gramscian theory), they and their communities already had a stake in engaging in, and even in impelling, discourse about the issues that were represented in *The Grimace of Macho Ratón*. I was particularly intrigued by Clifford's allusion to "a utopia of plural authorship that accords to collaborators not merely the status of independent enunciators but also that of writer" (Clifford 1986: 51) and invited the individuals with whom I worked in Nicaragua the opportunity to write about issues of concern to us both and to include their written work in the book. But as Lassiter (2005) noted, my experiment in co-authoring *The Grimace* ran into insurmountable problems because of power differences between the Nicaraguan organic intellectuals with whom I worked and me, the author with the final word.

I wanted to try to supersede those limitations in this work. As in Nicaragua, the California Indian individuals and communities with whom I worked were ready and willing to invest time and energy in shaping the representation of their perspectives about sovereignty and identity. In several cases, I was told that the discussions we were having about abalone narratives, foods, regalia, and so on fit in with the research work Indian leaders and intellectuals were already doing. Having worked with federally unrecognized tribes such as the Muwekma in assembling and analyzing ethnohistoric and ethnographic materials to prepare a petition for federal acknowledgement, I was already accustomed to developing research and analyses in close conjunction with, and often under the direct supervision and guidance of, tribal councils and chairs. This experience prepared me to shape a book not only in which there are many more voices than my own, but also in which debate and difference emerge from those voices so that it becomes impossible for readers to simplify or reduce them all to a single "indigenous voice."

In my work, challenging the authority of anthropologists and of the anthropological discipline in order to produce polyphonic ethnographies is not a gratuitous act of self-flagellation, as seemed to be the case during the heyday of the postmodern critique. Likewise, engaging in collaborative research and writing does not mean asserting the authority of a unified indigenous voice, since that entity has never existed. Certainly in the history of anthropology's engagement with Native North American Indians, there are important, well-known, and deeply prob-

lematic collaborative research relationships, such as the Franz Boas–
George Hunt and Alice Fletcher–Francis La Flesche duos. Moreover,
the goal of creating collaborative, multivocal methods, epistemologies,
and research goals generated the research for and subsequent decades of
controversy around "the Fox project" (see Bennett 1996; Foley 1999;
Lurie 1973 for a sampling of different views). Acknowledging this history
and the path blazed by other Native and academic intellectuals, I move
in this book from discussions of the struggles of unacknowledged peoples to those of those of historically recognized tribes, from material
culture to narrative to ecology and back again, which underscores the
multifaceted nature of indigenous intellectual production in contemporary California Indian communities. In the process, readers will encounter a challenging series of different sorts of textual renderings.

The audience for such a challenging text should be twofold: anthropologists, a growing number of whom are exploring the methods and
consequences of conducting collaborative ethnography and writing
polyphonic texts, as the Field and Fox volume underscores; and researchers, leaders, and intellectuals in Native communities, a growing
number of whom are using anthropological tools for Native goals (see
Field 2004) and are most inclined to employ collaborative methods and
epistemologies in those pursuits.

American Indian Sovereignty and Identity Now: The Struggle and the Stakes

For Native Americans in the United States, sovereignty is inseparable
from official federal recognition of tribal status. As I have written elsewhere, sovereignty means that

> federally recognized Indian peoples hold onto a sharply circumscribed but
> nevertheless always potentially valuable set of properties which include
> land and resources, as well as collective and individualized claims upon
> various parts of the U.S. federal bureaucracy. Even Indians who do not
> currently live or were not born on reservations but are members of feder-
> ally recognized tribes can return to those reservations and make claims to
> resources. By the same token, Indian individuals belonging to recognized
> tribes who do not reside on reservations and do not intend to live there are
> still able to make claims on certain resources from the federal government,

such as those having to do with education and health. These resources are certainly in the main quite substandard, but they are nevertheless significant. While the U.S. state has since 1934 occasionally tried to renege on the sovereignty arrangements initiated by the Indian Reorganization Act, these arrangements have been maintained into the 21st century and Indian peoples are currently engaged in an often contradictory struggle to achieve both economic viability and revitalize their cultural identities on the remnant resources left to them on reservations. For these reasons, being an Indian in the United States has become an identity which is closely policed. (Field 2002: 10)

This description of Indian sovereignty corresponds to what Thomas Biolsi has called three of four kinds of "indigenous space" in the United States: tribal sovereignty within reservation territories; "generic (supratribal) indigenous rights within an inclusive space that ultimately spans all of the contiguous United States"; and "hybrid indigenous space in which Indian people claim and exercise citizenship simultaneously in Native nations and the United States" (Biolsi 2005: 240). The American Indian struggle for sovereignty, Biolsi says, has focused mainly on the rights that federally recognized Indian tribes seek to exercise in their reservation territories, as well as the rights individuals Native Americans can thereby claim via their membership in federally recognized tribes. Nevertheless, he argues, Indian people, like other racial minorities, still maintain overriding interests in the struggle for civil rights in the United States as a whole.

While I agree with him, I focus in this book on the exercise of sovereignty within reservation territories. For federally recognized tribes, the effort to expand and deepen sovereignty over reservation space constitutes the condition for exploring cultural revitalization. For unrecognized tribes, the goal of the struggle for federal acknowledgement is precisely attaining the space and claims to resources that will make possible the exploration of cultural revitalization. These, then, are the struggles over sovereignty at the heart of the book and the stakes involved in those struggles. But if sovereignty potentially creates space for cultural identity, what do we mean by identity?

In the abstract, I consider identity "the constantly transforming and always incomplete production of, knowledge about and ways of expressing self and social being, under stratified systems of power" (Field 1999a:

1). But in the case of Native Americans in the United States, identity has been constructed and constrained by a historically unfolding dynamic played out among three distinct forces. First, there are Indian struggles to survive in the face of more than five hundred years of European colonialism and yet to maintain Indian identities that have changed and continue to do so. Second, the variously cold and hot wars waged against Indian peoples by the U.S. state, having failed to eliminate Indians, have produced persistent state-led efforts to define the meaning of Indian identity and to police the boundaries of that identity through federal recognition. Finally, anthropologists in relationships both complicit and contentious with both Indians and the U.S. state have also claimed and defended their authority to define Indianness. In this spiral of dialectic (perhaps "trialectic") relationships across the many years, Indians, the federal bureaucracy, and anthropologists alike agree that Indian identity has something to do with the following characteristics: historical relationships to and presence on particular territories; narratives about place, phenotype, kinship as substantiated through blood quanta; kinship as traced through descent; residence and locality; language; and ritual/ceremonial lifeways. The degree to which any and all of these characteristics is accorded relative importance vis-à-vis the other characteristics is, of course, what the struggle is all about.

In the past two and a half decades, many anthropologists, some of whom work with American Indian peoples, have reevaluated the role played by anthropology in the analysis of identity. Certainly, Benedict Anderson's landmark work on nationalism (Anderson 1983) must be included in any description of such efforts, and in the anthropology of Native North America, Clifford's classic "Identity in Mashpee" (in Clifford 1986) also marks an important opening salvo. These works helped to introduce anthropology to a debate that was to consume the intellectual energies of many for the next two decades, although anthropologists will never have the final word precisely because of the other interlocutors (Indian tribes, the federal government) involved. The debate posed, on the one hand, a constructionist point of view (exemplified by Anderson and Clifford) that understood all identities as historically imagined and created, against, on the other hand, a view that certain traits, such as language, kinship (as both blood and descent), and ritual and ceremonial ways defined specific identities in timeless and essential ways. I have written about and been frustrated by anthropologists' struggles with and against the constructionism-versus-essentialism debate (see Field 1999b; Field Forthcoming), in an effort to show how very different kinds of anthropologists work with various kinds of Indian leaders and intellectuals around these issues.

Like Clifford (2004), Samuel R. Cook (2000), Eva Garroutte (2003), Gerald Sider (2003), and Circe Sturm (2002), all working in North America, and Charles Hale (2006) and Rappaport (2005), working in Latin America, I favor an anthropology that transcends the self-imposed limitations of binary concepts such as essentialism and constructionism. I hinge such an anthropology of Indian identities on finely tuned historic and ethnographic work that makes transparent the relationships with Indian peoples and specific individuals in Indian communities and is scrupulous in avoiding both romantic and reductionist accounts of Indian identity. In this book, there is no general analytic reconciliation between cultural traits and their construction into historic Indian identities, because that process—so precious and vital—is exactly what the people with whom I have worked are engaged in creating in so many diverse and unpredictable ways. The stakes in taking this approach potentially liberate anthropologists from their own conceptual shackles but, more important (in my experience), open paths toward collaborative work with Indian communities and individuals.

Argument and Structure of the Book: How to Read *Abalone Tales*

The research for and writing of collaborative ethnographies, I assert, is not simply an interesting experimental enterprise. It serves broad epistemological, theoretical, and, indeed, political goals. A book composed of multiple narrative and analytic voices such as this one must therefore be structured carefully to bring readers into the middle of the multilevel discussion. At the same time, readers are invited to participate in understanding and analyzing the interaction between these diverse voices. I have tried to extend as far as possible the idea that certain animals— abalone, in this case—really do function as complex, multilayered symbols that provide insight for understanding Native identities and struggles. This is a convention, as I have said, that is common in both Native and non-Native discourses. Over the course of the chapters of this book, I query the extent to which the theme of abalone is my own construct, a shared construct that emerged through the process of collaborative research, or an a priori symbol of importance. My deeper argument is that collaborative research does create new forms of knowledge that hinge on co-created symbols and analyses. In terms of methodology, this co-creation is what Bruce Mannheim and Dennis Tedlock (1995) have referred to as "the dialogic emergence of culture" that results at the points of contact and communication between anthropologist and interlocutor. In theoretical terms, Rappaport (2005: 27) has called this dialogue "co-theorizing [which] involves the forging of connections between indigenous-created concepts and the theories and methodologies that politically committed academics draw on from their own traditions."

Research about the multifaceted significance of abalone provided a forum to explore diverse struggles over sovereignty and identity, and the collaborative form of research facilitated the emergence of multiple and diverse perspectives about and analyses of these struggles. I have grouped the six chapters of this book into three parts, each of which presents multiple perspectives. In each part, I pursue an argument about Native identity and sovereignty through the lens of abalone, but other purposes and goals are being served in the words and writing of Native individuals.

Part I, "Artifact, Narrative, Genocide," couples the contemporary histories of two very different Native Californian peoples (one unacknowledged, one recognized), both of which have suffered genocidal assaults on their identities. In the first case, I narrate a search for cultural history and identity through patrimony, making an argument about the struggle for federal recognition. In the second case, I ask a tribal leader to write about whether a classic telling of the northwestern California abalone story has anything to do with the tribe's post-genocide cultural rebirth and identity.

Chapter 1 considers the historical and cultural relationship between abalone artifacts and the struggle for federal recognition by the Muwekma Ohlone Tribe, the contemporary tribal entity of Ohlonean-speaking peoples. The chapter reflects my concern with an issue that the leadership of the tribe, engaged in very drawn-out and expensive battles for recognition, has seldom had time to consider: the material-culture patrimony of the Ohlonean peoples. Written in consultation with the tribe's chair, Rosemary Cambra, and other tribal members, the chapter focuses on interpreting archaeologically and ethnohistorically identified abalone artifacts in the context of the Ohlones' struggle for political sovereignty through federal recognition and for cultural revival in the face of their erasure from both anthropological and bureaucratic legitimacy. The voices of Muwekma tribal members are embedded within the narrative I have written in a relatively conventional format. The content of the chapter challenges the role played by anthropologists in Muwekma history on several fronts. The chapter also makes plain how in my work with the Muwekma I first came to consider the importance of abalone to them and to wonder about its importance in other areas of native California.

The second chapter moves northward to the Wiyot tribe of Humboldt Bay, who have only recently begun to recover from their genocidal history, particularly the 1867 massacre at Indian Island. That process of healing has hinged on both regaining control over at least part of that aboriginal territory, as well as reviving cultural practices such as basket weaving and World Renewal dances. From 2000 to 2003, I spent many days discussing Wiyot genocide and healing with Tribal Chair Cheryl Seidner and her sister, Leona Wilkinson. Both of them spoke about the ethnographically recorded story of Abalone Woman among the Wiyot as having historical and contemporary relevance to these processes. When I asked Cheryl to elaborate her ideas about this issue, she produced a three-part prose-poem over the twelve month period between 2002 and 2003. I have juxtaposed a résumé of Wiyot history with one of the textualized versions of the story of Abalone Woman in this chapter, both of which preface the interpretations Cheryl elaborated in her prose poem. Cheryl's consideration of the contemporary significance of the abalone story has "the last word" in this chapter.

Part II, "The 'Meaning' of Abalone: Two Different Abalone Projects," is composed of two chapters that recount contrasting research trajectories. Both chapters address my larger concern with abalone as a cultural trope for Native California peoples. In the first, I approached a very knowledgeable Native leader with ideas for researching the centrality of abalone among her people and, in doing the work, discovered on repeated occasions just how mistaken my ideas were. In the second chapter, I approached an equally knowledgeable Native intellectual and asked that he write about his own research on the abalone narratives and their central place in the broader scope of narrative among his people. In both cases, the theme of sovereignty formed the foundation for the work of the individuals with whom I was collaborating. Together, the chapters underscore the complex and often contentious nature of collaborative work, on the one hand, and the tight linkage between cultural "work" and tribal sovereignty, on the other.

In chapter 3, the first chapter in part II, I focus on the life of Florence Silva, Point Arena Pomo elder. From her maternal grandfather, the widely renowned and influential Bole Maru Dreamer John Boston, and her mother, the healer Annie Bigioli, she inherits a detailed knowledge about abalone as a creature eaten for food, an entity in narratives, and as a singular material for the production of regalia. I approached Florence in 1998 and asked her to help me to understand the meaning of abalone in her people's experience. But the focus of collaborative work with Florence changed repeatedly over the course of four years of frequent conversation. Florence's words and concerns infuse this dynamic narrative about the interpretation of abalone narrative and regalia, as she repeatedly redirected my attention to examples of cultural change and continuity, her own critique of the historical legacies of ethnography in Point Arena, and, above all, a focus on the struggles of her people to retain control over their land.

In chapter 4, the Karuk scholar, artist, linguist, and performer Julian Lang offers his analytic perspectives concerning the significance of abalone narratives within his larger project of reassembling and revitalizing the narrative cycles of Karuk culture. Soon after I contacted him in 2000, Julian established that our discussions and the opportunity to write about his analysis of Abalone Woman stories provided an opportunity to advance his larger project. Julian's chapter elaborates theories about historical and contemporary culture by referring not to anthropological literature, but, instead, to Native histories of struggle for identity and territory. In this way, it is not only "Native voice" that is expressed but the development of Native epistemology and scholarship.

Part III, "Cultural Revivification and Species Extinction," constitutes a departure from the larger question regarding abalone as a complex symbol for Native Californians and a re-focus on particular questions regarding the use of abalone in regalia and narrative, on the one hand, and as food, on the other. In one chapter, my role is exclusively to edit and arrange the textualized voices of others, and in the other chapter, I am the sole narrator of a text that follows a single argument. In both cases, questions do get answered about abalone's present-day significance in both cultural constructs and biological contexts.

The texts that make up chapter 5 are all situated on the Hoopa Valley reservation. When I went to Hoopa in 2000, I was forced to concede that I would not be able to establish anything beyond superficial knowledge about Hupa ceremonialism, symbolism, and narrative. I decided instead to find out whether those with real expertise would talk about a number of topics connected with abalone's role in Hupa story and ritual and discovered individuals who found my interest in these subjects meaningful and important enough to spend significant periods of time discussing them. The chapter includes one distinctive telling of the Abalone Woman story by Vivien Hailstone and Darlene Marshall; two interviews about Abalone Woman and abalone regalia with Callie Lara and Bradley Marshall, respectively; and summaries of conversations with Merv George Sr., who for the past few decades has organized the most important ceremonies conducted by the Hupa. I have arranged these different elements thematically to highlight the mixtures of traditional and innovative interpretation of regalia and narrative in the context of resurgent cultural expression in the Hoopa Valley.

Chapter 6 is a historical ecology of abalone that explores the decline of abalone species in the twentieth century against the backdrop of the trope of "extinction," an important political and cultural issue for California Native peoples—especially unrecognized tribes. The perspectives of Native peoples, among whom many individuals have extensive knowledge and experience on the coast, have seldom been considered among the more vocal opinions of white fishermen and marine biologists. The chapter explores the range of views among Native individuals and contemplates the resonance between discourses of abalone's extinction and the discourses of extinction for Native peoples in California. Chapter 6 therefore represents an attempt to combine Native and anthropological interpretation in theorizing the fate of a vital marine resource, abalone, over which Native sovereignty has been systematically extricated.

The different strands of collaboration and co-theorizing that characterize the entire volume are both maintained as separate and brought together in the conclusion to the volume. I begin in Humboldt County, on the shores of the Yurok coast. The Cultural Committee of the Yurok Tribe co-authored the text discussing the importance of abalone in Yurok narratives in the context of the relationship between Yurok people and the sea. Narrative, resource utilization, sovereignty, and identity —in short, all of the book's themes—come together in this discussion of Yurok people, places, and culture, embracing abalone as the trope of cultural persistence and the rejection of extinction. These themes are elaborated from a final theoretical perspective that I offer in closing.

Each chapter composes an "abalone tale," although the chapters do not offer the same kinds of stories. Nor, I reiterate, do opinions and ideas among the contributing individuals together constitute a single indigenous perspective. Yet among these narratives, anthropological analyses, and scientific explanations, all must be told, and someone, as always, must do the telling. As I and others render and craft these heterogeneous tellings here, these are tales that weave abalone, a multidimensional entity, into the past, present, and future of California Indian existence and experience. A common theme in each chapter tracks the ways anthropologists were sometimes historically involved in processes of cultural loss and the erosion of Indian identities, or in other cases were greatly constrained by their own analytic limitations. With the historical backdrop of rupture that California Indian peoples experienced, and the complex roles anthropologists played in those disjunctures, each chapter also describes the ways contemporary California Indian people have appropriated the tools of research and analysis once deployed only by anthropologists to serve the goals of their Native communities: sovereignty, cultural revitalization, and community integrity.

I

Artifact, Narrative,

Genocide

Anthropological scholarship focusing on genocide is a field that unfortunately is expanding in scope with each passing year, and that is a trend that is likely to continue (see Hinton 2005 for a superb recent example; see also Nordstrom 1997). The Ohlone and Wiyot experiences, described in chapter 1 and chapter 2, respectively, provide illustrative examples of two forms of genocide history in California. The Ohlone experience was shaped by missionization, urbanization, and anthropological complicity, while the Wiyot experience embodies massacre and cover-up in an area of primary importance to post-statehood Anglo-American resource exploitation.

I approached the leaders and other individuals in these tribes with a measure of understanding gained from growing up in a Holocaust survivor family, a fact about which I was quite forth-right in my relationships with these individuals. After numerous years working for the Muwekma Ohlone, as a result of which I first identified the Native relationship with abalone as important and worthy of research, I felt secure in suggesting to the tribal leadership that I pursue an investigation of cultural patrimony, particularly abalone necklaces. Because of many years of substantive work with the tribe, I also felt it was appropriate to reach conclusions about the relationships between patrimony and the tribe's struggle for federal recognition based on research about the abalone necklaces. I wrote this chapter and asked for critical comments from Rosemary Cambra, the tribal chair, and Alan Leventhal, the tribe's archaeologist, both of whom I have worked with since 1991.

By contrast, I first came to know individuals in the Wiyot Tribe through the process of proposing to do research on the contemporary significance of well-known ethnographic textualizations of the Wiyot version of the Abalone Woman story. Through this process, I came to know about and understand the tribe's historical experience and contemporary struggle. But in this case, I felt it was far more appropriate for the Wiyot individuals with whom I worked to have "the last word," as it were, because my question to them—about the contemporary significance of Abalone Woman—really was open-ended. I did not, in other words, invest in arguing in favor of any particular analytic approach to this question, as I had in my research with the Muwekma Ohlone. The result in chapter 2 is a text that is substantively shaped by Cheryl Seidner's decision to respond to the question with an extended prose-poem, which she sent to me by e-mail and read to me over the phone over the course of a year's time (2002–2003).

These two chapters therefore represent two different, contrasting sorts of approaches to collaborative research. In both cases, the symbol of abalone generated dialogic discourse about Native culture and identity based on the pre-existing importance of abalone to these Native peoples. It remains difficult to separate how much collaborative research highlights a symbol's importance from how much that importance is created by the dialogue involved in the collaboration.

with Rosemary Cambra
and Alan Leventhal

1.

The Old Abalone Necklaces
and the Possibility of a Muwekma
Ohlone Cultural Patrimony

In this chapter, I discuss the identity of the Muwekma Ohlone, an unrecognized tribe, from the perspective of the erasure of the tribe's cultural patrimony. I begin the chapter by elaborating two events that permit me to unfold current conditions among the Muwekma and the kind of work I have done with them. First, I describe an Abalone Feast that took place in 2000, the first of its kind in decades, which created an opportunity to consider the Ohlone relationship with abalone. Next, I describe an archaeological excavation that took place in 1992, in which many abalone artifacts were uncovered, stimulating my involvement and interest in the importance of such artifacts in Ohlone cultural history and identity. This leads to the heart of the chapter, an extensive discussion of several nineteenth-century abalone necklaces I went to European museums to inspect and an analysis of how to understand the putative relationship between these artifacts and Ohlone cultural history. I then explore the conceptual limits bounding any discussion of such artifacts, using materials from research elsewhere in California. The argument guiding these explorations is that research about Ohlone cultural patrimony—indeed, about Ohlone identity—hinges on the reestablishment of Ohlone sovereignty. This is significant because the process of achieving federal recognition actually assumes the reverse.

Alfred Kroeber, central figure in the establishment of the Department of Anthropology at the University of California, Berkeley, and the anthropologist whose life intertwined so deeply and importantly with the life of the man called Ishi, published the *Handbook of the Indians of California* in 1925.[1] This massive and encyclopedic summation of California Indian societies and cultures casts a long, long shadow over the identities of tribes and individuals in this state's Indian country. There are no Indian people for whom this is more true than the peoples Kroeber declared extinct in the tome. In addition to suffering the onus of an anthropological extinction sentence, such peoples have also suffered from official erasure, since none of them were accorded federal or state recognition. Between the work of anthropologists and the machinery of the state, California's unrecognized tribes have endured many decades of collective social and cultural invisibility. Among the peoples declared extinct by Kroeber and lacking federal acknowledgment are the Ohlonean-speaking peoples. The contemporary reorganized tribal entity of these peoples is called the Muwekma Ohlone Tribe.

The Muwekma Ohlone Tribe are members of multiple lineages whose ancestors inhabited the five county region on the San Francisco peninsula and the South and East Bay, as well as interior regions around modern-day Stockton and farther inland. Most of these ancestors spoke mutually unintelligible languages in the Ohlonean sub-family of the Penutian family, although the inland ancestors also spoke Yokutsan and Miwokan languages. The ancestral peoples were all incorporated into the mission-presidio system instituted by the Spanish Empire in the late 1700s, a system that maintained control over the area until Mexican independence in 1821. That system incarcerated Native peoples in barracks-style living, instituted massive changes in diet and daily life, and initiated ecological transformations in floral and faunal communities across the landscape. The result for missionized Native peoples like the ancestors of the Muwekma Ohlone was a demographic collapse and profound hemorrhaging of their cultural, linguistic, social, and economic structures and systems. That hemorrhaging is also evident in the dearth of surviving material culture and knowledge about daily lifeways, including, diet among Ohlonean-speaking peoples during the initial contact period and in the decades immediately following missionization.

The older people among the Muwekma remember eating abalone until the 1970s, and so do older members of the of the Ohlone Costanoan Esselen Nation, the contemporary reorganized entity of the Esselen-speaking people of the Monterey region, another Native people declared extinct by Kroeber. Rudy Rosales, Esselen chair during the late 1990s, on several occasions reminisced with me about eating abalone. "When there was nothing in the house, Mama would tell us to go down to the pier [at Pacific Grove] and get some abalone." Rudy and his brother would use crowbars to pry the abalone off the big wood pylons of the pier. There was no need to get nostalgic about it, he told me. "It was poor people's food, not some delicacy like now." But Rudy did miss eating abalone: It was a taste from childhood.

I asked Rosemary Cambra, the Muwekma chair, whether the tribe would want to have an Abalone Feast. She was in favor and arranged to hold such a feast at the completion of the third of three leadership-training seminars the tribe was holding at Alameda in the East Bay. As part of their efforts to become a federally recognized tribe—a Herculean and tremendously expensive process that had already been going on for two decades—the tribal council had been holding events to bring about increased interaction among the members and especially between the elders and the younger generations. The leadership seminars alternated oral-history projects with information-sharing sessions that had all been very well attended. Over the years, so many tribal members had uncovered artifacts made of abalone that several members had also put together a weekend workshop to learn how to fashion abalone into ornamental objects. Rosemary intended the Abalone Feast to crown the year-long intensive series of such workshops and projects.

On December 2, 2000, the Muwekma Ohlone held an Abalone Feast on the shores of San Francisco Bay. Among the forty or so members of the tribe who gathered to shell, clean, slice, pound, fry, and eat abalone, some had not eaten this food for decades—or ever. The California Department of Fish and game donated twenty-three large (more than eight-inch) abalone that had been seized from poachers and used as evidence in trials and were sitting in freezers in Sonoma County. Using some of my grant money set aside especially for this event, I purchased fifty four-to five-inch "domesticated" abalone from a local abalone farm.[2] The East Bay Regional Park District had provided the site at Alameda, just east of Berkeley, located right on the shoreline, equipped with kitchen and outdoor facilities.

Several of the elders immediately took charge of shelling the big wild abalone, trimming off the viscera and other organs, cleaning, slicing, and pounding the resulting chunks of meat. The younger generations did not hesitate to join in. Women wearing diamond rings and designer clothing were suddenly coated up to their elbows in puce green, half-digested kelp from abalone intestines. Children were entirely covered. Everyone wanted to use the mallets to pound the strips of abalone so they could be dipped into egg and bread crumbs. Soon the tenderized abalone was frying.

On a nearby bench, Hank Alvarez, an Ohlone elder with whom I have worked for almost a decade, chewed on a morsel of abalone and told me this: "Back, must have been in the '20s, we lived in Santa Cruz, real near the beach. There was a cliff over the ocean. My mom used to get up sometimes, real early, walk over to the cliff. She'd be looking down, lookin' at 'em. Abalones. She'd go there, she told me, 'cause she liked to look 'em, and see they was still there." I suspect that Hank was thinking that the Abalone Feast showed the world that the Ohlone were still here, too.

Archaeology and Abalone

Among the strategies the Muwekma Ohlone have employed to confront and rectify the widely accepted verdict of extinction that had been passed on to them, the tribe formed its own cultural-resource-management firm in the 1980s. This firm—Ohlone Families Consulting Services (OFCS)—responded to the vast quantity of archaeological remains unearthed as a result of the Bay Area's accelerating post-1970s economic-development boom and has been the vehicle for several social, political and economic processes. First, the OFCS, as a minority-owned and -operated enterprise, was able to secure a number of contracts from the city of San Jose, Santa Clara County, and the State of California that generated income for individual tribal members and tribal operations. Second, active involvement in cultural-resource-management work was a public manifestation of the real and continuous existence of Ohlone people and Ohlone sociality that directly challenged and undermined the extinction narrative that had been accepted by the public, anthropologists, government officials, schoolteachers, and others for decades. In this way, the OFCS both financed and provided data for the Ohlones' ultimate goal: federal acknowledgment. Finally, in a broader sense, the OFCS provided a means for Ohlones to actually take control over their own past by both excavating it and interpreting it in the reports written for each excavation. Parts of these reports were then expanded and published in a number of different widely disseminated journals (see Field and Muwekma Ohlone Tribe 2003; Field and Leventhal 2003; Field et al. 1992; Leventhal et al. 1994).[3]

In 1992, the OFCS excavated a major site just south of San Jose where Highway 101 was connected to Route 82 adjacent to Coyote Creek. The Army Corps of Engineers mandated that a catchment basin be dug at the intersection of these two roads in the event that Coyote Creek were to flood. In the summer of 1992, the idea of a flood seemed ludicrous, as northern California was suffering from its fourth year of a severe drought. But the very next winter, it rained torrentially, and the basin filled up (see Field and Leventhal 2003).

Alan Leventhal, the tribe's staff archaeologist, and several members of the tribe, including Susie Rodriguez and Arnold Galvan, showed me how to mark out a burial, document the strata, and use excavation tools. It was very hot work in the summer sun. Members of the tribe unearthed the skeletal and artifactual remains of their ancestors, which were buried in a cemetery featuring two line of burials, one dated to 1,500 years B.P. and one to 3,000 years B.P. The Muwekma called the site (Ca-SCl 732) Kaphan Unux, the Chochenyo Ohlone term for Three Wolves, because the remains of three wolves, in addition to a number of other animal remains, were ritually interred among the human burials. I personally unearthed a number of both human and animal skeletons in the three-thousand-year-old cemetery, many of which had been buried with olivella-bead necklaces and bracelets. Large round abalone ornaments circled the torsos and waists of several individuals. The abalone may have been thousands of years old, but its iridescence had not dimmed.

The beauty of these artifacts moved me to wonder about the meaning of abalone for the Muwekmas' ancestors and the manner in which abalone has maintained its role in California Indian regalia to the present day. I knew that it would be difficult to document the material culture of the post-mission Ohlone area, because early post-contact, nineteenth-century, and modern Ohlone material culture are all very difficult to find in California museums (see Shanks 2006 for a very recent and thorough photographic assemblage of Ohlone basketry). After many discussions with Tribal Chair Rosemary Cambra, I decided in the late 1990s to pursue research on the tribe's behalf about the material culture of Muwekma ancestors at the time of contact with Europeans and whether, in particular, abalone artifacts had been collected by early European explorers. If such artifacts existed, where were they now? Could Ohlone people lay claim to a cultural patrimony anywhere? If they could not, how did and would that affect their struggle to achieve federal acknowledgment? These queries themselves derived from my dawning realization that unrecognized tribes such as the Muwekma had no cultural patrimony to speak of—that, in fact, being an unrecognized tribe went hand in hand with losing the substantive historical depth embodied by material culture.

The many questions I ask about Ohlone material culture focus on objects that were observed and collected by one early European visitor to the Bay Area, Georg Heinrich von Langsdorff. But these questions are complicated by the diverse ways such inquiries bear on the Ohlone petition for federal acknowledgment. To elaborate those complications, I describe the manner in which the Bureau of Indian Affairs (BIA) has interpreted data about Ohlone history in its recent dealings with the tribe. Then I discuss possibilities for interpreting old abalone necklaces collected by an early European visitor in light of the erasure of a specifically Ohlone patrimony. These interpretations, meant to support the ongoing Ohlone social and cultural revitalization, hinge on two points. First, recognizing the shared material-culture heritage of a broad region of central and northern California signals the possibility that the idea of patrimony—that each assemblage of artifacts can be thought of as pertaining to one particular cultural group—might have to be reconfigured. Second, I acknowledge the inadequacy of non-Native interpretation of the meaning of patrimonial objects, as exemplified by my attempt to understand abalone necklaces. By contrast, the development of Native epistemologies around issues of repatriation constitutes a centrally important strand in the reinterpretation of Native objects. For the Ohlone, I conclude, such reinterpretations of material culture and patrimony depend on the restoration of their recognized status and of the sovereignty over their cultural identities that this would mean.

Early European Collectors and Ohlone Material Culture

Spain may have sent the priests, soldiers, and settlers that formed the first European communities in the territories of Ohlonean-speaking peoples in what is now the San Francisco Bay Area, but it was the actions taken by other early-nineteenth-century Europeans that preserved the little that remains of the material culture of the peoples of the Bay Area. The Spaniards may not have cared to collect such objects, and in cases where they did do such collecting, those who became responsible for the objects did not see fit to preserve them.[4] Thus, the vast majority of the very few objects that are now attributed to Ohlonean-speaking peoples are found in museums in Germany and in St. Petersburg, Russia, with several objects in England, because of the visits to the Bay Area by a number of German, Russian, and English seafaring explorers whose ethnographic collections were sent back home.[5]

Among the very earliest of these explorers, Georg Heinrich von Langsdorff, a German doctor and natural scientist, joined the first Russian scientific voyage around the globe in 1803–1807. During 1806, von Langsdorff spent considerable time in the San Francisco Bay Area, visiting Mission Dolores, at the tip of the San Francisco peninsula; Mission Santa Clara, in the South Bay; and Mission San Jose, in the East Bay. In the many pages of his journals that describe his interactions with the indigenous peoples in and around the missions, von Langsdorff blasted the Native people with invective and simultaneously praised their material culture. "All of the people we got to see [at Mission Dolores]," he wrote, "were under five fuss [sic], poorly built and had such a miserable, dumb, dark, foolish, slovenly appearance that we all had to agree that we had never seen a race of human beings on a lower level" (von Langsdorff 1993: 95–96). Yet two paragraphs later, he wrote:

> I saw among their household utensils very skillfully woven little baskets made from the bark and fiber of trees. They are so watertight that they

can be used to hold drinking water and as soup bowls and even as frying pans. . . . Many of these little baskets or bowls, which require a great deal of time and care to make, are decorated with the bright red feathers of Oriolus phoeniceus and the black crest feathers of the crested Californian partridge [quail] (Tetraonis cristati), as well as with mussels and coral. (von Langsdorff 1993: 96)

Repeatedly and without any consciousness of the apparent contradictions thereby engendered, von Langsdorff denounced the people he met in the most excoriating terms but immediately afterward praised their manufactures, for both their technical and their aesthetic accomplishments:

However dumb and simple, dirty, ugly and repulsive these people may be, they do have a great fondness for adornments and games. They have all sorts of adornments which they make partially from feathers, partially from mussels, that is from a species of sea ear (probably Haliotis gigantea) found frequently along the coast there and near Monterey. It is scarcely inferior in the magnificence of its iridescence to New Zealand's Haliotis Iris. They use a kind of mussel, which I did not get to see, for little rings that are of such admirable exactness that they are all of the same size. Without the use of iron instruments, they bore a hole through the middle. These rings look something like our glass beads and are strung together to make necklaces. (von Langsdorff 1993: 96)

Praising the skill in the making of such objects and their great beauty while refusing to acknowledge the intelligence, expertise, and sensitivity of those who made them, von Langsdorff made sure to obtain such objects when he could at Mission Dolores by trading "European glass beads, silk ribbons, knives, and other objects" (von Langsdorff 1993: 97). Later, at Mission San Jose, von Langsdorff again admired the "adornments made from mussels, feathers, coral, etc." donned by indigenous people preparing for a dance. Like many Europeans of his time, von Langsdorff repeatedly made note of the nakedness of indigenous men and women, affecting shock but always attentive to physique, musculature, and genitalia in the former case, and to facial and corporeal attractiveness in the latter. At Mission San Jose, he was less offended by the appearance of the indigenous people he met but no less fascinated by their material culture.

Native bodies and the objects they made were recorded by von Langsdorff in writing, and both frequently appear in the engraved plates that accompanied his text. Plate 36, "Objects from New California and Norfolk Sound" (figure 1), displays nine objects from California, including two kinds of regalia worn on the head, a basket, two abalone necklaces, a string of clamshell discs, and a bow and two arrows, as well as two baskets from the Norfolk Sound area of southeastern Alaska that von Langsdorff visited after his sojourn in California. In the case of the objects from California, it is not clear at what mission von Langsdorff collected which object. The fate of these objects of such great beauty embodies the problematics of Ohlone cultural patrimony because of the great uncertainties their existence underscores. Is there any way to specify their origin and the identities of those who made them and similar necklaces collected by other Europeans who visited the San Francisco Bay Area during the mission period? What were the meanings of these necklaces and of the abalone in them to those who made them; how can such meanings be discerned; and what is the significance of those meanings to the descendants of those who made the objects? How does such cultural attribution, or the difficulties encountered in making cultural attribution, play a role in the history of Ohlone peoples and their current situation?

My anxiety is that the attempt to grasp the problematics of Ohlone cultural patrimony, such as the historic abalone necklaces collected by early European explorers in the Bay Area, cannot be successfully settled —and by this, I mean that is may be impossible to regain an Ohlone cultural patrimony. I have wondered whether this scholarly worry over the origin, fate, and meaning of old abalone necklaces might therefore negatively affect the Ohlone struggle for federal recognition. As I have written elsewhere (Field 2002), when anthropologists work for unrecognized tribes, the "power relations" that are frequently invoked vaguely in many ethnographic texts are not only very real, but also extremely proximate, in the form of the BIA and its Branch of Acknowledgment Research (BAR). This discussion therefore proceeds under the shadow of the BAR and the federal acknowledgment process, given the way the BAR has deployed the recognition regulations in response to the Muwekma petition (see Field and Muwekma Ohlone Tribe 2003).

Rupture and the Federal Acknowledgment Process

Since the Muwekma Ohlone first began assembling their federal acknowledgment petition and sending documents off to the BAR, the tribe and those who work with its members have noted certain patterns in the ways BAR scholars deal with "the data." These patterns were sharpened after the BAR agreed in 1996 that the ancestors of the Muwekma had been a federally recognized Indian band, called the Verona Band, in federal Indian censuses until 1927. In doing so, the BAR set for the Muwekma the task of showing historic continuities between 1927 and 1982, the year the contemporary tribal organization as the Muwekma Ohlone was initiated. In my collaborative research with the Muwekma concerning this period, I have found a dense network of extended families, linked through kinship, and marriage and fostering/adoption relationships. Led by a succession of strong, informal leaders who reaffirmed the existence of an Ohlone people by facilitating these links, as well as decades of collective enrollment in federal Indian censuses, these factors composed the "glue" that held the ancestors of the Muwekma together until 1982. That was particularly true after the destruction of their residential community at the Alisal *rancheria* in the late 1920s.

BIA/BAR regulations that adjudicate federal recognition have proved especially inadequate, confusing, and capricious for peoples such as the Muwekma, who were previously unambiguously recognized in the twentieth century. Although BAR submitted a preliminary finding on the Muwekma petition that was negative in 2001, and then a negative final determination in 2002, Leventhal and I have shown that the BAR actually substantiated sociocultural continuity of the Muwekma ancestors from the date of the last unambiguous recognition in 1927 through the 1930s and 1940s until approximately 1950. BAR also admitted the continuity of the Muwekma lineages and their sociocultural network from 1965 until the Muwekma Tribe was organized in 1982. If this is true, how did BAR arrive at a negative determination? My review of its work concluded that BAR de-legitimated the Muwekma petition by opening new ruptures in the dialogue between the Muwekma and their historical cultural identity.

To accomplish these new ruptures, BAR simply dismissed the two most important sources of information that document the twentieth-century cohesion and identity of the ancestors and organizers of the Muwekma Ohlone Tribe: first, the field notes of John P. Harrington, which describe the stories, beliefs, practices, and sociocultural identity of the Muwekma ancestors at the Alisal rancheria near modern Pleasanton in the East Bay in the late 1920s and early 1930s (that is, immediately following the 1927 census, the date at which the BAR had conceded the previous unambiguous federal acknowledgment of these ancestors as the Verona Band); and second, the records and publications of the American Indian Historical Society (AIHS). This scholarly and activist organization, composed of both Native and non-Native individuals, documented and supported initial attempts in the 1960s and early 1970s by the Ohlone families to organize themselves in accordance with federal law, since, notwithstanding their disenfranchisement, they had maintained their identity as Ohlones and their cohesion through kinship-defined relationships. BAR's strategy was aimed at finishing off the work of erasure by severing the relationship between the most recent and detailed historical documentation of the Ohlones' immediate ancestors and the descendants of those ancestors who are the contemporary membership of the Muwekma Ohlone Tribe.[6] When I realized what lay at the heart of the BAR strategy, it resonated with another rupture that had successfully severed the relationship between early post-contact material culture, such as the abalone necklaces, and the succeeding generations of Ohlone people. If my critique of BAR's strategies has been aimed at undermining the most recent rupture, then, needless to say, my analysis of the earlier rupture is likewise meant to confront rather than support that outcome.

The Von Langsdorff Necklaces

Let us return to a discussion of the abalone necklaces collected by von Langsdorff and others and explore issues of identification, cultural attribution, and historical relationships with contemporary peoples that offer possibilities other than rupture for peoples such as the Muwekma Ohlone. This discussion could never have been written without—and, indeed, is in large part derivative of—the work of the scholar, curator, and master craftsman Craig Bates, formerly the Curator of Ethnographic Collections at the Yosemite Museum. Bates made available to me his entire, and very substantial, archive; his considerable explorations about this and related subjects, some of which remain unpublished; and the many photographs and slides of these objects that he has collected over the years. His scholarship sets a very high standard, indeed.

Plate 36 of von Langsdorff's engravings (figure 1), which I have already mentioned, depicts two abalone necklaces. One is composed of four rows of beads; from the engraving it is impossible to determine the material from which they are made. Below this band of beads are attached more beads of a similar kind, arranged in pairs to which are attached eighteen pentagonal abalone pendants. The other necklace features a band composed of two rows of beads, beneath which, once again, pairs of beads are arranged to which are attached only seven, much larger pentagonal abalone pendants.

Craig Bates (n.d.), Thomas Blackburn and Travis Hudson (1990), and, according to Bates, Brian Bibby all had assumed that the eighteen-pendant necklace which is in the collection of the Museum of Anthropology and Ethnography in St. Petersburg, Russia, was von Langsdorff's (figure 2). The curators at the museum, according to Bates (personal communication, 2002), confirmed that view. The visual correspondence between the necklace in St. Petersburg and the one in the engraving is striking, and I assume it is the obvious similarity that led these scholars to the same conclusion. For the same reason, von Langsdorff's seven-pendant necklace is considered to match a necklace in the Staatliches Museum für Völkerkunde in Munich (figure 3), notwithstanding a missing pendant in that specimen. Discussions with Bates and my encounter with the necklace in the Adelhausermuseum für Natur und Völkerkunde in Freiburg, discussed later, suggest problems with these identifications, centering on the nature of the beads used in each necklace.

Bates's descriptions of the necklaces in St. Petersburg and Munich, which he identified as von Langsdorff's, make clear that the beads used were clamshell (Bates n.d.: 31–32). The production of disc-shaped beads made of clamshell was an important industry in the territories of speakers of Pomoan and Coast Miwok languages in what are now Marin, Sonoma, Mendocino, and Lake counties. Trade in clamshell beads was also widespread. Making these beads required a great deal of technical skill, which included the boring of holes into the beads using a specialized flint micro-drill (see Hudson 1897, the classic reference concerning the production of clamshell beads; see also Loeb 1926). But apparently these beads were not produced by Ohlonean-speaking peoples, who instead made small, circular beads from olivella shell. In the same prior discussion of old abalone and other kinds of necklaces, Bates (n.d.: 33–34) seemed to imply that the use of clamshell beads would make attributing an object to Ohlonean-speaking peoples less likely, while the use of olivella-shell beads would render that possibility more likely. In either case, soon after contact with Europeans, Native peoples up and down the California coast began using white glass beads instead of beads made out of any kind of shell.

Based on a consideration of the beads used in abalone necklaces, it may be possible that von Langsdorff's necklaces reside elsewhere. Blackburn and Hudson's guide to California Indian objects now in European and other foreign museums mentions an old abalone necklace (figure 4) located in the Adelhausermuseum für Natur und Völkerkunde in Freiburg (Blackburn and Hudson 1990: 104), which, according to Bates, neither he nor Hudson ever saw or considered in their analytic work. I visited the Freiburg collection in 2000 and examined that necklace. The beads used in it are clearly olivella, and the material used to string the beads and the pendants was an older Native-produced vegetable-fiber cord rather than the commercial cotton string Native peoples soon adopted after contact with Europeans. The Freiburg necklace features seventeen pendants rather than the eighteen pendants depicted in both von Langsdorff's engraving and present on the St. Petersburg specimen, although it is very possible that the Freiburg necklace could have lost one pendant over the years. Looking at figure 4, it appears that one extra pendant could have been placed between the first and the second pendants to the viewer's left of the central pendant, if the second pendant were slid up toward the third. However, the abalone pendants on the Freiburg necklace are of graduated size, going from large central pendants to small peripheral ones, whereas the abalone pendants in both the von Langsdorff engraving and the St. Petersburg specimen all look roughly the same size. Nevertheless, on the basis of the use of olivella-shell beads alone, Bates (personal communication 2000) conceded that the Freiburg necklace could just as well be von Langsdorff's. Another factor that could contribute to identifying the Freiburg necklace as von Langsdorff's is the fact that he retired to Freiburg in 1831 and lived there until his death in 1852. The final deposition of the artifacts he collected on his voyages has never been precisely determined (see the introductory essay by Pierce in von Langsdorff 1993: xxii). Unfortunately, the Freiburg museum was unable to provide any supporting acquisition documents that would warrant such an argument.

Similar considerations could bear on the location of the seven-pendant von Langsdorff necklace. A specimen in the Cambridge Museum of Archaeology and Anthropology (figure 5) features olivella-shell beads rather than clamshell beads. The necklace therefore seems to be quite old; however, the beads and the abalone pendants are strung on commercial cotton string, according to Bates, and there are ten rather than seven abalone pendants. Similarities and differences among these necklaces and between each of them and what is displayed in the von Langsdorff engraving create considerable ambiguity and room for multiple interpretations. Moreover, it is worthwhile to entertain the possibility that each item in von Langsdorff's engraving represented an assortment of such items (i.e., abalone necklaces, baskets, etc.) that he encountered with frequency in his dealings with Native peoples on the California coast. In that case, each engraved item is a generic representation of a type of object rather than a specific representation of a particular item. It would be very possible to find among the few surviving abalone necklaces from the early nineteenth century an assortment of materials used, reflecting local preferences and technologies, that all share very similar iconographies and design features.

Other abalone necklaces in the St. Petersburg collection have been linked by Bates, Hudson, and others to Russian visitors who came after the establishment of the Russian settlement at Fort Ross (1812–42), particularly the objects from the I. G. Voznesenski expedition (Bates 1983; Blackburn and Hudson 1990). The Voznesenski necklaces are unmistakably related to the earlier objects, as demonstrated by the very similar rectangular and pentagonal forms of the abalone pendants, the way these pendants are attached to and hang from beaded bands, and the overall composition of the objects. European explorers of note collected other objects that featured abalone ornaments, particularly baskets, during the early post-contact period. These explorers include German Admiral Baron F. P. von Wrangell; objects from his collection are now in Frankfurt. The collection of Ferdinand Deppe now largely resides in Berlin, and the respective collections of the British explorers F. W. Beechey and A. F. Belcher reside in the Pitt Rivers Museum and British Museum.

Continuities and Attributions

Trying to ascertain the present-day location of von Langsdorff's necklaces might be an entirely fruitless project if the purpose in so doing is to determine the cultural groups who made them. Bates pondered the provenance of both the abalone necklaces in von Langsdorff's engravings and of the necklace in St. Petersburg (figure 2), which he and others consider identical with one of the necklaces in the engraving:

> This necklace [MAE 570–23; see figure 2], with its pentagonal pendant of abalone shell, is similar to specimens in some American collections: historic Sierra Miwok examples [LMA 1–71833; see figure 6] are similar . . . archaeologically the form is found in widely scattered locales . . . in the Sacramento Valley, in the San Francisco Bay Area and intervening Delta region, and north to Marysville (Gifford 1947: 23). Because of this widely scattered archaeological distribution, and because such multiple abalone pendants have been reported for the Miwok, Maidu, Patwin, Nisenan, and Pomo peoples, it is impossible to ascribe a specific tribal origin to the piece. (Bates n.d.: 32)

The Sierra Miwok necklace (figure 6) Bates notes is a late-nineteenth-century specimen that now resides in the Phoebe Hearst Museum of Anthropology at the University of California, Berkeley. This necklace's pentagonal pendants and beadwork band cannot help but bring to mind the older necklaces collected by von Langsdorff and other Europeans at the beginning and the middle of the nineteenth century. Edward Gifford's exhaustive comparative monograph, "California Shell Artifacts" (1947), graphically portrays the widespread occurrence of pentagonal abalone pendants over a wide area of southern, central, and northern California during a very long period, stretching back at least four thousand years.

The implications of the broad geographic and temporal distribution of such iconography in abalone shell with regard to identifying the cultural origin of these objects is further complicated by the tribal names and boundaries that Euro-American explorers, administrators, and, ultimately, anthropologists have used to refer to Native Californian peoples. The making of ethnic monikers, or ethnonyms, in Native America is in general a politically saturated practice (see Castañeda 1996 for the case of the Mayans of Guatemala), wholly linked to European and Euro-American observations and perceptions of the critical importance of place, dress, and language among Native American others. Anthropologists' maps of California Native peoples, from Kroeber's time and since then, draw lines around linguistic groupings. Such maps are ahistorical in that, while the boundaries reflect only the distribution of languages spoken at a particular point in time when the anthropologist was conducting fieldwork, they have been treated as demarcating actual tribal territories both at the time of contact with Europeans and since. This welter of ethnic naming and boundary making by anthropologists, I have argued, has played an important role in federal Indian policy (Field and Muwekma Ohlone Tribe 2003) and has necessarily been internalized by the Native people who are the objects of such policies and of the anthropological knowledge deployed about them. I have a sneaking suspicion that the ethnolinguistic mapping of Native California by early-twentieth-century anthropologists, and the making of these multicolored maps demarcating territories of myriad named groups, each with their own specific ethnonym, more than anything else reflects the world those anthropologists lived in. When I see those maps, I am reminded of the post–World War One reconfiguration of Europe—the break-up of the Ottoman, Austro-Hungarian, and Prussian empires into new, independent ethnic nations in which language, nationality, ethnicity, and ultimately race all became coterminous. It would be another twist of reality if California Native peoples must live in the shadow of yet another European obsession with race and identity.

The case of the San Francisco Bay Area Native peoples is quite to the point in these respects. The Spaniards called the peoples of the region *costeños*, which means simply "coastal dwellers." Apparently misheard and then mispronounced by early Anglo settlers as "*costanos*," anthropologists transformed the term once again to the absurd "Costanoan," perhaps believing this sounded "more scientific." The term "Costanoan" was then applied to the peoples who had been interned in the three missions around the Bay Area (Dolores, Santa Clara, and San Jose), as well as to the peoples similarly incarcerated at missions just to the south of the Bay Area (Santa Cruz and San Carlos Borromeo de Rio Carmelo, on the coast, and San Juan Bautista, inland) whom linguistic anthropologists identified as speaking related, although mutually unintelligible, languages in the Penutian family. In addition to speaking related languages, these peoples were loosely affiliated with each other, and with other neighboring peoples who spoke much more distantly related or completely unrelated languages, through intermarriage, trade, and annual ceremonial cycles long before their internment in the missions. Nevertheless, the application of the term "Costanoan" to disparate peoples on the basis of European perceptions of geography and language obscures how these peoples understood and named their identities before and at the time of contact.

"Ohlone" refers to the same Native groups as "Costanoan," all with similar post-contact histories shaped by the demographic collapse caused by missionization and the subsequent regrouping during the Mexican period. In the East Bay and South Bay, Native peoples have referred to themselves as "Ohlones" for at least a century, and in the East Bay Ohlone communities, the term "Muwekma" was also used into the 1930s (Leventhal et al. 1994). The anthropologist C. Hart Merriam was the first to use the expression "Ohlonean" languages in the early decades of the twentieth century, which Richard Levy (1978) elaborated into the widely accepted seven-branch Ohlonean language tree. The term "Ohlone" may have originated from "Oljon" or "Olchon," a village that was located on the coast of modern San Mateo County. Many versions of this term can be found in the records of Bay Area missions, as well as in the journals and other texts of Euro-American visitors to the region starting in the 1820s. Since the early twentieth century, the Muwekma Tribe's ancestors have described themselves as "Ohlone" and "Ohlonean" in their official dealings with the BIA/BAR. Even though the derivation of the ethnonym "Ohlone" originates in the colonial history that reshaped identities and boundaries in the Bay Area, I am not alone in considering the use of the term "Ohlone" a form of resistance to the absurdity of "Costanoan" (see Margolin 1978).

The argument I have been making in no way proposes either an essentialism—the idea that the ancestors of today's Muwekma had a "real" name and identity that Europeans and Euro-Americans simply destroyed—or a romantic antiquarian nostalgia for a pristine Ohlone past. All cultural identities change, transform, and mutate over time, and all cultural identities are historically constructed. Yet in the case of California Native peoples, such as the Ohlones, the two hands of anthropological practice and federal policy working together greatly complicate attempts to understand pre-contact identities. In that light, and given the widespread use of abalone-shell iconography, the identities of those who created the necklaces in von Langsdorff's engraving become ever more elusive.

But let us entertain another possibility based on Bates's analysis and the historical time depth provided by Gifford—that is, that the existence of shared materials, iconographies, and symbols by many peoples across a wide area of what is now California resonates with other such sharings across the continent. Pottery techniques, materials, and iconographies, not to mention architectural forms and design, have historically been shared, and are still shared, among peoples who speak vastly different languages, such as the peoples who are known collectively as "the Pueblos." A broadly configured material culture related to hunting and processing buffalo was historically shared among the "Plains Indians," a heterogeneous mix of peoples who spoke many different languages. One could cite other relevant examples, such as "Pacific Northwest art" and, closer at hand in California, categories of material culture such as "Pomo basketry," across linguistic and geographic boundaries. The point is that these categories of shared culture, as elucidated by anthropologists, federal and state governments, popular media, and, indeed, Native peoples themselves, are not considered inimical to the tribal sovereignty of the many particular peoples who find themselves classified under each different category, such as "Pueblo" or "Plains." There are in each case specific histories of treaty-making and conflict that shape the acknowledgment status of each tribe, such that these shared artistic and material heritages do not affect or hinge on that status. The need for or claim to a particular patrimony, such as the von Langsdorff necklaces, becomes especially important for unacknowledged tribes, such as the Muwekma Ohlone, on whom the onus of showing a continuous and specific history is laid to obtain official status. I came to that realization after talking to friends among the Gay Head Wampanoag (Massachusetts), whose tribe had achieved federal recognition at the same time its cousins at Mashpee had not. Our conversations focused on the role the Gay Headers' rich material culture and better-documented oral traditions had played in their successful petition. But the ways these factors play into federal acknowledgment are hardly a secret in Indian country.

If the issue of continuous patrimony is put into the context of broadly shared material cultures across the continent, it might be possible to understand sovereignty as the necessary condition for substantiating heritage and patrimony rather than burdening unacknowledged tribes with identifying a patrimony as a way of legitimating their history, and thus their case for sovereignty. In this case, ruptures in the continuity of material culture, and the loss of knowledge about cultural patrimony such as those I have discussed with respect to old abalone necklaces, are not threatening. Rather, they highlight the opportunities for research and interpretation recognized status would afford a people such as the Muwekma Ohlone. To argue this point in the face of BAR/BIA regulations and review processes clearly would be an uphill battle. It would be better to confront these issues directly, however, rather than let the silences undermine acknowledgment cases, as I believe they have done, at least, with the Muwekma and other unrecognized tribes in California.

But such opportunities themselves await a discussion of other problems that attend the interpretation of objects made by Native peoples.

Animation, Sentience, Agency

An additional complicating factor to this story became clear to me as I looked at more and more abalone necklaces and talked about them with Native people up and down the California coast. About this "wrinkle" I cannot write in any sort of authoritative way. Although I can perceive that profound discontinuities between Native and non-Native views of and beliefs about objects such as abalone necklaces exist, about the former I do not and cannot have an insider view.

My emphasis on the primacy of the Native view in these matters derives from my own grappling not only with the meanings of Native sovereignty over representation (see Field 2003), but also with the recognition of the inadequacy of many scholarly approaches to sacred objects and places and their tendency to silence Native interpretations. The growing field of ethnoaesthetics offers interpretation of objects that does not silence Native voices. Eliciting and elaborating Native standards of craftsmanship, beauty, proportionality, symmetry, and utility (among other qualitative measures), as Lila O'Neale (1932) first demonstrated among Native groups in Northern California, has transformed anthropological approaches to and understanding of non-Western aesthetics. Mari Lyn Salvador (1997) and Carol Hendrickson (1995) provide excellent recent examples of ethnoaesthetic work among the Kuna of Panama and Kakchikel communities in Guatemala, respectively, that resulted from collaborative research projects between anthropologists and Native artists. Ainu intellectuals and leaders contributed their own texts to the final volume edited by William Fitzhugh and Chisato Dubreuil (1999). Yet for all the strengths and insights of ethnoaesthetic work, the pot I am stirring here is not entirely composed of aesthetic ingredients, and it is important to deploy an eclectic approach. From the materialist angle, Marxist approaches to material culture often hinge on the concept of "the fetishism of commodities." This concept has generally been used in a reductionist, even dismissive, manner that does not help to illuminate Native concepts about sacred objects. By contrast, Jean-Paul Sartre's notion of "interanimation" explains that when individuals and their social groups focus emotional and symbolic energy on material objects, the objects may in turn come to be seen not only as repositories of that energy but also as capable of reflecting that energy back upon and to human beings. Sherry Ortner (1979: 96, 98) calls such objects "summarizing symbols" in that they are clustered, condensed, and saturated with affective meaning and "synthesize or 'collapse' complex experience, and relate the respondent to the grounds of the system of the whole."

The elegance of such approaches notwithstanding, Keith Basso's work with sacred places has called for anthropologists and others "to come to grips with the indigenous forms" through which sacred objects or places are understood and experienced and the "shared symbolic vehicles" that shape Native understanding of objects and places and "facilitate [their] communication" (Basso 1996: 109). Basso appears doubtful that anthropologists have had much success in that endeavor heretofore. Likewise, Victor Turner (1982: 18) has expressed a pessimism about non-Natives' attempts to analyze Native concepts of place and object, observing that sacred objects can be "impenetrable to total rational understanding," no matter how appealing ideas such as "interanimation" and "summarizing symbols" may be for academic minds. Nevertheless, anthropological and other scholarly fascination with Native concepts of object and place has not diminished. In that light it is impossible to overestimate the allure for non-Native scholars of newer approaches, which appear to determine once and for all that Native symbolic systems can be understood as naturalizations of social constructions. The disjuncture between Native and non-Native scholarly worldviews has been eloquently summarized by the Lakota scholar Craig Howe (personal communication 2003), who asks: In the absence of human beings, would sacred objects (or places) have power? Howe argues that the non-Native response would inevitably be "no." He adds that the Native response, by contrast, would be "potentially."

In the case of Native Californian regalia, the people with whom I have worked very much insist that the objects called "regalia" do much more than reflect and voice the intentions and emotions of their human animators. Regalia are themselves beings for California Indian people, and what is more, they are sentient beings with agency and destinies linked to yet distinct from the humans with whom they cohabitate. The interviews with Bradley Marshall and Merv George Sr. in chapter 5 offer authoritative, as well as eloquent, representations of Native views on this subject. As a result of specific interactions, I gained some insight into this issue; these experiences derive from ongoing conversations with Florence Silva, the person on whom chapter 3 focuses, about two abalone necklaces.

The first necklace belonged to John Boston, Florence Silva's grandfather, and is described and depicted in Cora Du Bois's *The 1870 Ghost Dance* (1939; see figure 7). This icon assumed a central role in the Dreamer religion (Bole Maru) rituals Boston practiced, particularly the Abalone Dance, and its fate has been of some concern to many people. I have heard from several individuals from other Pomo rancherias that Boston's necklace was buried with him, which Florence denies. Nevertheless, all concerned agree that the power of this necklace, its very being, was intricately interwoven with John Boston himself. Once he died, no one else could touch, much less use the power of, his necklace, and its role in the Dreamer religion ended. This was the case for all regalia used by the followers of the Dreamer religion. An individual item of regalia belonged to only one person—the person who dreamed that item. Yet, as tied to its dreamer as each piece of regalia was, these icons also were alive and sentient.

Between visits to Florence, and as I tried to balance my own fetishization of Boston's necklace with an inability to understand its nature (discussed in greater detail in chapter 3), I encountered another abalone necklace in the ethnographic collection at the University of California, Davis (figure 8). This extremely beautiful necklace, collected by the early-twentieth-century anthropologist C. Hart Merriam, was composed of multiple rectangular and drop-shaped abalone pendants, suspended from a clamshell-bead band. Because of its beauty, I suspected that it might have been used by a dreamer as regalia. I was able to locate where it had been made, and by whom.[7] Joe Miller, a Pomo man who lived in Lake County in a famous village named Shékum (also spelled "Cigom" or "Shigom"; see McLendon 1998) on the northeastern shore of Clear Lake, had made the necklace. My partner Gia Scarpetta photographed Miller's necklace, and we showed prints to Florence when we visited her next.

Florence unambiguously told me that Joe Miller's necklace could not have been a "spirit necklace" used, or made, or dreamed by a dreamer. Instead, she called it a "personal necklace," used in dances but never as a dream necklace. Miller's necklace was an ornament, not regalia: not a being. Florence told me that she was completely sure because Miller's necklace did not have either a star or a cross in its overall design.

I had been deceived by the beauty of Miller's necklace. Clearly, I had no way to distinguish necklaces that were regalia—sentient beings inextricable from the dreamer who owned them—from those that were "only" beautiful jewelry. The importance of the distinction was impossible to exaggerate, Florence had made clear. As I remembered the old necklaces collected by von Langsdorff and other early European explorers of the San Francisco Bay Area, I wondered which were regalia and which ornaments, and how could anyone know?

Sherrie Smith-Ferri, an anthropologist, director of the Grace Hudson Museum in Ukiah, and a Dry Lake Pomo, has observed that contemporary Native people transmit and relate unevenly to different layers of their historical past (Smith-Ferri, personal communication 2003). To paraphrase her words: In discussing the ritual and artistic traditions of the past, you may be able to reach only the proximate last layer in time, not two or three epochs before that. She offers the example of the relationship between present-day Pomo peoples and the Dreamer religion and that between contemporary Pomos and the religion that was extant at the time of contact and preceded the Dreamers. She points out that the Dreamer religion, with its roots in the Ghost Dance phenomenon of the 1870s described by Du Bois (1939), is today considered "traditional" by Pomo peoples. Yet the Dreamer religion itself differed vastly from the older religion and represented a radical intervention spurred on by the epidemics and other demographic catastrophes that smashed the foundations of the older religion. Smith-Ferri proposes that it is possible to maintain and strengthen a dialogue between present-day people and the legacies of the classic Dreamer period, during which John Boston worked at Point Arena and Annie Jarvis preached at Kashaya. Hence, Florence's discourse on the necklaces, as well as much of the ongoing Dreamer religion activity at many Pomo rancherias, are possible. But such a dialogue is not possible—or, at least, poses significant difficulties—with respect to the beliefs and practices of the older religion that preceded the Dreamers. The upshot of Smith-Ferri's observations, I think, is that Native knowledge systems, like all epistemologies, embody specific historicities. Therefore, one must pose historically plausible rather than impossible questions to material culture.

In that vein, one cannot argue that the relationship between contemporary Ohlones and the old necklaces such as the ones von Langsdorff collected permits questions about cultural continuity. That continuity has been severed in multiple ways. By contrast, contemporary Muwekma can, and do, maintain and explore the ethnographic work of John P. Harrington (1931) and the less extensive, yet still important, ethnographic work of other anthropologists of the early twentieth century. That ethnohistoric record shows that the immediate ancestors of the Muwekma were also exposed to and involved in the Dreamer religion that was so important northward into Pomo country and eastward toward the lands of Maidu- and Miwok-speaking peoples. Gifford wrote that, at the Sierra and Plains Miwok rancherias where he worked in the mid-1920s, "there appeared . . . teachers of dances who came from the west" (Gifford 1926: 400). Those teachers included Yoktco, a Maidu; Sigelizu, a Plains Miwok; and a Costanoan (Ohlone) man named Tciplitcu who preached among the Plains Miwok. Reestablishing the connection between contemporary Muwekma and the history of the Dreamer religion, dreamers such as Tciplitcu, and the regalia that plays such an important role in that religion can be facilitated by further ethnohistoric research. But even more important to achieving such a connection are decisions contemporary Muwekma must make regarding their "reachable heritage" and its material culture. Those decisions bring the discussion back around to the issue of sovereignty.

Recent examples of the repatriation of objects considered cultural patrimony, or sacred regalia, from museum collections emphasize that repatriation is a central arena in which Native peoples are exercising sovereignty. The repatriation of sacred objects in recent years has included the return of the Omaha Sacred Pole documented by Robin Ridington and Dennis Hastings (1997) and the retrieval of many effigies of the Zuni War Gods from multiple museums and collectors, as described by William Merrill and colleagues (1993), both of which I have discussed elsewhere (see Field 2004). Important differences between the two cases should not be overlooked. The Zuni language and culture, for example, have been far less negatively impacted than is the general case among Native groups. The repatriation of the many War God effigies from museum collections enabled the Zuni to restore these objects to their proper purpose within the context of living, ongoing religious practices. By contrast, the restoration of the Omaha Sacred Pole itself constituted a central act of reaffirming and reanimating Omaha religious practices that had been eroded and corroded under the impact of reservation life and BIA policies. The differences between these two cases underscore that sovereign control over cultural patrimony and sacred objects, while made possible by the same Native American Graves Protection and Repatriation Act (NAGPRA) legislation, responds to different histories and accomplishes different goals for each Native people.

In a resonant case, the Ngati Whakaue Maori tribe repatriated a sacred *taonga* (ancestral object), a being named Pukaki, from the Auckland Museum in New Zealand. This outcome both resulted from and fueled processes of contemporary cultural revitalization (see Tapsell 2000). The significance of all of these cases for the Ohlone and other unrecognized tribes is that the process of reanimating the sacred can come only after sovereignty is reestablished.

Conclusion

While the makers of the von Langsdorff necklaces were quite likely speakers of Ohlonean languages from the greater Bay Area, we cannot know with any certainty which groups made the necklaces, how those groups self-identified, or what the necklaces meant to them. The relationship, or dialogue, between the contemporary Muwekma and these old necklaces speaks to the loss rather than the active continuity of cultural patrimony. The possibly sentient nature of the von Langsdorff necklaces is irretrievable. But acknowledging the broadly shared material culture and historical relationships among Native peoples of California, and addressing the inadequacies of much interpretive work about the meaning and significance of sacred objects, establishes the foundations for research, epistemology, and knowledge based within Native communities.

The struggle for federal recognition for unacknowledged peoples is therefore not simply a matter of securing official status from the U.S. government. It is also a struggle against more than two centuries of cultural dismemberment. It is an affirmation of dialogue in the face of erasure, and while that affirmation can never reproduce or resuscitate the living dialogue with cultural patrimony, it hints at other possibilities. While only Muwekma tribal members and their leaders can ultimately determine their relationship with their historical material culture, I would argue that there is sufficient precedent in the recent history of the Muwekma Ohlone Tribe to imagine the direction of that relationship. The excavation at the Three Wolves site comes to mind. The oldest burials date to circa 2,000 years B.P., and no one could pretend that cultural continuity between these ancient people and their contemporary descendants was obvious (see Field and Leventhal 2003) Nevertheless, the Muwekma elders and young people who conducted the excavation accepted responsibility for these remains in a profoundly spiritual and practical affirmation of their history, of the work of their ancestors, even though their relationships to that work have been severed. In the work of interpreting these remains, the tribe has also been able to make sure they are safe.

Reading over this chapter, Rosemary Cambra commented that my anxieties about the Muwekma Ohlones' cultural patrimony should be balanced by mentioning the processes of cultural renewal that are currently flowering. She emphasized the importance of the tribe's mounting efforts to bring its language, Chochenyo, back to life by establishing a circle of speakers. With specific reference to the old abalone necklaces, she observes that the tribe is reinventing the institution of the *capitán*, a respected elderly authority figure, which has not existed since the 1920s. Hank Alvarez is to be nominated for this position by the Tribal Council. The investiture of the new capitán, if it does occur, will be performed when Hank dons an abalone necklace, modeled after the old ones collected by von Langsdorff and others in the early 1800s. This re-establishment of "summarizing symbols" constitutes a potent reclamation of the social relations underlying Ohlone material culture and patrimony.

Taking charge of cultural patrimony in this way will increasingly characterize the Muwekmas' relationship to aspects of their history. This dynamic underscores two characteristics of Muwekma Ohlone identity that I have observed since I first began working with the tribe. First, absence and loss are as much a real part of heritage for the Muwekma Ohlone as presence and continuity, and only by understanding the former can the latter manifest. Second, the process of rediscovering their histories and patrimonies as part of the federal acknowledgment petition has been also the process of bringing into focus what they have become and are now. The means to conduct the struggle have been, and continue to be, identical to the goal: acknowledgment.

This chapter shows simultaneously that the Ohlone must establish their recognized status by reclaiming their cultural identity and that abalone is weaving itself into the making of this new–old Ohlone tribe. In the next chapter, the persistence of the northwest California story of Abalone Woman finds a changing new role for a story among a people, the Wiyot, that genocidal campaigns nearly extinguished. Abalone necklaces and abalone narratives are certainly both the products of the human imagination, but in chapter 2, the memory of a living narrative offers building blocks for a contemporary people's attempts to make sense of past trauma in a way the Ohlones' reclamation of displaced, historically ruptured abalone necklaces may do only at a future date.

1. Plate 36 from Georg Heinrich von Langsdorff's *Remarks and Observations on a Voyage around the World from 1803 to 1807*, vol. 1 (Kingston, Ont.: Limestone Press, 1993). The two abalone necklaces in the engraving were the focus of investigative work in several European museums.

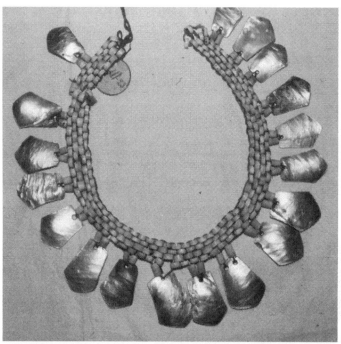

2. An abalone necklace on exhibit at the Museum of Anthropology and Ethnography in St. Petersburg, Russia (cat. no. MAE 570–23). This necklace is potentially one of the two depicted in the von Langsdorff engraving. Photograph by Brian Bibby; reproduced with permission.

3. At the Staatliches Museum für Völkerkunde in Munich is an abalone necklace (cat. no. 213) that more than likely is one of the two necklaces depicted in the von Langsdorff engraving. Courtesy Staatliches Museum für Völkerkunde; photograph by Gia Scarpetta.

4. An abalone necklace now in the collection of the Adelhausermuseum für Natur und Völkerkunde in Freiburg, Germany (cat. no. III-30), could be the necklace in the von Langsdorff engraving, rather than the St. Petersburg arti-fact, as previously supposed. Collection of Adelhausermuseum für Natur und Völkerkunde; photograph by Gia Scarpetta.

5. An abalone necklace in the Cambridge Museum of Archaeology and Anthropology in Cambridge (cat no. 1905.30) offers another perspective on the necklaces depicted in von Langsdorff's engraving. Courtesy of the Santa Barbara Museum of Natural History; photograph by Travis Hudson.

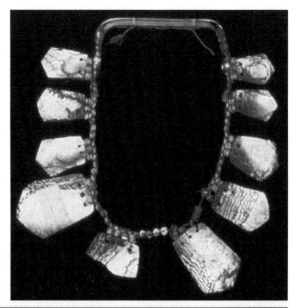

6. A historic nineteenth-century Sierra Miwok abalone necklace, curated in the Phoebe Apperson Hearst Museum of Anthropology, Berkeley, California (cat. no. LMA 1–71833). Courtesy of the Phoebe Apperson Hearst Museum of Anthropology and the Regents of the University of California; photograph by Gia Scarpetta.

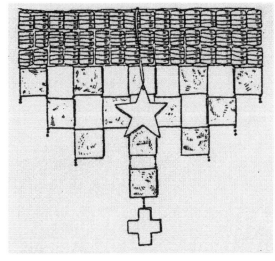

7. John Boston's pectoral, depicted in Cora Du Bois, *The 1870 Ghost Dance* (1939), is an essential piece of regalia in the rituals of the Dreamer (Bole Maru) religion.

8. Joe Miller's necklace in the C. Hart Merriam Ethnographic Collection, Department of Anthropology Museum, Davis, California (cat. no. CHM-1509). Courtesy of the University of California, Davis; photograph by Gia Scarpetta.

2.

Abalone Woman Attends
the Wiyot Reawakening

The far northwest of California, in modern-day Humboldt and Del Norte counties, is home to a number of tribes with perhaps the most vibrant cultural systems in the state. Even in a state distinguished by extraordinary linguistic diversity, northwestern California is remarkable: Wiyot and Yurok are Algonquian languages; Tolowa and Hupa are Athabaskan; Karuk and Shasta are Hokan. Yet these peoples, speaking languages as unlike as Zulu, Chinese, and Armenian, share many cultural practices, among them a cycle of dance rituals and life cycle–ceremonies, with accompanying narratives, that together compose what is often referred to (by both Natives and anthropologists) as the World Renewal religion. World Renewal, as Merv George Jr., organizer of the dances among the Hupa explains later in this volume, brings the animal and human worlds back into harmony, assuring that there will be enough food to eat during the year to come and that individuals' behavior will promote the well-being of the entire community. The peoples of northwestern California have also historically shared and continue to share basket-weaving techniques and styles, subsistence technologies and diets, settlement patterns, and domicile architecture. The fate of each people during the periods of white settlement, early statehood and the Gold Rush, and the military occupation of Indian lands diverged, however. The Hupa ended up with the largest reservation in the state; the Yurok, with a long narrow reservation following the path of the Klamath

River that was formally titled to them only in the late 1980s; the Karuk, with only a few small parcels. The Wiyot also have a small reservation at Table Bluff south of the modern city of Arcata, a very tiny remaining portion of their old aboriginal territory that once spread around the shores of Humboldt Bay. But the Wiyot population was punished far more severely during the period of early statehood than was the population of the neighboring tribes.

The Gold Rush, the very embodiment of Anglo-American territorial expansion in the name of natural-resource exploitation, began in 1849, not long after the territories that became California and many other Western states were expropriated from the Mexican Republic. For three decades, writes Jack Norton, "every conceivable and inhuman act that could be invented by the white intruders rained down upon the tribes of Northern California" (Norton 1979: 33). The Indian Island Massacre occurred in 1860, and more than sixty and likely as many as two hundred Wiyot men, women, and children were killed by six white men, "known to be landowners and businessmen" from the nearby city of Eureka (Kowinski 2004: D1). The Wiyot village of Tuluwat, exterminated and ultimately erased by the massacre, had stretched over a large area of what became known as Indian Island, located in Humboldt Bay. The Wiyot conducted World Renewal ceremonies at central villages such as Tuluwat, and the massacre was perpetrated while a large number of Wiyots had congregated at the village for their ritual dances. In the years following the massacre, the site was covered over by a shipyard. By the mid-twentieth century, it had become desolate, trash-strewn, and forgotten, except by the descendants of the survivors. Since the time of the massacre, the Wiyot people have not enacted the ceremonies of World Renewal. Much of the remnant population of Wiyot who survived the massacre, and the ravages of alcoholism and endemic poverty that followed, settled at the Table Bluff rancheria.

Under the leadership of Cheryl Seidner and her sister Leona Wilkinson, whose great-grandfather survived the massacre, the Wiyot of the late twentieth century have conducted a determined campaign to repurchase land on the island, including the site of the massacre, and heal the psychic traumas caused by their near-genocide through a cultural renaissance. The Wiyots purchased and rehabilitated just an acre and a half of the island in 2000, having raised funds through the Wiyot Sacred

Site Fund. In 2004, the Eureka City Council voted to return forty acres of Indian Island to the Wiyots, "the only city on California to return a sacred site to a native people" (Vogel 2004).

Cheryl, tribal chair, and Leona Wilkinson, who heads the tribe's Culture Committee, were willing to discuss the story of Abalone Woman, although initially they were unsure of what I was looking for. I asked them what the story meant to contemporary Wiyot, and they spent many hours with me discussing Wiyot history and culture and how they planned to make the island once again the center of Wiyot ceremony. Neither of them is a stranger to collaborative work with non-Wiyots. They have been promoting public remembrance of the massacre among the wider community in Eureka and Arcata for over a decade and, through extensive interviews with Ron Johnson, contributed to the important volume *Her Mind Made Up: Weaving Caps the Indian Way* (Johnson and Marks 1997). Cheryl and Leona have assumed very public profiles in pursuit of healing and remembrance, which also means that their feelings about the genocidal experiences of their people and their consciousness of the need to represent that suffering to the non-Wiyot world remain close to the surface. Their energy for their struggle is matched by sadness and realism, even as their campaign to heal historical wrongs garners success.

The Wiyot telling of the story of Abalone Woman is well known in both anthropological and Native circles in California. In discussions with both women, it became clear that they consider the story of Abalone Woman an important part of their recorded heritage, the significance of which is growing as the Wiyot repair longstanding historical traumas. What follows is a translation of the story of Abalone Woman, as told in the 1950s by Della Prince, Cheryl's and Leona's relative through marriage. The story was recorded and translated by the linguist Karl Teeter (Teeter and Nichols 1993; Teeter 1964). In response to my queries about Abalone Woman's meaning for contemporary Wiyot people, Cheryl wrote three installments of a prose-poem reflection on Hiwat (Abalone Woman), Wiyot history, and her own personal struggles and milestones over the course of our three-year discussion. The Wiyot version of the story features a violent relationship between Abalone Woman and her husband, who in this telling is referred to as Dentalium. Whether that characteristic violence reflects post-genocide trauma or actually predates the massacre cannot be determined. In any event, the violence and sadness of the Wiyot telling speak to Cheryl's sensibilities. Her running poem, which follows Teeter's translation, interprets Abalone Woman as a tragic figure, a symbol "of her people."

Abalone Woman : The Wiyot Story

TEXTUALIZED AND TRANSLATED BY KARL TEETER

I'm going to start to imitate Abalone. I'll tell you how it was. Abalone was a young woman. The young woman was in the south. In the north, on the other hand, was a young man. He was Dentalium. It never got dark, that's how it looked in the north, [because of] his standing outside. In the south also that's how it looked; that woman was the one who looked so nice. She didn't know what it was that looked that way. Then she, the woman, started out north. She carried a pack basket. She stuck in cooking sticks, on the pack basket. She had just about arrived there, to the place where she was going. The old man was home. That one, too, the woman, his mother [was home]. But the young man wasn't there. The next morning, he looked again to the south in vain, not seeing any more there what he used to see. The next morning, he looked again to the south in vain, not seeing any more there what he used to see. She, on the other hand, that young woman, knew it; she thought, "I guess I've arrived there, where I used to see it, that young man, the one who goes and stands outside." He goes out again in vain, that young man, he looks to the south again in vain, he doesn't see it there any more. He won't talk to her. He won't talk to her, that young woman. That old man, he tells him, "But won't you talk to her; that must be the one who came from the south before, the young woman. Not seeing any more what showed before, she must be the one." No, he doesn't talk to her. He keeps standing outside again in vain, he keeps looking again in vain. I don't know how long she stayed, perhaps one month. She told them, those old folks, "I'm going to start back again, to the south." In the morning she went out, she went out to bathe herself. She fixed her hair nicely. She started her pack basket nicely. The former cooking sticks were no longer, no longer cooking sticks; a woodpecker headdress is standing up there, where she stuck in what formerly appeared to be cooking sticks. After that the young man spoke to her, telling her, "You're not going back." She said, "I've stayed long enough, and I'm going back right now. I'm going to start back. " She starts to go back, the old people too think in vain, "She's going back." She starts to go. He starts to follow her, he starts to follow behind her. Crescent City, they started from there. Beyond Trinidad Bay he overtook her from behind. He caught hold of her there from behind. She said, "I'm not going back, I'm going to keep right on going this way." He caught hold of her from behind. He began to abuse her, her began to abuse her, she was abused with a knife, on the back he finally cut strips all over, on her back. That's the reason why now, later on, it looks like blood, abalone [like] blood, that's how it looks. That's the reason why now abalone is [plentiful] at Trinidad Bay, [because] that young woman stays there. He went back from there, that young man.

Abalone Woman

CHERYL SEIDNER, 2002–2003

I.

Is it possible?

Is it time?

Our story?

Through my eyes, my heart, my soul?

Can it be done?

Flying high over the U.S. thinking of what to write or how to write it . . .
    our story.

The written word only came to us within the last one hundred and 50
    years.

Not even then.

Our story was verbal, handed down from an elder of the family.

Told as a lesson to be learned, a purpose for our existence.

These stories are of our beginnings, how things came to be.

One such story is of Abalone Woman a beautiful woman of Wiyot
    Country.

One can only imagine that she was loved by her family, who also knew
    the ways and laws of the people.

A man from the North came and fell in love with her and she with him.

He asked her father to marry them and it happened.

He treated her well, lovingly.

He made his home with her in Wiyot Country.

He soon became homesick or longing for his country. One day they said goodbye to her family. He wanted her to meet his people, to learn to love his family as he had hers.

She was embraced with kindness; however, that did not last. Just within days, she was treated with disrespect, treated as a common servant. Her husband was the worst.

He beat her as well.

Abalone Woman asked to visit her family, she too was homesick. The answer was no. Finally one day she ran away. Abalone Woman's family embraced her and welcomed her home. She told them of their cruelty toward her.

They cared for her, restored her health and beauty.

Weeks had gone by, maybe months.

Then one day Abalone Woman's husband came. He apologized for how he treated her and for his family.

He stayed a long time. He treated her very well; again he was lonesome for his home.

He convinced Abalone Woman to go with him. Her family agreed, that she should go, that was her place as his wife. He promised that he would take great care of her.

Then they were gone again, he and his family treated her badly.

Again, she asked to go home and again the answer was no.

She ran away, this time he came after her.

He caught up with her at what was called Patrick's Point today.

She was crying as she walked along the shore, and her teardrops became the mussels. As she walked she prayed to the creator (above old man), that if she were to die, allow her death to be for the good of her people.

Soon her husband was upon her. He slashed her back then cut her up in pieces and threw her into the ocean.

Today when you see an abalone shell the back is red depicting the slash marks on her back.

II.

On another flight away up above California, 29,000 feet
Going to see some Indians
How can one think to write, flying so high, about one's culture.
I always dreamed I could fly when I was a kid . . .

Culture? What is it that which identifies who we are as a tribe?

From another's thoughts and perspective

Is that perspective a dangerous one or just one's memories formed into a culture?

I spent time with grandma Hazel at her knee as a young adult gleaning from her knowledge of the Wiyot people.

Gleaning from her wisdom of life.

My mother Loreta was another I spent time listening to. What she had to offer Her tribe through knowledge and memories.

She shared with me the Indian Island story and the massacre. She also shared about Hiwat, Abalone Woman.

This story was given to her by her father to pass on, not to be forgotten.

How does this story bring culture to the forefront of our lives today?

Culture is what we/you make it.

Sometimes new traditions happen.

Living each day in memory of the past.

Writing on a United Airline 29,000 feet over California on a United napkin.

Remembering my elders past in my daily life.

Dreaming the dreams of days passed, longing to know what they were really like.

Knowing it was a hard, but with laughter and good humor to last.

How does culture reflect on today?

It does indeed reflect upon our future.

It does begin to tell who we are.

So that we may emulate it now.

Only if we choose to experience it!

Only if we see the beauty of Hiwat and what she has to offer her people, the Wiyot.

III.

Feet planted firmly on Wiyot soil, surveying the small reservation, a remnant of what once was. Determined to seek culture, asleep, resting from Manifest Destiny, assimilation and termination. And something new and more sinister, paper bullets (genocide).

Awakening a sleeping culture takes its entire people. Why? If not, then what makes us stand out from all the others? Why have a tribe at all?

I believe the Creator had a purpose to have made each different and distinct. Capturing the essences of ourselves will be difficult. Our DNA cries: here we are. Yet no one sees the difference. Our DNA says English is our second language; however, it has been beaten into us, until submission. Our DNA quietly shouts that I am here, wake me. I'll show you the way. I've been there, let me gently guide your hand, your tongue, your dreams.

Let me show you the vision of your ancestors. Let me show you how to use modern technology to advance who we have become.

Hiwat, the beautiful Abalone Woman, surveys her people the Wiyot and says, "Here I am." "I am here, not lost to the ages. Here in your dreams ready to be awakened."

She is ready if you are ready to receive her vision. Are you up for the journey?

As I reflect upon my travels, mainly to Phoenix and to Oaxaca, Mexico, I begin to better understand what went before me, what is happening now, and what the possibilities are. I see the blending of cultures and am becoming more aware of the differences between cultures locally, nationally, and globally.

Oaxaca and Phoenix were a catalyst for me. Oaxaca showed me the beauty and richness of its culture, where the tribes in Phoenix showed me their blending of many cultures.

I sang my "Coming Home" song to Oaxacan students. The song depicts the Wiyot struggling to come home, trying to reestablish their culture, their very existence. Their culture, in Oaxaca, is established, without having to rediscover itself. They are already home within their aboriginal territory. The Wiyot are fortunate we are within our aboriginal territory as well. However, we are having to make discovery anew.

Are you ready to take that step? Are you ready to re-establish what was once rich and flourishing? This means we will need to work even harder.

What makes us different from the others is our once rich culture. If we do not have that, then assimilation has overtaken us and we have become that society we have been struggling against.

We cannot depend on Congress or others to bring the Wiyot culture or a remnant of it back. Congress once banned us from being Wiyot! It is up to us. Not 10 percent but 100 percent of all our efforts.

Someone asked what I could do for the Wiyot tribe. I ask you, "What will you do for your tribe?"

Some have already given their all, others have only recently begun in earnest. Where are you?

Hiwat is surveying the Wiyot countryside. Are you ready to fulfill the vision? Let it not be a fitful dream.

Further Thoughts

The Wiyot struggle to regain control of Indian Island and to seek public healing for the genocide they endured is not only a local story. It was also covered by the San Francisco newspapers and mentioned briefly in national media. The far more subtle ways the Wiyot community is (and sometimes is not) drawing together and remembering its history are much more opaque to non-Wiyot. There is an important milestone that the Wiyot are approaching in their future: the celebration of the World Renewal ceremonies. Once Wiyot people feel secure and knowledgeable enough to again begin conducting World Renewal ceremonies at the site of their ancient village, they will reestablish relationships with the regalia for these rituals, much of which incorporates the use of abalone. More tribal members will familiarize themselves with the ethnographic literature anthropologists wrote during the early and mid-twentieth century, encountering the texts and translations of the story of Abalone Woman. The anthropologists may not have intended their work to be used decades later for the purposes of tribal revitalization, but this is not infrequently the fate of much of the so-called salvage work anthropologists did in Native North America. In the Wiyot future, I would argue, Abalone Woman will live on in both text and telling.

II

The "Meaning" of Abalone

TWO DIFFERENT ABALONE PROJECTS

Early intuitions and questions exert an important influence over the course of an anthropological field project. I would argue therefore that the extent to which collaborative forms of research can really affect and change those early intuitions and questions says much about the depth of the collaborative effort.

I wanted to ascertain the meaning of abalone to Native California peoples: its symbolic value as a material, the significance of what it looks like. I had been greatly moved by the beauty of it when I excavated the abalone artifacts with the Muwekma Ohlone in 1992. The shimmering, opalescent play of multiple pastel colors in abalone shell appealed to me strongly, and I suspected that this quality must possess great importance and meaning to Native peoples who used it and wore it in their ceremonial regalia. As I began reading stories of Abalone Woman, I searched to find out whether those stories explained the meaning of the aesthetic qualities displayed by abalone, making clear the significance of the intense play of colors.

Good scholarship that deals with such questions has emerged in the study of the complex relationship between gold and pre-Columbian symbolism and society in Central America and South America. Interesting and allusive perspectives for the study of abalone in Native California abound. Nicholas J. Saunders writes:

From the Amazon to the Andes, and from Central America through Meso-america and the Caribbean to North America, different philosophies, symbolic associations, technological choices, and materials bolstered or reflected Amerindians' desire for the aesthetic of brilliance. Polished wood, iridescent featherwork, burnished pottery, greenstones, obsidian, crystals, gemstones, and a variety of metal and alloys were all favored variously, and to a greater or lesser degree across space and through time. Each shiny material possessed meanings whose cultural specificity was determined by availability, historical contingency, and varying degrees of technological sophistication; each also therefore became differentially embedded in language, mythology, ideology and socioeconomic reality. . . . Despite expected and complex differences among Amerindian outlooks, varying attitudes towards brilliant objects appear to have emerged from and cohered around a worldview that saw light, dazzling colors, and shiny matter as indicating the presence of supernatural beings and essence. (In Quilter and Hoopes 2003: 16–17)

Such an argument, brought to bear by Saunders and others in the Quilter and Hoopes volume, which seeks to find common symbolism and significance in the use of gold from Costa Rica to Colombia, is both attractive and worrisome. It is attractive because if it were true, so much could be clarified and generalized in the study of how and why gold and other brilliant materials, such as abalone, have been used. It is worrisome because an argument of this kind is necessarily derived from a great deal of speculation and second-guessing.

Based on references to the use of abalone in the ethnographic literature, there may be cause to extend such speculation about Native ideologies of brilliance to abalone, as well. Martine Reid, working from materials based on Franz Boas's work in the Pacific Northwest, recently wrote:

The longstanding symbolic association between the iridescent, white and blue-green abalone shell, traded up and down from the California coast, and light or the brilliance of the sun has established this substance of aquatic origin as a much favored element of decoration. Haida people, who painted crest designs on their faces for festive occasions, glued to their cheeks small pieces of abalone shell to symbolize sunlight. (Reid 2004: 58)

Yet for all the attractions of writing a book—or, at least, part of a book— about pan-Native ideologies of brilliance as manifested in abalone stories, regalia, and aesthetics, that is not the course of research and writing this volume took. I did want to know what abalone means and meant and how Native Californian peoples interpreted the iridescent brilliance of the shell in story and artifact. But I wanted the answers to my queries to originate in specific fieldwork collaborations, or "projects," rather than through an analytic review of the literature deployed as a context for understanding data from fieldwork. Nevertheless, I still had to come to terms with how my ideas did not necessarily match the concepts I encountered in working with cultural experts in Native California.

Chapter 3 presents a chronology, more or less, of dynamic processes I encountered in working with Florence Silva on the big questions I had about abalone's significance in her family's cultural and spiritual life. While I wrote the chapter, the fieldwork itself, over time, was increasingly led by Florence. All of the quoted comments included in chapter 3 are taken from notes I made during conversations with Florence rather than from reconstructed recollections after the conversations were over. I often asked her to repeat her exact words, because her wording was distinct and eloquent and I did not want to paraphrase what she had said. Where I do not directly quote Florence, I am using the notes I took during conversations, but am I am not completely sure I am using her precise wording.

By contrast, Julian Lang is the primary author of chapter 4. He has written his own articles, newspapers, and dramatic productions, as well as a unique volume (see Lang 1994). After the experience of working with the writings of Nicaraguans for my first book, it seemed natural to ask Lang, an experienced author, to write something for this one. He accepted the invitation without hesitation. While the ideas and the expression of them are entirely his, he wrote the chapter after many long conversations we had about these same big questions, during which time we established common parameters about the questions. In that light, I consider his chapter, like the others in this book, also the product of the experience of collaborative fieldwork and the co-creation of concepts and goals rather than a contribution to an edited volume that is topically (but not experientially) integrated with respect to central themes.

What is abalone a symbol for in Native California cultures? Is it a symbol? These two chapters provide very different answers to these questions.

3.

Florence Silva and

the Legacy of John Boston

Responsibility at the Intersection

of Friendship and Ethnography

John Boston's Abalone Necklace

In 1939, the University of California Anthropological Records published Cora Du Bois's study of late-nineteenth-century revitalization religions in California, *The Ghost Dance of 1870*. In the book, Florence Silva's grandfather, John Boston, is described thus:

JOHN BOSTON (1882 to 1930 or 1931)

> [Sealion White] About six years after George started, Boston began to dream and he kept on until he died two or three years ago. He said that the world was going to end in a flood but that he had stopped it with his prayers. He had no cloth costumes but he did dream a pectoral of clam-disk beads and abalone plaques. It had an abalone star on it. Drew, who dreamed after Boston, used the same thing except he added an abalone cross to it. . . . Boston's Maru dance was the Abalone dance (*wil*, abalone; *ke* dance). Men and women danced it together. They wore the pectoral. (Du Bois 1939: 97)

This passage describes a sacred object, a material manifestation that provoked many questions about the aesthetics and symbolism of abalone in conversations with Florence Silva, an elder at the Point Arena rancheria in Mendocino County. Her house stands almost at the end of the road that winds down a long hill through the middle of the 120 acre rancheria. Past a cul-de-sac of small, tidy BIA housing, past several broken-down trailers barricaded by wrecked cars, past a turn in the road, Florence's house sits in a large meadow that she keeps closely cropped along the north bank of the Garcia River. Fruit trees and flower-beds encircle the house, including varieties that are old and uncommon. Notwithstanding the severity of storms that batter the Mendocino coastline, Florence grows avocados and kiwi fruit in what would seem to be a microenvironment in the bottomlands of the Garcia River. Beyond Florence's house, the last structure on the road is the roundhouse, built by followers of the Dreamer religion in the early twentieth century and recently refurbished (see Jenkins and Theodoratus 1989; Theodoratus 1987). Point Arena, moreover, is situated along a particularly abalone-rich stretch of Mendocino coastline (Lundy 1997).

In this chapter, I will relate the work Florence and I set out to do and how our relationship developed and changed. This narrative will also intersect with other textualizations of Point Arena Pomo history and culture found in the anthropological literature.[1] The "Central Coastal Pomo" of this region were defined via linguistic and geographical parameters in which anthropologists of the twentieth century fit Point Arena people.[2] Similarly, the Dreamer religion, often referred to as the Bole Maru,[3] fits into a body of literature describing religious revitalization movements in central California during the late nineteenth century and early twentieth century. I came to look at these texts as derived from a simultaneous decontextualization of ethnographic information, divorcing data from the relationships between anthropologists and Native individuals that had shaped the disclosure of bits of information, and a recontextualization of those texts within an anthropological literature that has emphasized certain themes. Native individuals in these texts, I suspect, appear as partial people, their lives reduced to particular details or points that had utility for anthropological arguments. These sorts of arguments developed in the aftermath of immense population declines among the Native peoples of central California, caused by epidemics, forced relocation, and the brutal exploitation of Native labor during the period of early statehood. These multiple blows led to massive hemor-

rhaging of Native cultural systems that had previously been orally transmitted. Like Alfred Kroeber (see Buckley 1996), anthropologists working in this region seldom if ever came to terms with these histories and
their consequences and did not place such events in the calculus of their
analyses about Native culture. As I learned more about Florence; her
grandfather, the famous Dreamer John Boston; and her mother, the
healer Annie Bigioli, I wondered what my responsibility to Florence
might be. Considering that I was yet another anthropologist working in
Pomo country, should my role be to rectify that record in view of the
deficits I perceived in the anthropological literature? Or was I artificially
setting myself up as a purveyor of a "better anthropology" when in fact I
was repeating what I considered to be the errors of the past?

What Florence and I have talked about in the past four years has
changed, as our conversations became wide-ranging and open-ended.
During later visits, Florence laughingly asked me, "Well, what else do
you want to know?" In my mind, our friendship ultimately became more
important to me than the work aspects of our relationship. What I mean
by friendship in this case reveals, I think, problems with doing anthropological research about which other anthropologists have written (e.g.,
Mannheim and Tedlock 1995.)[4] The significance of the information
Florence told me, with respect to rectifying, improving, or adding to the
information found in the older ethnographies, eventually receded in
importance. Spending time with Florence became important to me regardless of whether we talked about those issues. In our conversations,
I no longer asked questions or brought up subjects on the basis of
an underlying research motivation, directed toward uncovering ethnographic points of interest. I wanted to talk with Florence more about
what she wanted to talk about. My friendship with Florence can in no
way be equated with insight into the cultural histories and traditions of
all the Point Arena Pomo, nor does our friendship provide knowledge
about the profound nature of the religious history of Pomoan peoples, of
the Dreamer religion specifically, or even of the legacies John Boston left
to contemporary adherents of the Dreamer religion. Because my friendship with Florence—a relationship of trust and camaraderie ultimately
not dependent on the revelation of ethnographic information—became
more important than ethnography, many aspects of what Florence told
me will remain private. This is not to say that Florence revealed con-

fidential aspects of her religion that were inappropriate for me to know; nor do I mean to imply that I became anything like an insider. Florence read this chapter as it was being written—indeed, reviewed all of my field notes as I produced them—and has had editorial power over them.

In outline, the agenda guiding my work with Florence changed course at least three times. I set out to explore the multifaceted significance of abalone. Then I tried to understand the legacy of her grandfather, John Boston. Finally, I decided to critically discuss the literature about her grandfather and the coastal Pomo region to rectify what I considered errors and oversights in that literature. The final change led up to a sense of the diminishing importance of all of these agendas in the face of our friendship, still maintaining the importance of honoring that friendship and the story of Florence's life.

The Parent of All Abalone

At first, I wanted to talk to Florence about abalone as food and about the decline in local populations and her explanations for that decline, and to ask her whether she knew stories—old stories—about this creature. As I began conversing with Florence, I was enthralled by the polychromatic scintillation of the abalone shell and by the appearance of purple, blue, pink, and green within the play of color. I wondered what significance Pomo people and other Native peoples who had historically gathered abalone shell placed on these colors, and I imagined a Native aesthetic of color and color combinations linked to traditional narratives. My central questions were: What does abalone symbolize to Florence and her people now and what did it symbolize to her grandfather and the Point Arena people in the past? Why was and is abalone used in regalia? Do specific colors or color combinations have specific spiritual meaning? To my initial questions about the importance of abalone to her grandfather, Florence responded with a series of narratives that I have called "the Parent of All Abalones." Florence accepted this title as appropriate as I continued to ask more about the story over the course of several visits.

In the story, two different accounts intertwine. In the first account, Florence told me about an enormous abalone her father discovered on a rocky promontory north of the Point Arena lighthouse. The discovery occurred during a huge -2.2 tide, which happens very rarely, she said. Her father ran home to tell everyone about what he had seen, and her grandfather, John Boston, was very excited and interested by the news. The huge abalone was never seen again. "It's probably still there," she told me, adding that she does not want to go out and find it. "It should just stay there." The second narrative breaks in at this point, in Florence's telling. According to her grandfather, the Parent of All Abalones was neither male nor female but could produce offspring. "It was very big, and it was the first abalone. The first abalone was the first creature to live in the sea. When it dies it will let out a cry that everyone would hear," according to her grandpa. "If the first abalone ever died," Florence added, "that would mean all the abalones had died, all of the creatures. It would be like the end of the world." I asked Florence to repeat these words; I wanted to get this right.

In fact, I returned to this story many times over the course of subsequent visits. The story stayed pretty much the same—or, better said, the two stories stayed the same. I asked Florence whether the abalone of the old story, the one her grandfather talked about, and the one her dad actually saw during the low tide, were the same. Maybe, she said. We moved on. John Boston knew other things about abalone. Florence recalled the way her grandfather would thinly slice the abalone and dry and salt it so it could be eaten much later or traded to the inland people who would come to visit during the course of the year. When the abalones spawned, he had told her, they made a certain, distinctive sound. The sea urchins, which compete with the abalone for kelp, would come around when they heard that sound. John Boston would go down to the beach and smash the urchins to protect and take care of the abalone. Another time, she related that John Boston had carved a stick in a special way and would rub the stick on the abalone to get them to spawn more. He took care of the abalone like he took care of many things. "Take care of the earth," is how Florence described her religion and the religion of her grandfather. "No gods, no beings except the living creatures, which you've got to take care of," she said. As for his pectoral (figure 7), it had been stolen out of the roundhouse where Florence had left it, "as a token," many years ago. Florence quietly urged me not to focus on this bit of the past, both because the symbolism of the regalia could not be discussed and because its loss was a particular hurt for her family. When she reread early drafts of this chapter, Florence reminded me that "the meaning of each piece [of regalia] is only for that dreamer." Once the dreamer dies, that regalia loses its meaning and cannot be inherited or used by others.[5]

Anthropologists and John Boston

During the time between visits to Florence, I tried to find all the references to and descriptions of John Boston in the anthropological literature concerning "the Pomo" and other Native peoples of Northern California. At this point, I was reading this literature to "get information" toward an emerging notion that my conversations with Florence about Boston could serve to amplify, not to mention rectify, the record about this important person. Treating the literature in this fashion became immediately an untenable practice, since all of the "information" I was getting was enmeshed in very particular sorts of anthropological narratives. This meant that nothing written about Boston should be taken at face value.

For example, Du Bois (1939) provided a rather detailed description of the rituals and regalia linked to Boston's dreaming within the context of an analysis that argued that the Dreamer religion functioned as a transitional religion between the ancient Native spirituality and Christianity. Du Bois conducted her research from 1932 to 1934 under the auspices of the Department of Anthropology at the University of California, Berkeley—specifically, under the direction of Alfred Kroeber, "at whose suggestion this project was undertaken" (Du Bois 1939: vi) One might observe that even though she worked under Kroeber's supervision, Du Bois's work on historical transitions marks a departure from Kroeberian discourse. Thomas Buckley observes that

> Kroeber was aware of the effects of the white invasion on Native Californians but for him the invasion was most pertinent, not as a moral problem, but as a force that disrupted the integrity of cultures. Thus, for example, Kroeber sought to recapture the reality of Yurok Indian culture "before the white man came and irreparably tore the fabric of native culture to pieces." That the white man also tore a considerable number of Yurok men, women, and children to pieces may have been personally disturbing, but it was not a matter of professional concern. (Buckley 1996: 277)

Du Bois also emphasized the sharp sense of irremediable cultural decay among Native Californians that forms the narrative backdrop to Kroeber's 1925 tome. For example, "the influence of leaders [such as Boston]," Du Bois wrote,

> was everywhere different and individualized, yet on the whole they seem to have been instrumental in reshaping shamanism, in furthering the development of the Bole Maru, or breaking ground for further Christianization. Their influence has made possible the introduction and acceptance of the many marginal Christian sects which now flourish among the Indians of this region. (Du Bois 1939:2)

Conceding the "preliminary and tentative" nature of both her data and findings, Du Bois nevertheless insisted that the Dreamer, or Bole Maru, religion, and other religions of the post-1870 period, acted to advance the Christianization of Northern California Indians. It is indeed undeniable that affiliation with Christian churches increased among Pomo Indians and other Native peoples of Northern California throughout the late nineteenth century and early twentieth century. Nevertheless, the putative relationship Du Bois highlighted between this trend and post-1870 Native religious phenomena (such as the Dreamer religion) seems "true" at least as much because of the domination of assimilation narratives in anthropology, which meshed with and supported the racist narratives of white America (see Baker 1998). In the same vein, Du Bois also used her data to contribute her own views about the diffusion of cultural traits, a debate occupying center stage in anthropology during the first half of the twentieth century. Such analytic practices are neither uncommon nor shocking.

In the appendix to her book, Du Bois included brief evaluative descriptions of her informants. While she described some with terms such as "dull," "uninformed," "careless," and "self-important" that appear to demean the people with whom she worked, she also considered other informants "intelligent," "alert," "friendly," and "well-informed." I wondered how her informants saw and evaluated Du Bois. In Greg Sarris's (1993) critique of Elizabeth Colson's ethnography of Pomo women, he is attentive to the quality and timbre of relationships between anthropologists and Pomo informants earlier in the twentieth century. In light of Sarris's work, Du Bois's evaluations may indicate the inequalities that defined her relations with these individuals. In retrospect, these individuals perhaps resisted Du Bois's project through tactics that she interpreted as personality defects.[6]

More to the point, Du Bois's characterizations of the religious traditions of particular people and families, such as Florence's, have important implications. For example, in Du Bois's narrative, Bole Maru's decline among the Pomo and their assimilation into Christian churches occurred when Dreamers such as Boston died in the early twentieth century and were not replaced by new Dreamers in the next generation. The next generation, Du Bois wrote, featured healers but not Dreamers. When Du Bois considered Boston's two daughters, Annie Bigioli[7] and Susanna Frank (Florence's mother and maternal aunt, respectively), as healers or curers rather than Dreamers, she did so in a fashion that emphasized a distinction between the two. Du Bois admitted that Boston "doctored" some but remarked that his daughters' "efforts are usually interpreted in terms of curing rather than pure Bole-Maru religion" (Du Bois 1939: 104). Such a distinction, I learned, did not at all correspond to how Florence understood these transitions and relationships. Du Bois's overall view of the Bole Maru, or Dreamer religion, along the Mendocino coast elaborates the distinction she made between healers and Dreamers. "In the course of fieldwork," Du Bois wrote,

> one receives a distinct impression that, at least within the last three generations, the religious ideology of the north-central California Indians is vague, confused, and contradictory; in other words, it seems not to have been formalized and categorized for the social group as a whole. An occasional individual may attempt an ordering of religious concepts, but that seems to be a purely individual feeling for clarity and system which has not the validity of "type" for the group as a whole. In my opinion, the formalization which ethnographers in the area have presented is based upon such occasional individuals. None such was found among the Pomo. (Du Bois 1939: 101)

In developing her assimilation/acculturation narrative, Du Bois acknowledged that traditional Pomo religious practices had dwindled under the impact of white settlement, or "encroachments," as she calls them. Terms such as "encroachment" remind contemporary readers that Du Bois, like other anthropologists of her time, had not fully come to terms with the demographic collapse of California Indian populations and the effects of colonial transformations of local ecologies on the viability of Native subsistence and economics. Likewise, Du Bois also recognized that many of the individuals in the Dreamer religion were reticent about talking about their religion with white people. But here, too, Du Bois did not fully appreciate how, among Pomoan peoples, knowledge of all kinds had been historically considered a kind of property that was not freely shared or easily disclosed. I therefore consider Du Bois's evaluation of the Bole Maru and its theology as a reflection of her own incomplete data and partial framework. In general, Du Bois's remarks suggest a certain isolation from existing anthropological work, such as Bronislaw Malinowski's, that treated non-textualized religious creeds far more carefully—or, at least, complexly. Her feelings toward some of her informants perhaps reflect complex strands of partnership and inequality that characterized better-known relationships between Native informants and anthropologists such as the Franz Boas–George Hunt partnership described by Judith Berman (1996) in all of its ambiguous profundity.

Later anthropologists who conducted ethnographies of the Dreamer religion have not seen eye to eye with Du Bois's interpretations. C. W. Meighan and F. A. Riddell, writing about their observation of inland Bole Maru rituals, state:

> As outsiders who were not able to spend lengthy time in the community, we were not able to obtain all the symbolism and meaning attached to the rituals. Hence we observed the ceremonies as an uninitiated or untrained Indian would observe them. As in every religious activity, there are participants at the lower levels of understanding, and we were part of the "congregation." The philosophical background and framework of knowledge within which the belief system operates were not open to us except in a limited way. But the mere persistence of Maru ceremonialism into the modern era when so much of native culture has disappeared is an indication that it has deep and powerful meaning for the people concerned, and that there must exist a codified system of beliefs as a rationale for Maru ceremonies. (Meighan and Riddell 1972: 3)

Florence provided additional comments after she reviewed an earlier draft of this chapter that are instructive with respect to the silences and incommensurabilities in anthropological texts. She observed that Boston relied heavily on his wife, Louisa Maria, in his interactions with the many different Native peoples whom he doctored and worked with, and she emphasized Boston's work as a healer. Louisa Maria was a very quick study with both Native and European languages, and she greatly facilitated his work by translating from languages Boston found unintelligible into his own language and into English. With respect to the way Du Bois discussed the Dreamer religion, Florence plainly stated: "He [Boston] didn't go in for any kind of religion. He didn't consider his way religion. It was his way of life." Her comment reminds us of the well-known incongruities in anthropological approaches to "religion" for peoples such as her own, whose languages, for example, did not even have a word for that concept before Europeans arrived on the scene.

Writing much later, Dorothea Theodoratus widened the gap between the analysis of curing or doctoring and the analysis of dreaming with additional distinctions. Boston was a Dreamer and a curer, wrote Theodoratus, but his daughters were only curers, because as "doctoring became less associated with the Maru cult . . . it was not necessary for these doctors to know how to give a Bole-Maru ceremony, nor to know much about the Maru" (Theodoratus 1971: 139–40). I certainly do not know nearly enough about the Dreamer religion to refute such a general conclusion, but Florence's discourse belies such distinctions. Her reports are, of course, hers, and they reflect her personal memories of her mother and her grandfather as their beloved child and as one of their cultural protégés. Thus, what she has to say cannot be understood to simply contradict any given anthropological interpretation, such as Du Bois's characterization of Bole Maru as both "a substitute" (Du Bois 1939: 137) for older religious practices and a stepping stone to full Christianization.

Black Widow Spider Silk

Florence stressed continuities between the teachings and practices of John Boston and Annie Bigioli, telling me that her mother had been trained by her grandfather to be a healer. In our conversations, she actually never differentiated between her grandfather's and her mother's teachings and beliefs: "Our religion is taking care of the earth. Don't ask for anything in prayers, just be thankful for all that you're given. Don't take more than you need." On several occasions, Florence said clearly that the practices of both her grandfather and her mother were "a projection of the mind" intended to heal the spirit and body, very much linked to the use of plants. Moreover, Florence emphasized that her mother's skills as a midwife had been very highly valued by people throughout Mendocino, Sonoma, and inland counties, a service she provided and a skill she knew that was at least as important as any other.

In this way, healing became the central theme of Florence's discourse about both Boston and Annie Bigioli. Annie had wanted to go to medical school, but that was not possible for women in rural California in those days. She did get training as a nurse in addition to her training from Boston. On several occasions, Florence elaborated a story about her father's car accident, in which his back had been broken. Annie raised black widow spiders specifically for their silk, which she used for delicate operations such as the one she carried out on her husband. "I was only fourteen," Florence said. "I watched her sew him up, all the tissues and nerves, the tiniest blood vessels and sinews." The doctors said he would never walk again, Florence said, smiling, but a year later he was walking.

Our conversations over coffee around Florence's long, elegant dining-room table expanded. We talked about her life and the lives of her mother and grandmother in a historical and inclusive way that no longer focused on only their Indianness, their Pomo cultural traits and practices, or other ethnographic motifs. But we also continued to talk about abalone and the many ways it fit into patterns of life and meaning for Florence. Whenever the subject of the Dreamer religion arose, I tried to grasp the large framework from which whatever Florence told me derived. I became convinced that the ideas, practices, and knowledge that the Dreamers had elaborated did cohere, and did compose a system, just as Meighan and Riddell had intuited. Everything Florence said made it impossible to think about the Dreamers, their practices, and their beliefs as a degeneration of an earlier, pristine spirituality. Instead, she depicted herself and her ancestors as doing all they could do to survive in the dominant Euro-American society, adapting to cultural disruption and the consequences of extreme demographic disasters. Meighan and Riddell made sharply resonant observations in the inland areas where they had worked several decades ago:

Since the days of Stephen Powers various observers have had casual contact with Maru ceremonialism. Often these observers have felt that they have seen the very last observance which retained aboriginal features, and for at least 50 years, the Maru cult has appeared to be due for extinction at any moment. However, the Maru cult still functions, despite the fact that nearly all Pomo speak English, attend the local white schools, and are certainly as sophisticated as the majority of their white neighbors. The Maru cult should therefore be viewed not as a simple "primitive" survival, but as a cultural phenomenon which satisfies a very real need in the Pomo community. This is not to say that this need cannot be fulfilled by other means, but the fact remains that this cult does meet certain demands of the people attending the ceremonies. (Meighan and Riddell 1972: 79)

All of this talk about the Dreamer religion, and the legacies of her grandfather and mother, as well as the cultural significance of abalone, were nestled within the ongoing events of the days we spent together. We talked about abalone, talked about Boston, and then switched on the television to watch the wild machinations and manipulations of the 2000 presidential election, the end of the Clinton era, and the continuing political and social scandals and outrages on the Point Arena rancheria. Laughing about being lifelong Democrats, Florence and I found that we agreed a great deal about political issues, from local to global.

The broad sweep of Florence's life encompassed so much more than a one-dimensional focus on her as a "Pomo Indian" or a practitioner of a Native religion. While Florence grew up speaking the Coastal Pomo language to her grandfather and often with her mother, she communicated with her father in the Sicilian dialect of Italian that he spoke. Her family had owned and operated a dairy farm at Point Arena, but after Annie's tragic death from a car crash, they bought a bigger farm south in Bodega. The new farm had three hundred cows: One hundred were the responsibility of her father, while she and her older brother took care of one hundred cows apiece. Hard work did not prevent Florence and her brother from taking adventures. They made several extended trips to Hollywood, where they earned money driving inebriated movie stars home from parties and studios.

Learning to co-manage a dairy, Florence dreamed of going to law school at the University of California, Berkeley, but insisted that she had been turned down for a scholarship not because she was Indian but because of her Italian last name. In the mid-1960s, she and her Portuguese American husband moved to the Bay Area. Florence became a police officer in the city of Hayward, where they lived until 1970, when they returned to Point Arena. During several visits, Florence and I did not manage to talk at all about anything Indian or Pomo. We were too busy talking about her memories of the late 1960s in the Bay Area, her observations of the hippies and flower children, and exploring her perspectives as a policewoman. For a while, I actually perceived Florence as a former representative of law enforcement rather than as a "Pomo elder."

But we continued to discuss abalone, its uses, and its fate as a creature. I had prepared a list of possible reasons for the decline of abalone populations, including overfishing, pollution, habitat erosion, and introduced diseases. Florence advised me that poaching had to be included in the list, and that poachers were probably the single most menacing threat facing Mendocino abalone populations. We drove up and down the coast so that Florence could show me where she and her family had been accustomed to harvesting abalone, as well as places poachers had recently been caught and arrested by the California Department of Fish and Game. Our conversations about abalone harvest and decline developed over several visits, and as I spoke to marine biologists, abalone farmers, and a few non-Indian fisherman about these topics (see chapter 6), I wanted to ask Florence what she thought, as well. White fishermen on the Mendocino coast were convinced that Native people had purposely hunted otter, one of abalone's most voracious predators, precisely to maintain abalone populations. Florence did not give that argument any credence. Her ancestors, she said, hunted animals to use them, and while otters had nice pelts, no one cared to eat them. Many authors writing about Native management of edible animal populations suggested that rituals associated with each animal acted to restrict harvests and maintain their populations (as in Blackburn and Anderson 1993). According to her grandfather, "there was always plenty of abalone." But this perspective must be contextualized. Boston was raised in the wake of severe over-hunting pressures on otters and consequently during the long period of growing abalone populations that continued to expand throughout the late nineteenth century. People did not overfish abalone, she said, because they placed great value on a varied diet. According to

Florence, eating many kinds of foods and enjoying many flavors composed what she did not hesitate to call traditional cuisine among the Native coastal peoples. Moreover, Florence stated that, unlike the fishing of salmon and the hunting of deer, the harvest of abalone was not accompanied by an elaborate ritual that controlled how many people went out for abalone and how much they took. She confessed that while abalone tasted very good, it had never been the favorite food of her people—salmon topped that list.

On several occasions, Florence talked about how the inland peoples used to come down to trade obsidian for fresh salmon and dried salmon, fresh abalone and dried abalone. Relationships with inland folks had nothing at all to do with their being "Pomo" or speaking a Pomo language. It seemed to me that Florence wanted to make sure I got that point: Each family and village on the coast had its own relationships with inland families and villages, and speaking a common language had nothing to do with it. Likewise, Florence answered other "anthropologist" questions I got around to asking eventually, with the intention of making sure I got it right, regardless of what I was reading in books. Both men and women went out for abalone; it was not a job for just one gender. Women did not hunt usually, not because they were not allowed, but because they had other things to do. It was true that possessions and wealth had been passed down matrilineally from mother to daughter here on the coast, but some families were wealthier than others "because they worked harder to get all the different foods, and to make fine tools." Before the white people came, she said, such differences between families or between men and women had to do with the talents and abilities of individuals and the energy with which they pursued their occupations and lives.

Harvest of abalone not only was and still is a question of obtaining food but also always related to the use of the shell in regalia and in symbolism. Florence emphasized that she and her family looked for certain species of abalone—red (*Haliotis rufescens*), green (*H. fulgens*), and pink (*H. corrugata*)—in certain places along the coast. Each kind of abalone was used to make specific shapes used in regalia. Stars, crosses, and circles were the most important shapes crafted out of abalone shell and used in the regalia dreamed by John Boston and other Dreamers. But I was very much mistaken to think of the use and aesthetic of abalone in only visual terms. As I later learned working with Bradley Marshall, and from people from tribes farther north, abalone is used in dance regalia because of the sound it makes when a person wearing it moves. Abalone sings. "The movement of the abalone," Florence said, "itself is music."[8]

Our discussions pursued other facets of abalone. Florence hung abalone shells around her house because "it was a pure pleasure, like a painting, a beautiful painting, except a person didn't paint it, it's from the earth and doesn't have anything to do with people." John Boston taught that abalone is used in Dreamers' regalia because it was the first creature to inhabit the ocean. Because of this, Florence said, "when you wear it, you are not cheating, not stealing spirit. You're united with spirit: the abalone and the person." I must have looked dumbfounded when Florence told me this. She asked me if I understood, and I responded that I was trying. She said: "It makes all things part of your spirit. You are one on one. We don't walk alone. We have to walk with everything all around us. We need the help of everything all around us." I asked about the abalone cross in Boston's pectoral, and she said that it signified the four directions, the food chain, and all the animals. The five-pointed star, she added, "is the light that looks down upon you, that does not leave you; it's always returning."

These remarkable conversations once again underscored an alternative understanding of the Dreamer tradition as a whole system, rather than as a set of vaguely connected fragments or as a step along the way to Christianity. I confessed as much to Florence, and she responded with this metaphor: Imagine the difference between picking a flower, enjoying it, and then throwing it away, versus growing a flower in a garden where flowers are always regenerating, so that there are always more of them. "Taking care of necessity," she emphasized, pointing to the fields behind her house that border the river, "don't destroy the grass, keep reseeding it." Florence also repeatedly stressed that Annie Bigioli's way of healing—"the projection of the mind"—could only work for people who were part of their cultural tradition. "You can't heal someone if they don't ask for it," Florence said, "and they have to believe: that's the old way. Even your own children need to ask to be healed."

I told Florence that I was glad that the Dreamer religion had not simply faded away and made room for Christianity. She laughed a little, saying "No, I'm not Christian, but my husband was." Practicing the healing and ceremonial ways of the Dreamers in her family could never be viewed only as a question of religious affiliation. But there was a bigger point she wanted to make in this conversation. "You do what you need to do to defend your land," Florence said sharply. That comment raised my awareness again of the inseparability of all of her practices: gathering food, healing people, taking care of animals and plants, interacting with spirit, and, indeed, the struggle to maintain Native control over the few remaining scraps of land. Florence's family and the other Pomo at Point Arena had faced those threats throughout the twentieth century (see Theodoratus 1971), including the federal government's efforts to terminate official recognition of Pomoan peoples in the 1950s and '60s.

Florence herself had been elected tribal chair of Point Arena during the 1980s. As chair, she had proposed an innovative plan to seed abalone hatchlings in a particular sheltered area of coast just south of the lighthouse. She explained her plan for a type of wild mariculture of abalone and more ideas for sustainable harvest of other marine foods during drives we took along the coast. She stopped to show me the results of ecologically harmful ways seaweed and other resources were being stripped from their environment. Florence made clear that the Dreamer tradition was a means of defending land and community, as well as constitutive of the very meaning of land and community, and of the ways her family lived those values. Back at home, her eyes pointed to the acorns drying in her dining room, reminding me of other discussions we had had about the ways she helped to propagate desired traits in species she harvested for food, a sophisticated practice that anthropologists had begun writing about in the 1970s (see Bean and Blackburn 1976).

On many occasions, our discussions of her grandfather led us to talk about Florence's current effort, along with other elders from other Pomo rancherias, to construct a museum of Pomo culture and history called Boh-Cah-Ama. This museum would be entirely under the direction and control of the participating Pomo communities, and during the last years, progress toward its construction has advanced considerably. It would be very difficult, based on our conversation, to separate this project from Florence's sense of spirituality and heritage—they have always formed different parts of her overall life's work.

After such conversations with Florence, I became more intent than ever to uncover the way I suspected anthropological texts had reduced the multiple facets of individual lives to one or two traits useful for making a point and moving an argument along in the anthropological text. Notwithstanding the insights Meighan and Riddell had offered in the early 1970s, earlier anthropologists' characterizations of the Dreamer religion retained considerable iconic value. It was against the domination of such portrayals in the "Pomoan" literature that Greg Sarris reacted, offering up instead the genre-busting biography of Mabel McKay, *Weaving the Dream* (1994). Sarris was—or, at least, became—a real insider in his project, which I never did and never could. My further efforts to "rectify the anthropological record" not surprisingly ran into real problems as I brought other texts to Florence's house for discussion.

Encountering Samuel Barrett's "Pomo Myths" (1933) in the Grace Hudson Museum, thanks to Sherrie Smith-Ferri's continuing efforts to educate me about the Pomoan literature in anthropology, I set out to find narratives to discuss with Florence.[9] Smith-Ferri's masterful essay about Barrett (in Barrett 1996) describes his journey from basket trader and marketeer to becoming Alfred Kroeber's very first graduate student in the Department of Anthropology at the University of California, Berkeley, to making a career as a scholar widely respected among both Pomo peoples and anthropologists. I photocopied stories in Barrett's volume told by people from the central coast region, figuring that what they had told Barrett might also be familiar to Florence. Upon looking at my copies, Florence quickly discarded all of the stories that featured Coyote as a character. "We didn't tell Coyote stories," she said laconically. "We told Bear stories." We ended up focusing on two particular narratives, in both of which Thunder was an important character.

But if I thought that our conversation would consist of Florence elaborating, or even retelling, the story, it became apparent that would not happen. Instead, Florence's comments focused more on the storytellers than the stories themselves, and what she said undermined the textual presentation of the entire volume. I was particularly interested in the story "The Abode of Thunder under the Ocean," because it specifically mentioned Point Arena and nearby places:

[Thunder] went on till he came to the ridge north of Brush Creek. He stopped on this ridge at the site of the old village of Kodalau. He rested here for a little while, then went down across Brush Creek, past the old village of Pda'hau [sic]. From here he went westward, passing along the south side of a big lagoon just west of the town of Manchester, to a small lagoon west of this, near the shore of the ocean. . . . The place where he went out of sight is the point farthest north of the Point Arena light-house, where you can see breakers and white foam now at all times. Before he went out there, there never were any breakers at this place and no white foam. It was always smooth before that. Whenever you hear thunder, it always starts from that place and some people think that Thunder was the man who went down there. (Barrett 1933: 188–89)

Florence had many times mentioned the old village of P'dahau, located on the ridge north of her house, where her grandfather John Boston had grown up and where the ancient roundhouse had stood. I myself had seen the foamy turbulent point north of the Point Arena lighthouse. The vivid abalone-like imagery used by Bill James, the storyteller Barrett consulted, was also an appealing part of the narrative:

This man [Thunder] has a big house at this point. It is made of a sort of glass-like substance. You can see right through the side of this house and see everything that is going on inside. There are many fish in here and they jump and strike against the walls in their endeavor to get out. . . . The Garcia River flows directly to this house and he [Thunder] is the one who sends the fish up the river. He has a big lever, as large as a redwood tree, which, when he pulls if down only a very little, lets millions of salmon out, so that they may run up the river. . . . Inside the house, thunder has something which acts as a kind of reflector and shows him what the whole world of doing. It shows him all the people and he can see what is going on all over and what everyone is doing. . . . Whenever he moves any part of his body, even when he rolls over it makes a great noise. Under his left arm, he keeps a square piece of a glass-like material and when he takes this out and moves it around, it flashes and makes the lightening. If he were to hold this out for any considerable time, everyone would go blind and the whole world would burn up. . . . No one dares to go out where Thunder lives, not even a shaman may venture so much. (Barrett 1933: 189–90)

With Sarris's deconstruction of Colson's work (Sarris 1993) providing an example of how to critically read ethnographies of Pomoan people, I was aware of the highly edited quality and character likely inherent in Barrett's tale telling. Florence's reading was another kind of deconstruction, in which she decoded the many different agendas and underlying histories behind each story. The Thunder story by Bill James "is really all about him," she said, and his part in one facet of the Point Arena rancheria's history. During World War One, Florence told me, her grandfather had allowed a number of Native families (inland Pomo, Wailaki, and speakers of other languages) from the Round Valley reservation in Covelo to settle at Point Arena. He had probably done so because a great many coast people had died from disease, and Boston felt sorry for the people who had been interned at Round Valley. Bill James was one of "the Covelo people," and in his story Florence detected a number of unsettling elements that actually described his relationships with the other people at Point Arena. Likewise, a particular subtext of the story entitled "Flower-Man Kills Thunder" was the main feature of the story to which Florence paid attention. This story, she told me, concerned the medicinal power of certain plants, but Bob Pot, the storyteller, did not want particularities to be known. So the story was told in certain generalities so nobody—not Barrett or anyone else—would know which flowers were used for which purposes.

As we reviewed several other narratives in "Pomo Myths," Florence focused on the multiple stories attached to each teller, their relationship to and with Florence, and the motive behind the story. Our conversations kept disrupting the possibility of reading "Pomo Myths" in the way I would have otherwise, forcing me to acknowledge a certain quality of flatness in the entire volume. Each story was presented in an identical textual manner, collated and grouped into categories such as "Myths of Creation," "Myths of the Sun," and "Trickster Stories," which hid the disjunctures and differences Florence emphasized. In effect, a parallel and very different volume—about how to tell the stories, the storytellers' lives, the local histories of each Pomoan community in which the storytellers lived—was conjured and referenced by Florence in our conversations. But this hypothetical volume has not yet been written down and may not be susceptible to textualization. It may be a future project for Florence's family and other Pomoan families like hers.

The sharpest and most personally embarrassing incident of disjuncture between text, Florence's knowledge and understanding, and the hubris entailed in my idea of rectifying the anthropological record occurred when I brought photocopies of passages from Edwin Loeb's "Pomo Folkways" (1926) to Florence's house. Loeb had also been Kroeber's graduate student, and joined a team of these students conducting extensive ethnographic investigations in Eastern Pomo communities in 1921. He also worked with two informants from P'dahau–Point Arena: John Boston and Drew Shoemaker, both informants for Du Bois and, later, Birbeck Wilson (1968).

Loeb was not interested in the Dreamer religion, and his research agenda and thematics had nothing to do with assimilation narratives and the inevitability of Christianization that so concerned Du Bois. Instead, Loeb was concerned about recovering as much knowledge as he could retrieve about the older religious traditions, referred to as "the ghost ceremony religion" and "the Kuksu religion," which had preceded the Bole Maru. In that light, Loeb extensively described John Boston's initiation into the ghost ceremony by his maternal grandfather, because "the ghost ceremony was held in its most original form by the Coast Central Pomo" (Loeb 1926: 338). In that light, Loeb devoted several pages to specifically describing Boston's initiation into the Kuksu religion as well (see Loeb 1926: 356–59).

I was very excited to discuss these pages with Florence and mailed her photocopies a week or so before I had a chance to drive back over to Point Arena. I arrived during a birthday party for one of her granddaughters and ate dinner with a few family members I had not met before. The first time I broached the subject of Boston's initiations, Florence said simply that she had never heard anything about that. The subject seemed closed, but I nevertheless brought it up again later in the evening. At that point, Florence told me quite seriously that the topic was something for the men, something men did, and that she as a woman would not have been informed about such things. It would be hard to exaggerate how abashed I felt at that moment. Clearly, it was very embarrassing for Florence, and doubtless others of her generation, to read such accounts. I realized that anthropologists, even one as informed and empathic as Loeb, might never have realized how mortified family members could feel reading such descriptions of their own elders when knowledge about such ceremonies and rituals had historically been transmitted in ways structured and constrained by age, gender, and status. Loeb was not the only problem. My enthusiasm for the project of rectifying the anthropological record had led me to the point where I was also quite capable, however inadvertently, of also transgressing the dignity and privacy of my friend.

This incident, in retrospect, marked the end of the rectification project. By focusing exclusively on John Boston and his legacy to Annie Bigioli, I had simply reproduced the very same reduction of individual lives and families that I had wanted to rectify. In truth, Florence and I had talked about *all* of her ancestors, not only her grandfather. Florence was just as interested in tracing the heritage of Boston's wife, Louisa Maria, the daughter of the sea captain Stephen Smith, who had owned the first lumber mill in Bodega and had married a woman from Peru. Most of all, Florence had spent a great deal of time finding out about her own father, an immigrant from Sicily. In fact, she made a point of photocopying all of the application forms she had used to get materials from Ellis Island so that I could request materials about my own immigrant father and grandfather. It was not possible to downplay or dismiss the parts of Florence's family and life history that did not conform to the mold of "Pomo elder."

Concluding Thoughts: "The Dreams Aren't Only about Spirit Things"

What, then, can be drawn from the collaboration between Florence and me with respect to my questions about abalone as a symbol for her, her family, and her people?

In the end, what I learned from Florence offers profound bases for understanding relationships between Native peoples and animals such as abalone. The story of the Parent of All Abalone is unique, it transcends gender, it links the fate of the ocean with a humble bottom-dwelling mollusk, and it positions that creature as the first inhabitant of the sea. The use of regalia made from abalone connects the nature of that creature with the "the projection of the mind," which Florence puts at the heart of the healing practices of the Dreamer tradition. Finally, Florence made clear repeatedly that her people's relations with animals such as abalone—whether as food, regalia, or in narrative—are inseparably linked to a defense of their connection to their ancestral land.

What Florence has shared in this chapter through an extended exegesis of the various meanings of abalone to her family helps to demystify the subject of California Indian religion from a very practical and political point of view. It should be very clear that protecting their privacy and dignity, rather than a fetishized secrecy, is a far more decent characterization of Native peoples' feelings about their spiritual practices and heritage. Certainly, it is impossible to separate the strands of practical day-to-day life, relationships with animals and plants, the struggle for Native sovereignty and survival, the world of the spirit, and the realities of the twentieth century in Florence's words and in her life. Reading this chapter, Florence admonished me: "The dreams aren't only about spirit things. They could be about events, the future, so you could tell what was coming and when. About the inhumanity of war and hate, to protect ourselves from these things."

Florence's living heritage, which she is passing down to her children, grandchildren, and great-grandchildren, thus is directed far beyond the boundaries of Point Arena, Mendocino County, or the State of California.

In the next chapter, Julian Lang offers a distinctive interpretation of the significance of abalone as a linguist, poet, performance artist, and leader among the Karuk people. While in this chapter the discussion of abalone's meaning for Florence and her family unfolded as a dialogue between us, in the following chapter, my voice is largely mute.

4.

Reflections on

the Iridescent One

Julian Lang's life and scholarship are focused on reassembling an integrated ritual and quotidian Karuk worldview and cosmography that
contemporary Karuk people can inhabit. His published work, particularly the volume *Ararapíkva: Creation Stories of the People: Traditional
Karuk Indian Literature from Northwestern California* (1994), and his
work as a performance and visual artist are manifestations of this focus.
He has played a key role in the organization and enactment of the World
Renewal ceremonies among the Karuk and is an important presence at
Yurok and Hupa ceremonies, as well. Unlike the Hupa, who inhabit a
relatively large reservation on a significant chunk of their old aboriginal
homeland, the Karuk control a few tiny parcels of rancheria turf that
represent a small fraction of their aboriginal territories. The work of
ceremonial, language, and artistic revival under such conditions presents particularly harsh challenges.

When I met Lang in the fall of 2000, he had coincidentally already
been pondering the role of Abalone Woman in Karuk narrative cycles
for more than a decade. Abalone stories had not been recorded by
anthropologists working among the Karuk as they had been in ethnographic work among the Hupa, Wiyot, and Yurok, yet through his
investigations Lang had concluded that Abalone Woman was as important a spirit being for the Karuk as for the other peoples. Abalone
Woman had become part of several projects Lang was pursuing among

his Karuk people, as well as with Cheryl Seidner and Leona Wilkinson of the Wiyot. My conversations with him offered him the opportunity to put concurrent lines of research and analysis together. In his research, Lang harnesses the methodologies of anthropologists and linguists for epistemological and analytic purposes that serve collective tribal goals.

This essay follows a braided combination of academic and Native fabrics of thinking. First, Lang introduces readers to the Karuk Spirit Beings, including Abalone Woman, in the context of the overriding paradigm of "repairing the world" that lies at the heart of northwestern California Indian worldviews. He then reviews the history of the colonial fragmentation of the Karuk worldview and its Spirit Beings. This sets up the problematic of his research: Amid the colonial wreckage of Native life, there are no recorded Karuk abalone narratives. Lang then relates how, through the making of an art installation in San Francisco, he concluded that Abalone Woman had been a central figure in Karuk narratives. The process of making the installation required him to go beyond the paradigm of bounded, discrete cultural entities central to the anthropology of California Indians. Instead, Lang explored the literature about many of the different Native peoples of the northwestern region of California, including a group that anthropologists had deemed extinct, bringing the anthropologists themselves into the purview of his installation. As he unfolds his answer to the question of how Abalone Woman is a key spirit being in the Karuk worldview, he refocuses on the Native value system embodied by the World Renewal ceremonies, which seeks to repair the world and, in Lang's case, heal the fragmentation caused by colonialism.

"Do like they did and you can't go wrong" (Lang 1992: 17). This sentence expresses what guides the Native peoples of northwestern California. The words are from the Karuk elder Violet Super—words of guidance to a younger generation assuming its new responsibilities for conducting tribal ceremonies. She could have said, "Do like the Spirit Beings did" and thereby express more explicitly the truth as we know it: In the beginning of the world, before our ancestors grew here, there lived a race of beings known in English as the Spirit Beings, the Immortal Ones, or by similar terms. By a process of trial and error, the Spirit Beings established the original instructions provided to our ancestors, which, they were told, when followed faithfully would maintain good in their world. If they do not follow the way, imbalance will reign in their world, causing sickness and every kind of affliction. It is a simple case of cause and effect: "Do as the Old Ones did and we can't go wrong."

Our knowledge of "the Old Ones" comes to us through oral tradition— through elders such as Violet Super, but especially through our mythology. For instance, there is a sort of manic drive that overcomes many of us to acquire "wealth": not the kind of wealth promised in the American dream necessarily, but the kind of wealth that was loved by the Spirit Beings in the beginning of our People. The first anthropologists wrote page after page about our unstoppable drive to seek indigenous currency: the pileated woodpecker scalps, the dentalium shell, the large obsidian blade. It is a drive that still infects us today. Young and old alike work hard to build their "treasure." Once one's treasure is sufficient, it suddenly becomes equally important to display one's wealth at the ceremonies. It was the tried and true way of the Spirit Beings, and when followed, the individual's prestige is mysteriously raised to great heights. While there is evidence that in the old days, some sought wealth by treachery or other dark means (e.g., death-price, double-crossing, etc.), ill-gotten wealth was never used during the World Renewal ceremonies, the most important ceremonies of all. Only wealth that was acquired through prayer, devotion, and self-denial is eligible to be used during these dances.

All of the traditional tribal institutions originated with the Spirit Beings. The period during which the Spirit Beings were living, our myth time, is called *Pikvahahirak* in the Karuk language. This was when they created our material culture, the World Renewal ceremonies, and the rituals to fix the Earth. The purpose, the prayers, and the sites to be included in the ceremonies were prescribed by the Spirit Beings. Once these institutions were created, they were accompanied with instructions to humankind to enact the practices. Today, many of the original communities and their descendants continue these pre-contact prescriptions given to our ancestors.

Wealth is partly at the center of our Indian world. Wealth is the regalia worn during these ceremonies originating in ancient times. From the first generation of human beings and since, the regalia were known to be the "playthings of the Spirit Beings." The playthings, *ikyamiichvar*, called toys in the Karuk language, reveal to us that the ceremonial dances had strong associations with pleasure for the Spirit Beings. Today we share, not vicariously but actually, their pleasure when we perform the White Deerskin Dance, the Jump Dance, the Brush Dance, the War Dance, and other ceremonials. The regalia's value is that it connects us directly with our primordial origins. Through this connection we experience feelings of spiritual exaltation, feelings that, in turn, are projected onto the onlookers attending the dances. And thereby, the ritual is complete.

True, the world we live in today is separated from the world of our ancestors by a gulf as big as the Pacific Ocean. Yet direct connections with that distant past persist. In some ways, the dances have evolved and reflect who we are today. Consistency with the past, nevertheless, rules.

Abalone is a Spirit Woman who is ever present during our ceremonies. The chiming of abalone pendants suspended from the ornately decorated dresses worn by the women still evokes strong feelings at every ceremonial. Multistrand necklaces of abalone are worn by both the men and women. She transformed long ago into a form of wealth for us; our belief is that she is the feminine form of wealth. She must be present at every ceremony. She is always front and center. We cannot understand or see a day when she will not be present.

The story of Abalone is both sad and hopeful. Her first mate was a huge mismatch for her. A myth story tells us that Pithvava, Big Dentalium, wanted to be her husband. This was not to be. But he, too, is always present with her in our ceremonials. Spirit Beings from the sea, they join with the sea lion, whose teeth are carved and then fashioned into the spiked headdress used in the White Deerskin Dance. Other shells are also used: the olivella shell, most notably, and a rare and small clamshell found only along the coast in the Tolowa country near the Oregon border. Our ceremonies are somehow incomplete without these "sea" spirits. Together they join with the large obsidian blades, the woodpecker scarlet, the flicker feather, wolf-hide bands and hides of the albino deer and the river otter, along with the juniper berry, the woven-basket quivers, and tanned deer-hide blankets. They were all used by the Spirit Beings in their "good times."

It is our job today to re-create the dances that the Spirit Beings performed in the beginning. It is how it is done on the Klamath, Trinity, and Smith rivers today. These are our teachings, and, we hope, they will continue.

A Brief History about Us

Our People have lived with the toxic fallout caused when local Native peoples came into first contact with Europeans. As happened across the country, this contact resulted in whole families' and whole communities' being wiped out. Locally, there was a massive death toll due to disease, murder, and displacement. The high mortality rates were followed by successive social and government policies designed to extinguish our spiritual identity and psychological well-being. It has been seven generations since the Gold Rush in 1849–50. Effects on local Native communities from the tragedy of first contact are evident daily. Many of today's Native leaders believe that the toxic fallout from the period of genocide is ongoing and that it still pierces the emotions of our people. It brought about profound change and upheaval to Native people of the region.

From a Native perspective, we see that the foremost compulsion for settlers was to clear the land, to kill or annihilate competitive species, to reduce the natural world's resources to nothing after having put a price tag on it all. Locally, farmlands were carved out of biosystems overflowing with hard- and softwood forests. Open land, always in short supply hereabouts, was quickly converted into fenced-in pastureland, into ranches and farms of every size and specialty.

Some of the local tribal groups found their rugged geography to be a sort of saving grace since it slowed settlement. Those living along the coast did not fare as well as those living in the interior. California's longest coastal plain was contiguous with Humboldt Bay, the largest naturally protected port north of San Francisco and south of Puget Sound. Violent repression against the Indian people living on this coastal plain culminated with the worst human massacre of the area, the Indian Island Massacre. Although the killing of women and children shocked the white gentry, the surrounding meadowlands continued to be converted into farmlands and dairy ranches.

A continuous stand of massive redwoods bordered the meadows to the east, forming what we call popularly today the redwood curtain. A poignant tear surely comes to the eye of today's local timber barons when they contemplate the sheer volume of lumber that was harvested in the early days. Three-hundred-foot-tall trees must have been jumping from their stumps and landing under the saw blades. The redwood harvest brings a tear to traditional Native leaders, as well. They were told since birth that the redwood trees were people—Spirit People who stand as reminders of the beauty and primacy of the creation of the world.

It took several generations for settlers to convert such natural abundance into product. A landscape of depletion was already evident by 1900. Wind and water erosion or seismic transformation caused the eerie, otherworldly beauty of a Grand Canyon or California's Mono Lake. The erosion caused by human beings lacks the beauty and creates wastelands. It is common practice today to hide the continuing desecration of old-growth forests with a buffer zone of trees. Behind the verdant buffer can be found a snapshot of Christendom's Armageddon. Heavy settlement in the area extended along the coast in Del Norte County (near the Oregon border) southward into Humboldt County—a distance of about 125 miles. The interior mountains were settled more sparsely, but with the advent of mechanization, the desecration extended in leaps and bounds.

Settlement has continued since the 1850s. Violent repression of Native peoples was over by 1900, a period amounting to only two twenty-five-year generations. The death rate for many of the traditional village populations as measured against pre-contact populations was 90 percent or more. Traditional life was shattered, and once proud and upright dance owners who hosted well-attended dances according to the highest indigenous standards disappeared.

To the east, the rugged mountains limited settlement. Today, there are still only a few small towns. There was untold damage to the region, nevertheless, first caused by waves of locust-like humanity seeking gold as they entered the river gorges. In the beginning, their work was done with only picks, shovels, and brawn. Machinery made it possible for irreversible damage to be done to the rivers and forests, extending to the ocean beyond. They came, they took, and then most quickly moved on. By historical or geological measures, the onslaught was short-lived. Each wave of opportunists left behind a disillusioned indigenous population facing disrupted lives. After adjusting to their losses, our ancestors slowly reestablished the ceremonies like grasses returning to a burned-over field.

It was on the rich coastal plains and in the river valleys that the most tenacious settlers set down their stakes and erected their fences. They took by force and with the support of the law much of the arable land of the Tolowa, coastal Yurok, and Wiyot peoples. Today the largest towns are found in this area.

Our indigenous way of life was previously extremely localized. Our belief system and lifestyle sustained a sedentary way of life—generation after generation lived in the same village as their forefathers. Many families lived in a house located on the exact same spot that their ancestors' houses once stood. Our ceremonial dances were held at the exact same spot that they had always been held. Our worldview insisted that we remember the exact locations visited by the Spirit Beings in the beginning, or at which they executed their mythic deeds.

Our lives were characterized by great diversity: languages from three completely unrelated language families were spoken within a very close proximity, for instance. I believe it was our similarities that in the end have been our greatest strength. The revival of the ceremonies after the devastating influx of gold miners was possible because of our collective drive to resume the original instructions proclaimed by the Spirit Beings in their stories and to honor the memories of our Old Ones.

A group representing dance families from the Hupa, Yurok, and Karuk peoples affirmed this point in June 2004. On that day, the City Council of Eureka returned to the Wiyot people, who are indigenous to the coast around the area of Humboldt Bay, a substantial portion of land on the north end of Indian Island, the place of the Indian Island Massacre of 1862. The dance family representatives publicly and unequivocally stated that they were each connected with the Wiyot people because of the ceremonial held on the island: the World Renewal ceremony. Each speaker related that he or she would be there to assist with material and spiritual support when the Wiyot people decided to resume their dances. The speakers went on to say that they were bound together like a family through the Jump Dance and White Deerskin ceremonials.

The white community developed industries to harvest the salmon stocks and to log fir, pine, cedar, and redwood forests. After 1910, vast tracts of land came under the control of the federal government and logging companies. Native-controlled lands dwindled, and the promise of the Spirit Beings to provide for them was denied by government policies. Working for wages became the new norm for many Native people. People began seeking paid work where they found it. This shift in livelihood contradicted the epochal cultural imperative to live localized, sedentary lives. And for several generations, our cultural ways suffered. The devotion to sustained ceremonial practice and reliance on traditional beliefs waned. Many families continued to live at their ancestral home sites, but many more moved away. The ceremonies suffered. Some believed irrevocably so. Many Indian people had become disillusioned with traditional life and sought a modern way to live.

What, we can ask, in view of this history has become of our Spirit Beings? What about our spiritual and psychic well-being?

Fixing the World

Today Native northwestern California is complex. Disillusionment and despair persist among many. Many of us have found a place within contemporary society: Success is not unheard of. In fact, many families have members who are professionals, lawyers, doctors, Ph.D.s, and Ed.D.s. The list goes on. Tribal governments are in place that are successfully managing forests and fisheries and providing public services that were unimaginable even thirty years ago. But what about our beliefs?

Recently, the numbers of individuals and families choosing to actively participate in our annual ceremonies have been growing. In Karuk country during the early 1980s, there were times when there might be forty-five to fifty persons present at a major ceremony, while today there might be three hundred persons or more. The number of ceremonies being held today has grown. It might be more correct to say that the number of ceremonies being held today is approaching the number that was held before first contact.

It is true that the early settlers disrupted the everyday and spiritual lives of our grandparents, our great-grandparents, and their grandparents in profound ways. But as we gaze on our own children singing and dancing unselfconsciously, we realize that *their* children will be able to choose a future that includes the ceremonial fixing of the world. It is a testament to the power and lasting resonance of our original instructions and to the efficacy of the Spirit Beings. It seems that we have resumed our inherent drive to be one with our creation and to assert, once again, our original instructions.

My people, the Karuk people, live along the mid-stretch of the Klamath River where there are three annual "Pikyaavish," the Karuk American word for the World Renewal ceremony. In the old days, this ceremony was the paramount step in individual and collective spiritual consciousness. The ceremonies occurred at the upstream and downstream ends of our world and at our world's center. It is a ritual stemming from the older "people's ceremonies": the healing ceremonies, the puberty rites, and the reparations, or settling-up, ceremony. The World Renewal is a communal ritual that reenacts the creation, re-creates and renews the Earth and the Spirit Beings of the Earth. It creates harmony and balance in the natural world. All three of these ceremonies are held today.

The Karuks' downstream neighbors, the Yurok people, held biannual World Renewal ceremonies at four places. The Hupa held biannual ceremonies, as well. The Wiyot had three ceremonies to fix the Earth. The Tolowa held their ceremonies on the Smith River and at sites on the coast near the Oregon border. Today, many of these ceremonies are being held again.

The people's ceremonies (healing, puberty, and reparations), as well as the ceremony to fix the Earth, were disrupted. In some cases, certain ceremonial sites were abandoned or destroyed. We can say today that ceremonials were suspended at one time or another by all of our local tribes. Some dances have yet to return, and, sadly, some may never return. Native leaders of today have actively sought the means to return the ceremonies and have successfully revived many.

Having been directly involved in work to return several World Renewal dances in the past twenty years, I can suggest that there are two main reasons for their successful return. The first is that they, the ceremonies, connect our fellow tribal members with the original instructions and the Spirit Beings. This drive to connect with the creation has never died. The second is, I believe, that we have a predisposition to participate in communal displays of regalia. It makes sense to us in deeply psychological ways. And once ceremonies are returned, tribal members travel for miles to participate in them once again, especially, I have noted, when their families were once possessors of the treasured dance regalia. Some families will bring objects to the dances that were hidden away long ago. We are witnesses to many dance objects as they are revealed for the first time in more than fifty years.

Amid all of this—communities reconnecting with the original instructions and the Spirit Beings, the return of communal displays of regalia, and the spiritual healing of the people and Earth—there is what can only be called an inevitable wall of vehement resistance to their return. The resistance amazes me because of the obvious good a ceremony brings to a community when that community works with the best intention to return a dance to its rightful place in the world. And yet, the resistance adds a certain symmetry to ceremony itself. It creates a time for the people to reflect on the needs being provided for by the ceremony and on its importance. After a few years, the vehemence is forgotten, and the ceremony becomes an indispensable part of us again.

The White Deerskin Dance at the old village site of Weitspus on the Klamath River is the most recent World Renewal ceremony to return. At times, its rebirthing seems to be governed by a whirlwind. At other times, bliss and timelessness reign. In the end, I believe that the community of Weitspus will be strengthened, and the world will become more stable. And by performing the rituals and dance, the Spirit Beings of the Earth there will help to heal the human beings living there.

The Abalone I Know Is Named Yuxtharan

I tasted abalone meat for the first time in the late 1970s. Without a doubt, it is the most scrumptious of all the shellfish. A group of Kashaya Pomo friends brought it to a community gathering and picnic. It was great fun, but I have mostly forgotten that time except for my first experience eating abalone. It was delivered already removed from its shell and sliced into thin steaks. The cooks lightly pounded the steaks and then threw them on a barbecue grill. Another cook was deep frying seaweed until nice and crispy. The meat was placed on a homemade tortilla. Seaweed was laid across the meat. A fresh, homemade hot salsa was dribbled across it all, and this was handed over to me. I remember the moment: bright sunny day, happy people, laughing and teasing cooks, and, me, transfixed into a gourmand's ecstasy—I love abalone!

My first experience with abalone was very positive, if a bit one-dimensional: All I ever did was eat it, so you might say that my relationship with abalone at the physical level was extremely good. About twelve years later, I discovered another side of abalone: Abalone Woman, the Spirit Woman from myth. After having met the Spirit Woman, I can say that at the emotional level my relationship with her is even better—or as good a relationship as can be had by a mere mortal with a Spirit Being.

I met Yuxtharan'asiktávaan, the mythic woman, in the early 1990s while creating a multimedia arts installation at the now defunct, and sorely missed, Capp St. Project in San Francisco. The installation was my first large-scale conceptual art piece designed to conjure "the other world," the indigenous spirit world. To be honest, Abalone Woman was not an element of the installation initially. She was not even significantly within my personal cultural consciousness at the time.

Early on, the art project became an historical de-constructivist piece. It was inspired by a six-and-a-half-minute audio recording that I had found in a catalogue of language recordings at the University of California, Berkeley (Haas 1982). It was of the last fluent Mattole Indian, Johnny Jackson. The find set off a spark of intuition. It began growing slowly.

I was raised in sleepy northwestern California. I attended elementary and secondary schools that were within a few hours drive of the Mattole River valley, where Johnny Jackson had lived in southern Humboldt County. I was raised to believe and did not question the fact that the Mattole Indians were extinct. I can recall hearing distinctly from those in our household and from grade-school teachers that the Mattole were no more. It was therefore a great thrill for me to be listening to a recording of the Mattole language. What hit me hardest was the fact that the recording meant that the Mattole were not extinct. The recording had been made in 1958. Were there other Mattole Indians about?

The concept for the art installation slowly came to life and included the office and workshop of a fictitious, chain-smoking female anthropologist seeking out speakers of lost languages. In the end, she was able to gather only fragments and ghosts of what once was. Adjacent to the anthropologist's workshop, with its maps, artifacts, filing cabinets, and anxiety, was a circular door. It recalled the round doorways at the front of the traditional plank houses of our region. Beyond the door was an interior space designed to present the sacred spirit world as it is known by the Indian people here in northwestern California. The space offered glimpses of the sacredness of the Earth as informed by the Native knowledge of the place we call home. I hoped to demonstrate that our spirit world exists well beyond the short human lifespan. I wanted to show that scientific approaches to knowing can sometimes confound, bypass, or ignore the sacred—a sacred world that coexists with the modern world and modern mind.

From the ethnographic recording, the Mattole Project was born. I learned later that the Native speaker, Johnny Jackson, had passed away a few short days following the recording. The installation's focus shifted from physical extinction to cultural extinction to cultural persistence. I listened often to the six-minute recording of Jackson. I studied the publication by Fang-kuei Li on Jackson's language, dryly titled *Mattole: An Athabaskan Language* (Li 1930). Though the publication is essentially a grammar, it contains a short collection of stories and texts that gave me my first look at the Mattole mind. Old Man Coyote was included in the selections, the ever present trickster who is found in the traditional stories of all of the local tribal groups. There were other animals, as well. Looked at together, one could see that the ocean was at the center of the Mattole life way.

Li's Mattole glossary, grammar, and collection of stories provided material for the art piece. My collaborator, the San Francisco–based photographer and builder Jo Babcock, took several trips to the mouth of the Mattole River. He returned with wonderful large-scale, otherworldly, solarized prints of the terrain at the river's mouth. After I had pulled together all of my research, the recording, the photographs, the construction plans, and the painting ideas, the piece lacked a fulcrum. There was no vortex. The piece, full as it was, did not move me.

One day, I received a large collection of northwestern California traditional music. The collection contained songs labeled "Mattole Songs" (Brainerd n.d.). I listened and earmarked several songs identified as girls' puberty songs, "flower songs," for potential inclusion in the piece. The installation grew sporadically—layers of meaning on top of layers. Months later, I found a very short collection of unpublished, handwritten field notes on Mattole ethnography by John P. Harrington, a noted anthropologist of his day. His prodigious fieldwork with numerous Indian languages has remained unparalleled, according to experts, and is likely to remain unmatched forever. In 1928–29, he was busy working with my people, the Karuk, far up the Klamath River. He took a break to buy supplies and made the long, dusty car trip to the coast, arriving in Eureka on the Humboldt Bay. While there, he interviewed several Wiyot Indians, including Dandy Bill, Amos Riley, and Birdie James. Harrington sent them through his now well-known grinding mill to extract their precious cultural information. While eliciting place-name data, he prompted them to identify place names outside Wiyot territory. My heart rate and breathing increased as I read their data on the Mattole, their southern neighbors. The Wiyot speakers told stories associated with many Mattole sites. The fulcrum for the art piece emerged.

Speaking generally, each and every art piece that an artist makes *must* have a "heart" for it to live and to breathe. The heart for the Mattole Project turned out to be the words of those old Wiyot people. They told about a rock that sits just offshore from the road that ran then, and that still runs, along the coast near what is called False Cape. "Footprints," they said, were visible on top of a rock there—perfect footprints! They said the footprints were those of a Spirit Being. "Her name," they said, "is *Hiwot* (hi:wo:t)." It was Abalone Woman. They also said, and this astounded me, that she was born and raised at the southern shore of the mouth of the Mattole River. This kind of specificity is almost too much, too good, for an Indian person from northwestern California to consider.

In the end, Abalone Woman, Hiwot, became the heart of the art piece for two reasons. Abalone Woman consolidated—in my mind, at least— several different stories and concepts from different local tribes that together defined northwestern California as a distinct cultural region. In addition, the voices of Harrington's Wiyot consultants affirmed my belief and assertion that the unequivocal spiritual focus for our indigenous ancestors was a strict devotion to and emulation of the Spirit Beings, the progenitors of indigenous humankind.

There are other Footprint Rocks in California and throughout the West, and they surely commemorate important events. But this particular rock was able to combine a certain place, the Mattole River, the focus of my thinking at that very time, with the promise that has guided all of my artwork: that we have inherited certain Truths about the world conveyed to us by means of our indigenous languages and myth. Through orthographic scribbles on a page, Harrington captured a moment that rang true. The reverence for the Spirit Beings, a reverence that I knew well, was present in the words of those old Wiyot people. The Mattole Project found its heart and its emotional weight after being for so long a product of the intellect. Culture, it can be said, combines art, mind, and heart.

One night I dreamed of a house at the center of the installation space. It was Abalone Woman's dwelling. Her house was circled by the Spirit Beings of the world as she meditated and sang away inside the house.

The dream solved for me my next Abalone problem. How was she going to fit into the piece? The dream house helped, but it also revealed a new, glaring problem: I had no abalone shells. According to the dream, her house was made of abalone shells. I was directed by friends to a Pitt River Indian man who loved to dive for abalone. I contacted him and told him about the installation, what it meant to me as an artist, and that I hoped to create a house of abalone. He listened and then said that he did, indeed, have some abalone shells. He said I could come to his house and pick them up if I liked. I offered to pay for the shells, but he said no. The art piece made sense to him somehow, and he wanted to donate the shells.

Jo Babcock, my collaborator, and I drove to Sebastopol from the Bay Area. No one was at home when we arrived, even though we had told the man that we were coming that very afternoon. There were no abalone shells. We looked and found nothing. We left empty-handed and then thought: It's a big yard; let's look again. As we looked here and there, we spied a black tarpaulin under a tree in the far corner. I was thunderstruck when I lifted up the tarp. There was a pile of more than one hundred fifty large abalone shells. We could not believe it. We had lowered our expectations—we might collect several shells here and several shells there. With the opening date looming, we figured we would go with what whatever shells we were able to collect. The gift of the Pitt River man made it possible for Abalone Woman's house to be of mythic proportions.

We returned to San Francisco with the shells. I cleaned them for hours and hours. Talk about tough! Then I began designing the house according to the specifications given in the dream. It was tepee in shape. My research revealed that this was the actual shape of indigenous Mattole houses. The several ethnographic photos of Mattole houses further verified the house shape as indigenous. In the dream, the outer surface of the house was sheer. The abalone shells were within the house. Our finished structure differed slightly. Instead of sheer, the house had a hard outer shell made to resemble the rough and hard outer surface of an actual abalone shell—multicolored and rough. After constructing the house, we focused on its interior.

The shells were placed inside the structure on the floor. We added directional lighting to accentuate the shells' natural pearly iridescence. The audio recordings of the Mattole puberty songs were played on a repeating loop from inside the house, as well. The vast room in which the installation was housed was darkly lit and cool. In each corner of the room, four large, solarized, full-color landscape prints were backlit, casting light into the space. Tall wall paintings representing Spirit People ringed the room, and they were illuminated by track lighting, adding a bit more light.

Visitors entered the space through the round door cut into the wall, with traffic naturally flowing to the right so that one circled the room in a sort of spiral course that ended up in front of the entrance to Abalone Woman's house. As one peered through the house's doorway, the lustrous gleam of iridescence was more impressive than I could have ever believed. Combined as they were with the visual impact of the glowing shells, the two repeating songs projected an eerie, otherworldly beauty. To this day, ten years later, I meet folks who visited the installation, commenting that they will never forget the experience.

I love Abalone.

Who Else Knows Her?

Abalone Woman is our own indigenous mystery woman. Known by all our neighbors. Her destiny, it seemed, was to marry Big Dentalium. Today, abalone and dentalium are what we call *araréeshpuk*, Indian money. She did not marry Dentalium, though. She married a young man who, the stories tell us, was born immaculately—a very mysterious man himself.

It is in a *Latsik*, myth story, from the Wiyot people that we meet Abalone Woman. The Bear River and Mattole River Athapaskan-speaking people also have myth stories, but it is the Wiyot story that is best known. The rest of us local tribal people know her less well. None of us possesses a myth story with her as its main character. She is, nevertheless, an important force in our myth storytelling tradition.

Karuk people do not possess a *pikvah*, myth story, of Abalone Woman. I have researched this topic for years and have found no published or unpublished story, nor have I found any Karuk elder who knows any such story. My own discoveries about her happened serendipitously. As I extended my research about her to include neighboring tribes, I began to see that there was a possible story cycle that included stories from the Hupa, the Karuk, the Yurok, and the Wiyot. Other neighboring tribes— the Bear River people, the Mattole River people, the Tolowa and Shasta groups—possessed stories that help us understand Abalone Woman, but to a lesser extent. What was clear is that she was a member of the highest echelons of the Spirit Beings.

Trying to understand Abalone and her position takes one down a labyrinthine path. The Yurok and the Karuk each possess a story about a Spirit Being named, in English, Dirt-Boy, He-Was-Dug-Up, Root-Boy, or some similar name. The boy possesses magical power. He grows to manhood quickly. He is also a trigger that manifests an important tribal prophecy. The Karuk represent him as a solitary figure, while the Yurok saw him as sociable and always willing to help others. Knowing Dirt-Boy is essential to knowing Abalone Woman.

I spent several years compiling the extensive handwritten and largely unpublished texts that Harrington collected from the Karuk people in 1928–29. My first real clue about a story cycle revealed itself in these ethnographic texts and data. By story cycle, I mean a series of stories found in the oral and published literatures of neighboring tribes that are unmistakably connected by character and plot. Separate stories, when viewed together, create a larger story that literally defines the indigenous world being considered. In this case, let us consider what is known. Abalone was born and raised at the mouth of the Mattole River. Dentalium was born and raised at Yontucket, far up the coast in Tolowa country. Dirt-Boy was born (immaculately so) and raised at the village of Panámniik far up the Klamath River in the mountains to the east. Abalone's and Dentalium's marriage did not happen. Finally, Dentalium beat Abalone Woman severely. The stories of the region agree on these facts.

Dirt-Boy became Abalone Woman's husband. More about him and

his origins is important to know if we are to truly understand Abalone Woman. The magical baby boy was dug out of the ground by a young maiden while she was out digging roots at the Karuk village of Panamniik (present-day Orleans). This was a large village amid a substantial river valley, with vast meadows running east and west following the course of the Klamath River. He was immaculately conceived. The roots being gathered were from the *xavin* plant, known locally in English as the Golden Lantern. Growing in the midst of these prolific plants, with their pretty bright yellow globes, the Panamniik elders knew there was one that grew to huge proportions. Instead of a root, the boy was growing at its base.

Strong admonitions were given to the young maidens not to dig up this huge, magical root. Attached to it was a prophecy. One girl disobeyed the elders and dug up the root of the magical plant. The Karuk medicine story reveals to us that the plant itself was the germ and seed of our most important Spirit Being, known to us all as Across-the-Water-Widower. In the Karuk language, he is Ithyarukpíhriiv; in the Yurok language, he is Wohpekumeu; in the Hupa language, he is Yimantuwiñyai.

Let us consider the creator spirit Across-the-Water-Widower. Ithyarukpíhriiv created most of the world as we know it today. He was very creative, and after completing his work, his sex drive became insatiable. After seducing many young maidens, a plot was contrived by his own son to trick him into going across the water to a spirit land from which he might never return. Spirit beings, it is said, have great powers of intuition, and Ithyarukpíhriiv knew of the plot to get rid of him. So he left behind his sperm in the form of the brightly colored yellow xavin plant so that the young maidens might admire and remember him after he left the world.

The young maiden Panamnih'ifápiit Veekxaréeyav, the Orleans Maiden spirit being, did not heed the warnings of the elder women and dug up the magical root, finding the baby, Dirt-Boy. The young maiden raised the boy, who grew quickly. She decided early on to raise the boy as her very own husband-to-be, to the dismay of all the elder women. They knew that the end of the era of the Spirit Beings was at hand his with the boy's unearthing.

The Great Transformation marked the time when all of the Spirit

Beings left this land. They transformed together as couples, male and female. Some of them became plants; others became animals; and still others became spirits who might remain behind to watch the human beings. The Orleans Maiden was frantic as the Great Transformation neared because the boy did not return home as the time to transform neared. In a flash of intuition, she knew that her husband-to-be was elsewhere and that they would not transform together. She found him and attempted to kill him with her long stone pestle, but only wounded him. He dove into the ocean and transformed into the Whale. The Orleans Maiden transformed in grief, and alone.

The Yurok have a story about a young man named No'ots. The name apparently refers to the numeral "2" but was the same young man who was dug up in the middle of the gathering field near the village of O'men, the Yurok name for the Karuk tribal village Panamniik. The Yurok story tells more about the boy and his many adventures prior to entering the ocean.

When taken together, the Karuk and Yurok stories provide the big picture of Dirt-Boy. The Karuk story and medicine formula tell of Dirt-Boy's origins. The Yurok story provides the story of his youth. The stories culminate at the time of the Great Transformation. The Orleans Maiden appears in both stories, and she attempts to kill the boy using her stone pestle. Large sea stacks sit offshore on the ocean's horizon to commemorate the story. The sea stacks are said to be the Orleans Maiden's stone pestle. Another rock sits offshore at the town of Yontocket (present-day Crescent City). Neither the Yurok nor the Karuk story tells us explicitly who Dirt-Boy became after transformation.

Our final clue concerning Dirt-Boy's identity and his ultimate marriage to Abalone Woman comes from a 1928–29 commentary by a Karuk man who was responding to the Karuk story about Dirt-Boy and the Orleans Maiden. Chitkas was an eighty-year-old man from the village of Sahvurum, several miles downstream from the Panamniik village. In response to the story, Chitkas recalled a Kick Dance song about "that boy":

Iii, Siytuum uuth pakunpíhtaakaranik
Oh, they swam westward from Pestle Rock
Iii, Ipara'ávan pakunpihtaakranik
Oh, [it was] Whale-husband [and together] they swam away westward.

The story about Orleans Maiden tells us that Abalone Woman and Dirt-Boy transformed together. They married.

The commentary concerning the story was a cathartic moment for me because it gives Abalone Woman her place within the world of the Spirit Beings. Her husband was Whale-man and not Big Dentalium, as one might expect. After all, both the abalone and the dentalium seashells became our indigenous currency, our "Indian money." But that was not her fate. Her true mate was Ípat, the Whale. We know through the stories that she was considered a rich woman. One Wiyot story tells us that she was also considered the most beautiful woman in the world. And as the stories not yet found will no doubt show us, she is at the heart of who we are.

Our reflections on Abalone are at an end. Her complete story is not yet told. More research and thinking is needed to complete the picture. What we know is that the mountains and ocean, creation and longing are just a few of the subjects that are somehow explained through her stories. Abalone Woman is a central mythic and spiritual force for me personally. That I know. I believe that for every person who comes to meet her, she becomes a mythic and spiritual force for them, as well.

I love Abalone Woman.

Afterthoughts

The reconstruction of spiritual wholeness Lang pursues through writing, performing, and creating art, on the one hand, and by organizing and carrying out the ceremonies and sharing his energy with Native communities throughout northwestern California, on the other, flies in the face of all that those communities have experienced since Europeans arrived. Lang's approach to understanding the place of Abalone Woman in Karuk narrative and worldview is based on both his conclusion that Abalone Woman was a central symbol before colonialism and his attempts to return her to that position. This is obviously a far more ambitious project than my own, although it dovetailed with my intention to understand the significance of abalone. If my work with Florence Silva showed me that collaboration meant I had to constantly adjust the motivations and goals inhering in my abalone projects, my work with Julian showed how anthropological research could be harnessed to a

9. *Abalone Woman Falls in Love.* Inspired by a traditional Wiyot story reinterpreted by Julian Lang. Abalone Woman sees the brilliance of Dentalium Man far in the distance up the coast to the north (by Trinidad, California) and falls in love. At the same time, Dentalium Man sees Abalone Woman's beauty of light and color reflected in the sky and immediately falls in love with her. Painting by Lyn Risling (acrylic on Masonite, 11" x 16" © 2001).

10. *The Chase.* Inspired by a traditional Wiyot story reinterpreted by Julian Lang. After Abalone Woman arrives at Dentalium Man's home to marry him, he ignores her, not believing she is really his true love. When she finally leaves to go back home, he realizes who she is, so he chases after her, becoming angry that she is running away. Eventually, he catches up to her. Painting by Lyn Risling (acrylic on Masonite, 11″ x 16″ © 2001).

11. *Transformation.* Inspired by a traditional Wiyot story reinterpreted by Julian Lang. After Dentalium Man catches up with Abalone Woman, who attempts to run away from him to return home, he stabs her in the back with his flint blade. At that moment, she transforms into Abalone. Painting by Lyn Risling (acrylic on Masonite, 11″ x 16″ © 2001).

more activist abalone vision. In both cases, abalone narratives and the multiple uses of abalone resources formed part of Native worldview that incorporated the politics of identity, sovereignty, and creativity. From the broad canvas of abalone's significance as a cultural symbol, I now return to more specific questions about the uses of abalone in California Indian life in the past and present.

III

Cultural Revivification and

Species Extinction

The biggest theme underlying this project, and the focus of part II, has been to ask whether abalone is an encompassing symbol for California Indian cultures both historically and at the present time. In part III, I beat a tactical retreat from that larger question after realizing through my work with Florence Silva that many of the ways I approached the issue were deeply flawed. From Julian Lang, I learned that the ramifications of my question took me far out of my depth, so to speak. I concluded that the breadth of knowledge and expertise that is necessary to ask about abalone's significance in these terms is not available to me and must be addressed, ultimately, by intellectuals from within the relevant California Indian communities.

In response to these lessons, the chapters in part III diverge sharply in their approach to more specific questions and issues. Chapter 5 presents responses to questions about the story of Abalone Woman, the nature of abalone regalia, and the revival of the Flower Dance among adolescent girls, from five members of the Hupa Tribe living on the Hoopa Valley reservation. Each of these individuals should be considered very much a cultural expert whose knowledge about these topics and whose active involvement in the cultural life of the tribe distinguishes him or her from most other Hupa, not to mention a non-Hupa anthropologist. While I have arranged the comments, interviews, and writings from these individuals in a fashion so that their responses to the questions are grouped together in separate, thematically oriented sections, my own comments and analysis are muted, even peripheral, to approaching these questions. I taped the interviews with Bradley Marshall and Callie Lara and present transcriptions of the audiotapes. With Merv George, I took notes as we talked and quote him when I am certain that what I wrote down at that time is exactly what he said. Otherwise, his comments are presented in a paraphrase of the notes taken during conversations. After her Aunt Vivien (Hailstone) passed away, Darlene Marshall wrote down the Abalone Woman story Aunt Vivien used to tell, in response to my persistent interest. Darlene is a well-known storyteller at Hoopa and in California Indian storytelling circles, has written children's stories, and was happy to take on the challenge of textualizing Vivien's story. The story presented in the chapter is exactly what she typed out and gave to me at Hoopa one winter day in December 2000.

By contrast, in chapter 6 I am the main analytic voice in an elaboration of ecological factors that have shaped the decline and disappearance of California's abalone species. A central purpose of this chapter is to include California Indian thoughts about changing abalone populations, which have in fact seldom been considered in the main narratives about the fate of abalone over the past century. But I have used comments from particular individuals in California Indian communities to advance certain ideas in a manner much more typical of how anthropologists use informants' comments in ethnographic research and writing.

By juxtaposing these very different sorts of approaches, my agenda is not to show the superiority of one over the other. During the research and writing for this project, both sorts of approaches become equally plausible—indeed, necessary—as I learned more and increasingly came to consider the nature of my own contributions and limitations. My intention is to show how collaborative ethnography paves the way for anthropologists to pursue different kinds of methods with respect to different sorts of questions and to validate these different methods' capacity to produce knowledge.

with Vivian Hailstone,

Darlene Marshall, Bradley Marshall,

Callie Lara, and Merv George Sr.

5.

Cultural Revivification in

the Hoopa Valley

Previous chapters discussed and analyzed abalone narratives among the Wiyot and at Point Arena and queried the relationship between the Ohlones and the Point Arena Pomo and regalia of various kinds and ages. The importance of ceremonies was made clear in the life and memory of Florence Silva, in the heritage of Ohlones and Wiyots alike; ceremonies were also of tremendous significance in the work of Julian Lang. In this chapter, these foci are explored once again among Hupa people living on California's largest reservation, Hoopa Valley.

As the largest piece of territory in California under the sovereignty of a Native people, Hoopa Valley would seem to differ from the rest of Indian country in the state. Much of the history of European and Euro-American colonial rule in Native California seems like an exaggerated version of what took place elsewhere in Native North America. For example, the genocidal campaign against the Wiyot is not without parallels, it is true, but given the relatively small population of California Indian peoples such as the Wiyot to begin with, such campaigns had far more devastating demographic effects than, for example, the Sand Creek massacre did on the Southern Cheyenne (see Sandoz 1992). Anthropological complicity in the creation of unacknowledged California Indian tribes, including the official erasure of Ohlonean and other central California Native peoples, also seems like an exaggeration, maybe even a parody of anthropology's colonialist legacy in Indian country.

By contrast, the history of the Hupa people of northwestern California much more resembles Indian histories in the rest of the United States, which is to say that it is still marked by considerable violence, harshness, and injustice. As described in Byron Nelson's *Our Home Forever: The Hupa Indians of Northern California* (1988), whose rendering is considered reasonably accurate by Hupa people today, the post–Gold Rush invasion of northwestern California by white Americans led to military occupation of the valley, attempts to force the Hupa to evacuate their homeland, and the eventual establishment of a reservation on a portion of the Hupas' aboriginal territory. Throughout the twentieth century, the Hupa experienced the same government programs that aimed to assimilate and de-Indianize their people that other Native peoples endured in the rest of the United States. Allotment of reservation lands, boarding schools, officially mandated agricultural and vocational training programs, aggressive Christian missionary activity, and the negative effects of well-intentioned white reformers were, however, unable to convince most of the Hupa to abandon their religion (at least, not entirely) or their predilection to fish and gather other wild plant and animal foods, or their concepts of value and beauty.

Yet the many facets of officially sponsored assimilation of Native peoples, and a hegemonic cultural climate in the United States that enshrined the notion that Indian peoples were vanishing and would soon disappear, conditioned much cultural loss in the Hoopa Valley, although less so than was the case among other California tribes. While the major ceremonies of World Renewal were maintained, other ceremonies dwindled and were lost. While Hupas still valued their magnificent baskets and regalia, during the twentieth century fewer and fewer individuals learned how to manufacture these objects, as the materials with which to make them became much scarcer. Like every other California Indian language, the Hupa language stopped being taught in the home, and while it is currently taught in schools in the valley, with the exception of a very few elders, it is no longer anyone's first language. Yet the past decades have seen many efforts to defend Hupa heritage. The making and use of regalia, the enactment of ceremonies and narratives about those ceremonies, and the creation of language programs are central features of cultural work in the Hoopa Valley.

This chapter is composed of the commentary of five individuals, all of whom are deeply involved in "cultural revivification," which describes processes of maintaining, reviving, and creatively reinterpreting rituals and other practices rooted in the Hupa cultural heritage. Some of their commentary is recorded from conversations with me, some of it transcribed from formal interviews, and one individual wrote an important telling of the story of Abalone Woman. The three main topics discussed and analyzed by these individuals are the story of Abalone Woman and its significance; the revival of the Flower Dance, the rite of passage for adolescent girls; and the living and sentient nature of regalia in its manufacture and use.

Callie Lara, whose interview is presented in this chapter, introduced me to the term "revivification." Callie is a major figure in the dances held in the Hoopa Valley and is part of a prominent family in both the Hupa and Yurok tribes. As related by Callie, the story of Abalone Woman is intricately involved in the revitalization of a rite of passage for adolescent girls, called the Flower Dance, in the Hoopa Valley, and in addressing issues around gender in contemporary Hupa society. Contrasting with Callie's version of the story of Abalone Woman is Vivien Hailstone's version of the story. Vivien was of mixed Hupa, Yurok, and Karuk ancestry, and it would be difficult to ascribe a particular tribal origin to her telling. I knew about the extraordinary basketry and jewelry Vivien made—it is impossible *not* to know about it, if one has even a passing acquaintance with contemporary Native arts in California—but first met her at the 1999 California Indian Conference. I bought a basket bolo tie from her and asked her about Abalone Woman. She said that she did have a story, but that she would not tell it to me then and there. I would have to visit her, she said, and give *her* some of my time. Unfortunately, before I could visit Vivien she passed away. Vivien's niece Darlene Marshall, also a well-known storyteller, lives in the Hoopa Valley and befriended my family and me. She offered to write down Vivien's version in her own way.

I also interviewed Bradley Marshall, a prolific and highly appreciated regalia maker who elaborates an articulate understanding of the nature of regalia in the past and present. My conversations with Bradley began not at Hoopa but in his apartment in the Castro neighborhood of San Francisco, where we first began to explore the life of regalia. In the sections that follow, I have added recorded comments from several years of conversations (2000–2003) with Merv George Sr., who has been responsible for organizing and leading the major World Renewal ceremonies in the Hoopa Valley for quite some time. These redacted conversations summarize the cultural revival among the Hupa and the way abalone stories and regalia are integral to those processes, hinting at the vast knowledge and expertise about these topics that Merv George has gathered over the years.

The Story of Abalone Woman

These two versions of the story are told, clearly, for different purposes. In both versions, a strained relationship leads to violence between a man and a woman. Callie Lara's version, told in response to questions I posed in an interview with her, becomes something of a parable for domestic violence and the way insults are redressed. For Vivien and Darlene, the story communicates a parting of the ways in which mutual respect and autonomy appear already established between the genders. The purposes to which this story can be put are thus multiple within the context of contemporary gender relations.

Callie's Version

Les: There's an abalone story that we were talking about before, that's told by Wiyot people, and that's also told by Hupa and Yurok people. Did you hear a version of that story growing up?

Callie: Well, yeah. The way that I had heard the story was, well, you see the Hupa people have generations, and I'm not sure the Yurok people, the Wiyot people, or the Karuk people do, but we have generations. And our first generations were those spirit people, all of the spirit people that were in the valley. And the second generation was animals that left all of these lessons and these stories and these characters. Everything was acted out through these animals that were here. And the third generation was the human beings, the people, that learned from the two before. It was during that first generation, when spirit people lived in the valley, they said that there was a really wealthy man, and he had a son. And they bought him a wife from farther down [the coast]. Some say from the Wiyot people, and some say even farther down. He paid a lot of money, and when you pay for your wife you're paying for the respect of the family and for the respect that is due to the children. You're not paying for property; you're paying for the respect that is due now to the new family that's coming and for the family where she came from. Because they did a good job in raising her, they're good people, they were whatever— you're paying for that. So he bought his son a wife and she had to leave her family. When he first took her home, he was kind of a young person and jealous and was not real wise about things. He began to get really jealous of her and jealous of her people longing for her and that she longed to be there. So he started cutting off her visits to home. Then pretty soon, he started denying her things that she really liked, certain foods, or certain places to go, or certain materials she liked to work with—he would deny her that, he was real restrictive. As time went on, she was getting sadder and sadder, and as time went on he was beginning to get very abusive. He didn't want her talking to other people in the village, and he didn't want her talking to other men in particular. He was just really jealous, which was something that was not done; you just didn't do that. So anyway, she left—she left one night because she was so sad, she was so homesick, she was abused and she was getting sicker and sicker. She fled more or less, and she traveled along the ocean. She could see her feet in the ocean, in the sand, and she knew he would follow her. So she started walking on the rocks, and she crawled on the rocks, and I guess she traveled for a long, long time. And her feet, she would cut her feet on the rocks, and her feet would bleed, and she would cry. Her tears would form these abalone shells on the rocks, and the blood would fall over that, and that's that red that you see on the back of an abalone. That's her blood, and those were her tears. Which goes back again, with the tears, to her good spirit, her inside, her over her shoulder, the irides- cence of her. So anyway, that's what happened. And it was never known whether she ever made it to where she was going, because that wasn't the point. The point was that that kind of marriage be- havior was not accepted, and it was paid for, by her, going along on those rocks and having that happen to her. So we use that story when we talk a lot about domestic violence for young people, because it was not something that was accepted. It helps young people to see that

that was never part of our way; a part of something that we thought was OK.

Les: Is she a person—a spirit person [named] Abalone Woman—who is thought about a lot, or does she just appear in that story?

Callie: She just appears in that story—where the abalone came from. And then every time we use that abalone, it's like that's paid for, that's why we don't accept that kind of behavior. That's why we look at the value of our teaching and our life, and of women, of women in our society. That's what tells us that.

Les: So it's being paid back every ceremony, every dance?

Callie: Well, no. Yeah, you could say that. . . . We have a system here, where if you do something wrong, and you offend people and you insult people there's a payment you have to make. When she left, and went along the rocks, she paid for that leaving. That's over, that's done, the violence is not accepted. Do you understand that?

Crane and Abalone

Told by Vivien Hailstone and written down
by her niece Darlene Marshall

Crane was a good man. He worked hard to provide for his family and he was very proud of his accomplishments. You could see him standing tall and stately, fishing on the Klamath River, congratulating himself on these accomplishments. Once, when he visited an area around where Point Bragg is now, he met a beautiful woman, whom he courted and finally persuaded to marry him and move back to his Country. She was Abalone and she was one of the things for which he congratulated himself. He stood there thinking, "My wife is by far the prettiest in the area; I'm sure there are those who envy me." Then he thought: "I am a good man. What a lucky lady she is to have me for a husband, such a hard worker and great provider." As if to prove what he was thinking, he gathered the day's catch, which was quite large, and headed home.

"Wife," he said, "here is dinner, and there is plenty for you and the children." He sat back and waited for her praise, then moved by the fire as she prepared the meal. When it was done and served, he noticed that his wife had eaten nothing. "You haven't eaten!" he said. "Are you all right?" Busy putting things away, she murmured that she wasn't hungry right then but would eat something later.

When Crane went to bed, he realized that he had never seen her eat, at any time. She was always going to eat later. He watched her without her knowing. Hmmm, he thought. She isn't losing weight, she looks good. He was puzzled. Whenever Abalone would look his way, he would pretend he was sleeping.

Finally, she went to the corner of the room and moved a large rock under which was a basket. She removed the basket and started eating. Crane could not believe what he was seeing. She was eating kelp, plain old kelp, and she seemed to relish it. Crane watched and was amazed by her enjoyment of the kelp. The more he thought about it, the angrier he became. Crane provided the best, or so he thought. He had been so proud that he could give her the best, and here she was enjoying kelp— anyone could gather kelp. Crane jumped out of his bed and said: "How could this be? I give you only the best and you won't even eat what I provide." He was so angry that he beat her, then left to cool off.

It didn't take Crane long before he started to feel ashamed. He hurried home to apologize, but it was too late. Abalone was a beautiful woman; he loved her, and it frightened him to think that he might lose her. Crane started following her tracks in the sand as she went south along the beach. There were several places where she had stopped to cry, and her tears turned into small shiny pieces of abalone.

At last, Crane caught up with Abalone. He apologized and asked her to come back with him. He told her that he loved her and didn't want to lose her.

Abalone looked sadly at Crane and said, "This shows how different we are. It is best that I go back to my people. What you call 'the best' is not what I need. On the other hand, kelp is what we think is best. I cannot go back. I will do something for you, though. I will send the children to you part of the year, and during the fall, you can send them back to me."

That is why geese, their children, fly south during the fall and north in the spring. We have only a few places this far north where you can find Abalone: those places where she stopped to cry. Her tears turned into the abalone found there.

The Flower Dance

In this section, I have excerpted conversations with Merv George during which I learned about the revival of the Flower Dance and its central importance to the reassembling of Hupa ritual. In another part of my interview with her, Callie elaborated on how the Flower Dance has had much to do with processes of cultural revivification at Hoopa Valley. Bradley Marshall, who had just arrived for his interview, contributed relevant commentary about Callie's role in bringing back the Flower Dance.

Conversations with Merv George Sr.

Merv George Sr. is a descendent of the pre-statehood Hupa elites. The famous ritual specialist Rudolph Socktish, who possessed tremendous knowledge about ritual, subsistence practice, and storytelling, instructed him. Rudolph Socktish was a primary informant for early anthropologists in the Hoopa Valley, such as Pliny Goddard (1903). For a few years starting in 2000, Merv agreed to let me study Hupa culture with him, and afterward he helped me to redact and edit the text of our conversations. We often met at his house, or at the house of one of his sons. Sometimes we drove around the valley, talking, ending up at the swimming area on the Trinity River called Tish Tang, where my family would be picnicking. We did not always discuss the Hupa religion or history; Merv played in a rock band, and had lived in Eureka and Arcata as well as on the reservation. Often, we ended up talking about the tribulations of raising children.

Merv's authority to lead the ceremonies and his spiritual power hinge on his performing his role and doing it well. Nevertheless, during the time that he has been organizing and guiding the dances, his words and direction have sometimes been disregarded by ignorant individuals, often young people who disparage his knowledge and his responsibility. But, he pointed out, his family and lineage have provided leaders for the ceremonies for many centuries. Over the years, Merv observes, he has shown that he knows how to make the rituals do what they are supposed to do. In 2001, Merv and his family held a Flower Dance for one of his granddaughters, the first one held at Hoopa for many decades. We talked about that at his house a few months after the ceremony had been held. The Flower Dance is the coming-of-age ritual for adolescent girls. It was not an easy task getting ready for this ceremony. Few people at Hupa are old enough to remember how the ritual was conducted early in the twentieth century, and it seemed to Merv that some of those few were not particularly interested in sharing their knowledge or memories. Merv wanted to share with me the importance of abalone in the Flower Dance.

Toward the end of the dance, the adolescent girl or girls (who have very recently had their first menstruation) jump up and look into the interior of a large abalone shell. "You look into it to see what you can see. See the future, see the beauty. Maybe, maybe you can see the beauty of your future," he laughed. The colors of the shell, Merv told me, do indeed matter, as they are part of how the vision the girl sees unfolds.

Abalone is important in all sorts of regalia. "You put it on at night, and the fire makes reflections on the abalone. The abalone lights up, and when you wear it on your chest, your whole chest lights up." Abalone has great beauty, but it also has its voice. Merv said: "It clicks and clacks; it's a special sound. Nothing sounds like that. You hear that, you know someone's going to dance."

According to Merv, abalone was very abundant at one time at Patrick's Point along the coastline of the Yurok people. "You used to take river otter pelts down to the coast to trade for it," he said. "You could harvest abalone also at Orick and at Klamath." But the abalone have been fished out for at least fifty years, he said. He also pointed out that the water was very cold on that coastline, which in the old times before the whites came had made diving for abalone on this stretch particularly difficult.

He remembered that the rim of the abalone is used as a back scratcher during the Flower Dance, since girls are not allowed to touch themselves during the ceremony. Men wear abalone in the regalia they use for the Jump Dance. They wear five or six strands of abalone that make the loud clacking when they dance. People give Merv large abalone shells as gifts, and many of the shells were lying in his garden. When he needs some for regalia, he breaks up the whole shell into pieces and shapes and polishes the pieces for what he needs.

Merv thought that it was true that Hupa people may have used abalone as a kind of money at one time. It is certainly true, he said, that the shell is still bartered extensively in Hoopa. He reminded me many times that regalia are for using, and for sharing. Regalia must be danced, handled, allowed to fulfill their destiny.

In 2003, Merv talked again about the Flower Dances that he has been helping to get going again in the valley, for his granddaughters and for other young girls, which have to take place soon after the girls "come in" (start to have menstrual cycles). Merv's family holds Flower Dances in the family's ancient house at the Hupa dance grounds, where the Jump Dance is held, as are Brush Dances. He recalled how the big abalone shells are held up by the girls at the end of the dance, and how the girls are supposed to see a vision of their future lives in the shimmering colors of the shells' interior. Merv talked about how many of the old people wanted to criticize but not to help get the dance started again. So Merv and his daughter researched and learned; they also made up new songs. This went to the heart, he observed, of how he understands and organizes the rituals—there are rules, to be sure, but there is also a wide range of possible creativity and innovation. Composing and singing new songs brings the dances to life, brings them into the present. "You wouldn't want to sing a song just because it was old, but because you wanted to honor the people who taught you that song and remember them."

Callie Lara

Les: I was wondering if you could say again, Callie, what you were just saying before, about the women's point of view with respect to abalone and the idea of reflection, looking over your shoulder

Callie: The way that I learned it when I was growing up was that we, women in particular, have a strong connection with abalone, and it's used in our Flower Dance ceremony, which is for women. Indian doctors, women doctors, use abalone; women dance with abalone. There's a strong connection between women and abalone. Because it's not only in the Flower Dance that you are looking at that. The vision at the very end, at the culmination of the dance, is when the girl looks up into the abalone, and she's asked a series of questions, and she answers them. Some say that they are looking at a reflection, and some say, well, they can see the vision in the iridescence of the abalone. What I was taught was that we didn't have [pre-contact] things that reflected, mirrors that were reflective, so the abalone, when you looked into it, what you were really looking for was to look over your shoulder, look over your right shoulder. Because we believe that's where your good spirit is, the spirit people, the ones that take care of you, are behind you. My brother used to tell us—he's an Indian doctor—and he used to tell us that when they were training, that was something they always had to do when they came up against something, what we call Indian devils or spirits that are not good things. That if he looked over his shoulder, there was his guide. So when we look into the abalone shell, we're looking for that reflection over our shoulder. Others say that they are looking into the reflection and in their mind they are seeing a vision of their spirituality or their destiny and those kinds of things, So those are kind of two, and there are other interpretations of how that is. But . . . all those interpretations complement each other. One doesn't contradict; it all complements each other. It's just depending on who's telling it.

Les: You were saying that from a doctoring perspective, it's a little different than from a dancing perspective.

Callie: Just that when we're talking about the abalone shell at the end of that [the Flower Dance], a doctor, or someone that is studying medicine, . . . might . . . see that and say, you have to look over your shoulder, that's where your good spirit person is, or the spirits are, that guide you. I don't know what another person's perspective might be. They might not even focus on that, but they do know that they're supposed to look into that shell. And it could be that for those that look into the shell and see a vision, that's the way that it comes to them. But the purpose of it, the way that I learned it, is that you look for that reflection, which you're supposed to see over your shoulder. Of course, you didn't see the brush, or this and that; you'd see those people or that guidance there. It guides you. We always believe that they [spirit beings] are our guide; they're going to let us know how to respond or how to act. And that's why we look to them. Christianity, I think, is real similar: They call on their God when they need help. It's kind of the same thing. Knowing that that's the cycle of life, that's what you draw on.

Les: Thank you, Callie. I can't imagine going into anyone else's house and their being able to sit down and give this amazing philosophical perspective when they're getting ready to go the bank!

Callie: [Laughter] Everything that we do—my family, and my grandmother's family, and my other grandmother's family—they always looked at the world that way. But that was a woman's responsibility:

to look at things in a philosophical way. Not to fear confrontation or all of those things that you work out. We've lost a lot of that. But the Flower Dance is really going to change the way youth are in the valley now. And it's only been coming back just lately. We've had this—what is the word now that Kishan [her daughter] uses?

Bradley: Revivification.

Callie: Revivification of the Flower Dance. In that, we're really looking for some positive outcomes. Those are the kinds of things you really can't measure in a short period. We're just going to have to see how it goes.

Bradley: That's been an interesting process, too. Because I think it came for me, about the abalone shell—looking in. It was a number of different people that came together, and Callie was one of them, the principal people, from my perspective, about bringing it back in. It seems like within our culture here, we've gone different lengths of time without doing certain things. But we've always kept it within our living memory. Someone within the tribe has the memories, or a combination of different people hold different parts. So I think that when we're out there doing research to bring something back, it's important to go to all these different people because they may all have a different take or a different part of it. But when you bring it all together, you have the whole again—versus going out and reading in a text on a ceremony and saying this is the way it is, this is the only way it is, because so and so wrote it, and they were writing exactly what they heard. And it just doesn't work that way for us. Callie was one of the ones that was principal in, I think, bringing it back as far as what she remembered.

Callie: It's funny how you remember pieces of things. Like I was telling the girls the other night, all of my life I said that I wanted to make bark skirts. Because . . . I used to peel bark with one grandmother, and then maybe three or four years later, another one would be weaving and I'd get to go over there and play with it. In my mind, I would think: How did they get this to this point?

Now I'm fifty years old, and it wasn't until two years ago someone said, "Do you want to go out and get bark with me?" And I was going—that's the missing piece, that's the part I never knew! And I said, yeah! It just takes a long time for those things to come back. So when we started talking about the Flower Dance, Salish [her son] was doing a lot of research, years ago, like ten years, he was really focused on it. Shortly after that, Melody [her daughter] started getting really interested, because she had daughters. It's taken all this time, but here we are. All those pieces that people had—the songs, the medicine, the sticks, the dresses—it all started coming together and it was, like, we didn't ever forget. But still, we know that even though we don't live in that day when we had certain things accessible to us, we're able to use things that are accessible that are similar, or maybe made in a different way, but still bring them in and perform that particular formula.

The tape had run out. The rest of this conversation focused on the significance of reviving the Flower Dance and how, without it, women had been excluded from the tribe's ceremonial life. Hupa women had been excluded by the Euro-Americans after contact, and Hupa men who had still consulted women had been belittled by Euro-Americans. Callie looks forward to the time when the Flower Dance is completely integrated into ceremonial life and is performed on the same regular basis as the other dances, for the Hupa and the neighboring peoples. Callie also discussed the process of interviewing Hupa women for the tribe's self-published book on the revivification of the Flower Dance and how men were also interviewed about the process of bringing the Flower Dance back. The book is titled *Do You See the Big Bird in the East*—something that the girl performing the Flower Dance says as she looks into the abalone shell.

The Nature of Regalia

In his interview, Bradley Marshall's discussion of making and dancing living regalia brought him to other topics, particularly the curation of Hupa regalia in museums and his views about museums as repositories of cultural heritage. Callie elaborated on women's special relationships with regalia. In our conversations, Merv George's consideration of the nature of regalia was inseparable from their use in the central ceremonies of Hupa ritual life, which he is in charge of organizing and leading. These topics for him also involved much thought about the relationship between all the tribes that participate in World Renewal dances (in his experience, Hupa, Yurok, Karuk, and Tolowa) and his views on the relationship between Native religion and Christianity.

Bradley Marshall

Bradley: Well, I should say this right off, that this is simply my perspective, and my perspective, I think, is more of an artist's perspective or a creator's perspective on abalone. The way that I was taught with this, my father always told me that when you are making something you have to be in a good place. You have to have good thoughts, because whatever you're feeling, whatever you're experiencing, it will come out in your work, it will show in your work. Whenever you're putting something together and sending that into the world, or into the dances, you don't want bad to be sent out. So that means that when I create something, whether it be to cut out a piece of abalone, to put together a necklace, or build a necklace, I have to have a good heart or be in a good place in myself, because that piece is going to go out into the world, and I don't want to send bad out into the world. Also with the pieces I create, I know they are going to outlive me. A life span is pretty short, when you think about it—we're only here for about eighty years or so. But the pieces I'm creating I know are going to be here for several generations. With the proper training and a stroke of luck, they'll be used by several generations beyond me. Our area in particular, and for us in Hoopa, contact [with the Euro-Americans] has only been for about one hundred fifty years, and so the things that we have now that are considered old are from one hundred fifty to two hundred years old, and that's still relatively new when you look at European society. But you look at us, and the knowledge that we've carried and what we've done, [it] is pretty much the same all the way through for thousands of years. And so what we create today we'll be using years from now, after we're all gone. After I'm gone, it'll still be here.

As far as the abalone is concerned, when cutting abalone, I look for the coloration in it, where am I going to get the best coloration, where am I going to get that reflection. If that's going on a piece of regalia, I'm looking for reflection in the abalone, the way the light's going to hit it. Within the dances, when we're dancing, in the Brush Dance, you have the fire that's in the middle, and at night you'll see the abalone stand out. You'll see the red of the fire reflected in the abalone. What I was told years ago—I don't even know by who anymore, it's been so long ago—is that the abalone's reflecting that fire and the abalone is what's haunting or scaring the bad spirit and chasing that bad spirit out. So you want to have abalone in your dances. So what I look for is, where am I going to get the most coloration, where am I going to get the most reflective quality, because the fire's going to be reflected in the abalone. And if you watch the Brush Dance at night, and you see all the quivers go around, the quivers are what stand out with abalone. When I'm cutting and polishing, it's a long process. And abalone dust is not healthy for us, so I try to do all of my work underwater. A long time ago, what the people would do is scrape the abalone on a rock, to get it down to a decent thickness, or use the rock or some sort of hard implement to put a hole in it. But today, because of the equipment that we have, I can actually produce the shapes that you're seeing—the small, intricate cuts or a pattern or design within the shell. And to me, it's a fun process, coming up with ideas of what, or the concept, which a lot of times I dream about ahead of time. And then I'll put it together. So I may see it in my mind, a full necklace or a design. And then the challenge becomes how to put it into a piece of abalone or how to form what I'm thinking of.

Les: Talk more about the process of making the regalia, if you can, and the whole idea of putting life into the regalia, and the regalia as living.

Bradley: Well, again it goes back to what I had mentioned on my thoughts, my feelings, my emotions going into that piece. I was taught that a piece of regalia is not alive until it's danced. So I can create a necklace, and it's just a necklace. Or I can create a quiver, and it's just a quiver. But as soon as that piece is used within any of the ceremonies that it's meant to be used in, then it gains a spirit. Or you could say that the spirits that were in the animals that I used come back into it and form a new life. One of the things that I've always been told is that the regalia that I make I don't own. Even though I've put the time, the money, and the effort into it, I can never own that piece. I'm just a holder. The difference between an owner and a holder is [that] a holder is going to be the person to take care of the item. Holder is the one to make sure that the item gets out to the proper ceremonies or is used in the fashion that it's meant to be—almost like a parent with a child. It's a parent's responsibility to make sure that child is taken care of, it's a parent's responsibility when the child is at a certain age to get to the places the child needs to go. And you find yourself running all over crazily with the child for years, all through adulthood even. Well, I kind of picture the regalia as children, because it's my responsibility to house them, to make sure that they're maintained, and to make sure that, if the string is getting worn, they're put on, to replace it, if there's something broken on it, to replace it. To maintain that piece of regalia. And then it's my responsibility to run that regalia all over, wherever the dances are going on, wherever it's supposed to be, it's my responsibility to make sure it gets to that place. So again it's in the same context of the parent with the child; that's how I look at the regalia that I hold. Also, because a parent can never own a child, because a child is his own or her own person. It's a life, it's a spirit, it's a living being, and we don't own other living beings. Regalia has the same sense. Once that spirit has come into that piece of regalia, it's a living being, it has its own spirit, and as such I can never own another spirit. It's just my responsibility to make sure that spirit gets to where it needs to go, or to maintain that spirit. So that's what it is, by living. But in the process of, I guess you could say, giving birth to the regalia, all of my emotions, all of my feelings—my essence, in short—is going in to create that piece of regalia. It's creating that piece of life, and it shouldn't be created with hate, it shouldn't be created with anger or with anything of that nature, because that's what you're going to be sending out into the world. And that's what will be out there long after we're gone.

Les: We talked several times about the sounds abalone makes when it's danced—its song. Can you talk about that?

Bradley: Well, the abalone itself, what I've found is that different pieces of abalone have different sounds. And the way it's cut, the way it's shaped, will also have a different sound. Kind of like a wind chime. On an abalone, if you take the rim of the abalone, it has more of a tinkling sound, almost like a cricket at some points. You take the under-part of the shell, right by the rim, and that has another sound. Then you take the heart of the abalone, and it has a deeper sound. And so, a lot of times when I'm creating something where the abalone [pieces are] going to moving against each other, I'm thinking what kind of voice I'm going to give that piece. Am I going to want a quieter, softer voice for that piece, or am I going to want a louder voice, a deeper voice for that piece? And so when I'm creating it—say, I'm creating a woman's necklace—I may end up using a softer tone for the voice, which means that I use the rims of the abalone to give that softer voice. If I'm making a man's necklace that I know is going to be used for jumping in the center—say, for the Brush Dance—and in there the man's going to be making a lot of noise, I want that piece to have a heavier voice, a stronger sound, so you can hear it; so that the shells, that piece is singing, as well. But I want that voice to be heard.

Les: So you're always thinking about the use that the regalia is going be put to, and what sounds you want to hear from them.

Bradley: It's like a voice. Again, with the children, what type of voice do you give your child? Are you going to have your child be quiet and not say anything, and just kind of be in a corner somewhere? Or do you want your child to out there and be heard? Or do you want your child to complement everything that's going on within the room? It's the same effect with abalone. I don't want my pieces to be tossed off in the corner and not be seen and not be heard. Yet I don't want them to overpower whatever's going on. It should intermingle and work together. So that's what I target, and that's what I look for.

Les: In your work in museums, when you see regalia at the Clarke [in Eureka] or in other museums, what's happened to the life of regalia once its put in museums, once its taken out of circulation as a piece of regalia?

Bradley: I think I told you the story [about] when I first went into the Clarke. This was probably a good ten, twelve years ago, maybe fifteen years ago. I went into the Clarke, and I stayed maybe ten, fifteen minutes within the museum, within the Native American section, and I actually left crying. And I didn't know why I was feeling so bad. I went in. It was a good day; I was in a good mood, but I didn't stay in the room too long where all the Native stuff is laid out without feeling bad, without crying. And I didn't really understand why. I knew there was something there, but I didn't understand it. So I started asking: Why was that feeling there? It was so strong. It just didn't make sense to me why I would feel that in one specific room. And what I was told was that there was a lot of regalia in that museum, regalia that was not being used and could not be used. In short, the regalia itself, that spirit, was taken away from its home. And when the regalia is taken away from its home, it cries to go back, it cries to be used. It's a spirit, it has that life in it and it wants to be among others, it wants that interaction, it needs that interaction to survive. When I looked further into it, I was told that if regalia is not used, it dies. And when it dies it'll disintegrate, its life leaves it. It's kind of like a human again, when we die we go back into dust. Well, a piece of regalia, if it's not used, it'll die and it'll go back into that dust. And that was what I was experiencing at that museum, was the crying of that regalia, to go home, to be used, to be interacted with again.

My belief on museums has changed over the years. At one point, I felt that anything in the museum that was ceremonial or created by a tribe should go back to that tribe. But over the years my belief system has changed. My belief system now is . . . well, what the museum argument has always been is that the Natives should be happy, we're preserving the culture for them, we've preserved this culture up to this point. If it wasn't for us, they wouldn't be able to look at any of these items or study these items. My argument to the museums is: How are you preserving a culture by removing it from that culture? I'm OK that the museums hold on to those items because I do think museums have served an important role in the preservation of certain items, in holding those items. But we, as Native people, to continue our lives occasionally will need to interact with those items, and for the life span of those items, they need to be interacted with, as well. They need that human contact. And so with museums, it also becomes difficult because so many collections have been contaminated, and it's been a build-up of contaminations over years. We've had areas where arsenic was the number-one pesticide back in the early 1900s, and then it went to another pesticide, then to another pesticide. Then we hit the late '60s, early '70s, when DDT was considered the best remedy for killing bugs. And so it was covered with that. So what we've found in museums is that you have a layering effect of poisons. And when you have a layering effect, all of these poisons are interacting with each other, and we don't know quite what the chemical build-up is going to do. We also don't know what's going to happen to the human populace once we use it. We can look at museums today, and we find that over the last couple of generations of museum workers, employees have come down with strange illnesses, left with bad health problems in a short amount of time. Now we find that the general populace, when they go view these collections, they're leaving with these same illnesses. And so, going back to the tribes, if tribes bring these items back, under, say, NAGPRA or whatever they're doing, what is it going to do to the populace? Are the tribes going to be actually ready to handle those kinds of items? And that's certainly up to the tribe for them to make up their own minds on whatever it is.

But I think that as a person that creates not only for my tribe but for other tribes in the local region, when I go into a museum, it's an open space for me to learn, it's an open space for me to do some studying, some research. And, granted, some places I need to cover up, at the Clarke, I'm lucky that we don't have the contaminants.

Les: Why not?

Bradley: Because of the nature of the private collections. The whole collection came in as privately owned, not as institutionally owned, collections.

Les: So they were not treated with those substances.

Bradley: Right. So the people kept them in their house, kind of like what you see around us today, where it's kept within the house, it's kept as a part of the family. [The Lara house has lots of baskets, regalia, and other Hupa-made items displayed in glass cases all around the house.] And we didn't need those pesticides. These [points at items around the house] are taken out and used, they're taken out and cleaned, they're treated as children or as a part of the family. Whereas once it goes into the museum, it becomes more of an object or a piece of art. It's a different feel. So with the museums and the pesticides, what happens if the person takes a headdress home and wears it in a dance? What is it going to do to that person? Whereas someone like me who creates these pieces can go into these institutions and look at them and then I can re-create them. I'm still considered Hupa. I'm also Yurok, Karuk, Tohono O'odham. I'm from a number of different areas, but my main affiliation is Hupa. So I can look at these items in a relatively peaceful environment. I can request to see whatever it is and study it in a way I may need to re-create. Whereas if they're in a family situation on a reservation, I may not be as comfortable with that family, or as you've seen with the regalia I have, it's . . . generally packed away in trunks, and it takes a while to get to a specific piece. Whereas you may request to see a white deer hide—that may be in a specific trunk that I know but it's buried under three other trunks that are full of other things. Or if I got it mixed up somewhere, I could be going through one trunk looking for a specific necklace that's in one of the other three or four trunks. You know, when you look at it from that perspective, you many not know where exactly it is, you have an idea, but you know it's within the dance stuff. Whereas with a museum, I can call ahead, I can make an appointment, and I can go in and look at the whole collection and see what they have. But when it comes to finding someone that actually has the time to go ahead and pull it out [of their private collection] and is willing to pull it out and let you examine something to re-create it, it's a different story. So museums I think are good in a certain sense, and yes, they have helped us with preserving our culture.

But by the same token, I don't feel that museums should be arrogant about us being thankful to them for saving our culture. I think that at the Clarke, since I'm on the Board, the argument I heard when I first went in was: You should be thankful because we're holding your culture for you, and you can come in and look. And yes, I am thankful. I have used it since I've gone on the Board for that purpose. But also, I realize that those items did need to go out and be used because they are spirits. So we've instituted a loan policy now for the items that are ceremonial to go back to the ceremonies and be used. But we also have our doors open for people like me that are creating or are looking for these items to research to re-create them and bring them back into the community in a greater abundance. It's an easy and accessible place for them to come in and view. If they call ahead of time and make an appointment, they can see anything they want, including the entire collection, and spend time. A number of people have gone through the entire collection, and since I've been there, it's been full of people. And also since I've been there and since we've had more interaction as far as people coming in—we've even had Merv George come in and sing to the deer hide. We've had girls come in and dress in the upstairs for the dress shows we've had. Trying on the hats, they're laughing, they're giggling, they're alive. The response I've felt from the items, being alive, is that its OK now, that they're happy, they're safe where they're at, they're being well taken care of. But they also have that human interaction, and they go back to the ceremonies.

After Callie walked back into the room, Bradley told us a story about her husband, Walt, going to a museum in Denver, where he saw deer hides. Walt started singing the Deerskin Dance songs, and the deer started dancing. Callie said the deerskins were behind glass. He sat down in front of the glass case and started singing, and the deerskins began to sway and move.

Callie Lara

Callie: Basically, abalone shells are a woman's; that's what she wears in a dance, that's what she carries into the dance, as part of that dance. All of those things that are used in the dance, from the otter hides to the woodpeckers, to the abalone shells, to the dentalia, they are all the spirit of all those things coming together, [which] is like the people that are coming all together. To wish well, to pray, and to bring good energy to the dance. Well, those things [are in regalia], too, and that's why we treat those things like they are a living thing—not exactly a living thing, but like a spiritual thing. We're careful with them, and we show respect to our regalia, as we would a human being, the same kind of respect is shown.

Les: So regalia is alive?

Callie: Yeah, regalia has its own spirit, especially if it's used in the dance. But we generally say that from the time the maker starts working on that, all his energy, all his thoughts go into that. And if he's had a bad day, that's woven right into that, or if he's had a good day, or if he's processing. Processing is a good thing, you know, if he's processing a bad day, and just working it out and coming to a good result, all those things go into that, into what he's making. So that's passed on—that's what he takes to the dance. Plus their own, the life that they came from, whether it was an animal, or a shell, or whatever, it was all a living thing, a life that was sacrificed to make that [regalia]. So that's one component: the maker, the regalia maker, all this energy is in there. And then it's taken into a dance, and it's collective, everyone's energy, and everything's energy that comes to that dance. So we don't believe that those things just dissipate, and they're no longer there. We think that it's cyclic, and so they are continual. And that's why we're careful with those kinds of things.

Merv George

Merv disagrees with those who maintain that it is possible to be both a Christian and a believer, if not a participant, in the Indian religion. Some in the Hoopa Valley really seem to struggle with this.[1] Merv's view about the big differences between Christianity and the Indian religion derives from the actual incompatibility between the doctrines and theologies of each religion, and from the continued and continuous hostility that the numerous churches in the valley display toward Indian rituals. Merv told me that the Adventists, the Pentecostals, and the Baptists in particular still tell their congregations that Jump, Deerskin, Brush, and other Dances are devil worship. The churches broadcast prayer and Christian singing over loudspeakers during the Dances, set up tents for their own Christian revivals near where the Dances are being held, and create an atmosphere of harassment and tension when key Indian rituals are going on. By contrast, Merv said, everyone is welcome at the Dances; no one is turned away, and no one who attends is forced to say or do anything. This shows, according to Merv, that the opposition between the religions does not derive from a kind of purism or exclusivity on the part of people who are believers in the Indian religion toward Christians.

Merv explained: "Anyway, what we are doing is praying to all the spirit beings, the people who went before us, the people from long ago. There's no word for God in Hupa or for the Great Spirit, or anything like that. We pray to the spirit beings in the rocks, in the river, the animals and the plants. Praying that the food will come back, maybe there will be more food, that the weather will be good for the plants and animals, the river will be OK, that everything will be in balance. We are praying to restore the balance. You can't pray for yourself in the Indian religion, you can't pray to get something or to get ahead. You can ask for the strength to do what you have to do, for help in being a part of getting everything in balance. And you know, it works. After a dance, everything seems quieted down, all the problems seem to get much better. Then six months or a year after the dance, everything gets riled up again, and that just keeps on until its time for the next dance. I guess that's why they set it up like that."

The Hupa had been instructed to carry out the rituals in certain ways by the spirit people, and that is the way you had to do it. If you did not do the rituals the way they were supposed to be done, or if you went where you should not go during the dances, it could be dangerous. Maybe, Merv hypothesized, that *is* one way that Christianity and the Indian religion could be theologically incompatible—that is, if Christians do not know or choose not to obey the rules set out by the spirit beings.

We talked about the interrelatedness of the different Indian peoples of the region on a kinship level. Merv, for example, is part Karuk; his wife is enrolled in the Karuk tribe; and his grandmother was Chilula, a people who, like the Hupa, spoke an Athabaskan language but whose distinct identity faded out early in the twentieth century. Yet he insisted that each people has a different tradition with respect to the dances and ceremonies. "They have a different medicine," he stated, with reference to the Yurok starting up the Deerskin Dance at Weitchpec after more than eighty years and to the Yurok celebration of the Jump Dance at Pecwan. "They can't use what we have here, how I put the dances on here. They do it differently, and it is their way. This is our way, my people's." This means that there is only so much that Merv can do to help the Yurok get their dances started up again, because their tradition is historically different, and needs to maintain itself apart, from the medicine practiced here in the valley.

One time, Merv drove us out to the Jump Dance grounds, next to the old cemetery, adjacent to the Brush Dance pit. This is also the site of a well-known, ancient village.

Merv told me: "This is where we started, where the spirit people dug us out of the ground, and where we emerged into the light. It wasn't no creator or Father who did it. We were in the ground and were dug out."

He recalled many memories of conflicts that had occurred around the time of dances. "You are *not* supposed to carry conflict into the dances," he said. "If you do, there can be really very terrible consequences." Merv recounted the many times that individuals who brought conflict and contention into the dances experienced terrible accidents or losses of life, either to themselves or to their families. He told those stories without self-righteousness or a sense of superiority but with a palpable sensibility of respect for the forces at work in the dances that cannot be avoided or defied.

Back at his house, Merv reiterated that Rudolph Socktish, his paternal uncle, had trained him. On his mother's side, he reminded me, Merv is Karuk, but he identifies completely with Hupa. About Rudolph, he said:

"I was instructed to do this [organize and lead the dances], and that's why I do it."

We talked for a very long time about wealth in both mainstream American and Hupa culture. Wealth in Hupa regalia is the opposite of material wealth with respect to the mainstream sensibility. Regalia wealth must be shared, used, displayed, and, especially, danced or you are suppressing the purpose of the regalia. The regalia are themselves living, sentient beings who must dance and be danced to fulfill the purpose of their lives. Regalia must be danced not only to fulfill their function, but also because of the sentient nature of these objects, their individual needs and destinies.

I asked Merv to further explain "the rules" involved in organizing and carrying out the dances. One example, he responded, would be what is and is not appropriate to share when the different peoples in the region participate in carrying out the most important of the central dances—Deerskin, Jump, and Brush. The dances, he said, are much the same among these peoples—the moves, the sequences, the regalia used. Reiterating what he had told me months before, he discussed why the medicine is different. The deep nature of the prayer among Yurok people, for example, is very distinct from that among the Hupa. So Merv will lend certain regalia to Yurok camps that are doing the Deerskin Dance at Weitchpec, but he will not give them "medicine regalia." In 2002, when the Deerskin Dance was danced among the Yurok at Weitchpec for the first time in many decades, he lent them a new deerskin that his son-in-law had given him when he had asked Merv's daughter to marry him. This was a beautiful new deer that had never been danced, and Merv was happy to see it get danced at Weitchpec, but it was not medicine regalia.

The intermarriage between Yurok, Hupa, and Karuk in fact help to facilitate the sharing of regalia and the attendance of individuals from each people at the dances of the other peoples. Yet at the same time, the way an individual was raised is the primary factor in the determination of his or her personal identity. At a recent Brush Dance held at Soames Bar, a Karuk place, one of Merv's young grandsons participated. Merv attended "not as representative from Hoopa [Valley], not as a part-Karuk asserting his claim to that ancestry, [but] just 'cause I'm the boy's grandfather." Therefore, he in no way tried to act as an expert based on his leadership role at Hupa; rather, he acted as a family member/participant. Merv is very careful always to make these distinctions—never to tread on the ceremonial turf of other peoples, and never to be an "expert-at large," since, in his opinion, he cannot and does not have the medicine to participate in a central fashion anywhere but in the valley. It is OK for individuals to offer a prayer for their own people when they are at someone else's dance, he told me, but not to pray for those who are hosting the dance, since the two medicines are different and not at all equivalent.

Another example of a "rule" that Merv said could not be changed is that the Brush Dance must be held at night and cannot be stretched into daylight hours much beyond sunrise. He felt very strongly about this and remembered that his uncle Rudolph also reminded people in no uncertain terms not to dance the Brush into the daylight hours.

Returning to the subject of regalia, he said: "It is alive; it does have a life of its own. When it's going to be danced, you have to blow smoke all over it, which helps to put the life into it." This life comes from two sources, at least. One source comes from the maker of the regalia, who, according to Merv, "puts [his] soul into it." When the regalia first gets danced, you have to see if "it works," if it really is alive. The other source of its life derives from the animals and plants who gave their lives to make the regalia—it is all made from "natural stuff" that was once alive in a different way. Merv reminded me of watching the deerskins coming down the path down to the dance grounds and how they looked at sunset, how alive they really are.

We also spoke again about the terrible effects of organized religion in the Hoopa Valley and in the world at large. Merv reiterated that Hupa and other Native people of the region had not had a concept of or a belief in a "big guy," a single all-powerful God. Instead, the spiritual life of the people of the valley was focused on the Kehenni—sometimes referred to as spirit people or spirit beings, the ancestor spirits, "the Immortals who dance forever," for whom and in front of whom the living people of today carry out their ceremonies. It was to these spirit people that Merv prayed and spoke before the Flower Dances of the past two years, and it was the spirit people who could appear to the girls inside the abalone shells at the end of the dance. Merv remarked: "This is the best dance we can do, with the knowledge that we have. We're doing the best we can."

And it seemed clear to him that they had done no wrong and had not incurred anger or disappointment from the spirit people.

As Merv explained the spirituality that guides his leadership of the dances, he told me repeatedly that he comes from a "skeptical family." He does not tell quaint "Indian tales"—or, at least, whatever tales he might tell are most definitely told as tales. Such telling is very different from his discourse about the ceremonies, regalia, the meaning of the dances. That type of information forms a coherent and multilayered worldview that sharply diverges from the Euro-American reality. He illustrated the difference between these two kinds of stories, talking about the "river monster" of the Trinity River, named Kaymoss. Merv thinks these stories derive from the enormous river otters that he has witnessed lolling about the sandbars in front of his house. He did not tell me this story with either condescension or humor; he mentioned it just as a "story" some families tell, a story that has nothing to do with the main features of World Renewal.

As our conversation drew to a close, a current of sadness in Merv's voice and words struck me. He told me how he had to pray before starting the cycle of dances, to pray for the right heart and mindfulness to bring about successful dances, to create the right atmosphere for the dances to do their work of healing. He acknowledged how the atmosphere at large in the world worked so much against that healing—how violence and warfare, greed and willful malfeasance were circulating in the air, in every person, in their bodies and words. This has been getting worse lately, he pointed out, and then showed me the hill on the east side of the valley where he would go to pray, saying that if you climbed up that hill and onto the ridge, you could see Mt. Shasta on a clear day. Mt. Shasta, he reflected quietly: spiritual center for all the Native peoples of northern California, and wellspring of the kind of energy that all the doctors and healers called on to try to do the work of healing in a very dangerous world.

Afterthoughts

In the early twenty-first century, the Hoopa Valley remains a geographically bounded place in which one Native California people and their culture control a physical and psychological space sufficient for maintaining certain forms of autonomy, especially by comparison with the tiny rancherias to which the majority of other California tribes are consigned, not to mention the landless limbo of unrecognized tribes. That same geographical boundedness made the Hoopa Valley a place the U.S. Army could easily patrol and militarize in the late nineteenth century, which all three of the Hupa individuals interviewed in this chapter wryly recalled. In the contemporary moment, the Hupas' land base provides, on the one hand, both vivid features of their past such as the old village sites with intact traditional houses, and on the other, the apparatus of modernity congealed in the valley's schools, health centers, administrative facilities, and commerce. This is the context for cultural revivification at Hoopa Valley.

Individual lives also straddle these facets of the valley's geography and its connections to urban California. Merv George's daughter looks into the abalone shell to see her future, and Merv's rock-and-roll band plays gigs in nearby Eureka. Brad Marshall first showed me the unparalleled collection of feathers and abalone shell that he uses to make regalia at his apartment in the Castro district of San Francisco, where he was living at that time. Native peoples' lives are indeed as multidimensional as any others. In this living cultural mix, there is a multiplication of the significance of Abalone Woman's transformations for Hupa people, of the making and dancing of regalia, and of the annual cycle of enacting the rituals of World Renewal.

Consideration of anthropology's contribution to current processes of cultural revivification at Hoopa Valley must be weighed in light of anthropologists' presence in the valley for more than a century. In 1903, Pliny Goddard, who worked with Rudolph Socktish, completed a comprehensive-sounding ethnography titled *Life and Culture of the Hupa*, which became the first volume in the University of California's Publications in American Archaeology and Ethnology series. His work is still regarded as important by many Hupa, including Merv George. In the late 1970s, Nelson's *Our Home Forever: The Hupa Indians of Northern California* emphasized the effects of colonialism on Indian society and culture from a perspective that derived from late-twentieth-century political activism in Indian country. In the early twenty-first century, the presence of articulate and highly motivated Hupa activist intellectuals, such as the individuals who spoke in this chapter, has changed the anthropologist's role. While the anthropologist may initiate research with her or his own questions, as I did, ultimately the research process must focus on those issues of importance within the Native community and give voice to multiple perspectives from that community. That is what I intended to do in this chapter.

In the next chapter, I return to research questions that sparked this project at its beginning: the fate of abalone species and Native involvement in and analysis of the fate of abalone.

6.

Extinction Narratives and Pristine Moments

Evaluating the Decline of Abalone

The Santa Barbara Museum of Man

In the summer of 2000, I visited the Santa Barbara Museum of Natural
History with my friend Tharon Weighill. Weighill is Barbareño Chumash, an unrecognized tribe whose aboriginal territory included the
museum grounds, the nearby historic mission, and indeed, the entire
city of Santa Barbara. Entering the museum, one can go down one hall
that exhibits a host of mega-fauna such as the tule elk, grizzly bear, and
sea elephants that have completely or mostly disappeared from Californian territory. Down the opposite hall, one can view exhibits of the
material culture of the Chumash, with accompanying text about the
extinction of their culture and its documentation by the early-twentieth-
century anthropologist John P. Harrington, chronicler of the Muwekmas' ancestors, as well. Weighill pointed out the discursive and symbolic
parallels between "the hall of extinct animals" and "the hall of extinct
Chumash." In both cases, the rhetoric of interpretation lets viewers
understand that *these* animals and *these* peoples are all part of a super-
ceded and irretrievable past.

Inherent in these museum phenomena lurks the romantic image of
the Rousseauian Indian and images of the vulnerable wildlife and Indians who require protection from the very white society that has destroyed their fragile "habitats." From the perspective of the work I have

done with unrecognized tribes, these conventions and interpretations create a "common-sense" acceptance of Native peoples as outmoded, outdated, done in, or, at least, done for. Critique of these phenomena cannot obscure what anthropologists such as Eric Wolf (1982, 1999, 2001) have been arguing for at least the past two decades: Both biological and cultural ecologies have been irrevocably transformed by the economic regimes leading to the historic emergence of industrial capitalism. The historian William Cronon (1983) blazed many paths in the imagining and telling of intertwined natural and cultural histories of Native and immigrant peoples in North America. In California, many scholars have published analytic work that intertwines environmental, cultural, and social histories (see Castillo 1978, 1989; Forbes 1982; Hurtado 1988; Jackson and Castillo 1995; Phillips 1997; Rawls 1984) and emphasizes the linkage between ecological transformations and the post-contact history of Native peoples in the state (see Bean and Blackburn 1976; Blackburn and Anderson 1993). As William Preston writes:

> The introduction of Old World pathogens during the Protohistoric period and the arrival of alien settlement during the Colonial period progressively removed native peoples from their uppermost position in the state's hierarchy of life. The weakening and eventual destruction of indigenous environmental relationships unleashed enormous ecological and cultural perturbations that directly influenced post-Columbian history. (Preston 2002: 136)

The work of all of these authors makes it possible to historicize Native utilization of animal resources, such as abalone, without necessarily becoming entrapped by the predicaments inhering in tropes of extinction and natural history of flora, fauna, and Indians. But this framework of historical analysis accrues its own hazards. The lure of reconstructing what once was, either conceptually or substantively, is predicated on the insupportable notion that there is a starting point, a moment of pristine biological and human nature from which all subsequent changes can be traced and analyzed. From a number of perspectives, I will discuss why that pristine moment, for all of its attractions and conceptual utility, never can exist (see Broughton 2002 and Neumann 2002 for even more fully elaborated arguments in this vein). As Donna Haraway (1989: 55) writes, "The concept of social relations must include the entire complex of interactions among people: objects, including books, buildings, and rocks and animals," and those social relations must be described historically rather than idealized.

In that light, is not possible to ignore the crisis endangering abalone populations in California, as reported by marine biologists, Native peoples, white fishermen, newspaper accounts, and other sources. The white abalone (*Haliotis sorensii*) is already practically extinct (Davis et al. 1992; *San Francisco Examiner* 2000; *San Jose Mercury News* 1999a). Pink abalone (*Haliotis corrugata*) and green abalone (*Haliotis fulgens*) have become quite rare. Several diseases, apparently brought to the area by the commercial abalone farms, have caused population crashes among black abalone (*Haliotis cracherodii*). All of these species are already considered "commercially extinct": Their populations cannot sustain harvests of any size; therefore, fishing for them in any quantity is completely banned and cannot respond to the market for abalone. Red abalone (*Haliotis rufescens*) is the only species whose population can withstand any degree of harvest at this point of time, and only along the coastline north of San Francisco. By 2004, the harvest of red abalone was limited to people licensed with a state tag, who were allowed to take three abalone larger than seven inches in diameter per day during the ever more curtailed assigned season.

To address my questions about the relationship between the fate of abalone and that of Native peoples in California, particularly those deemed "extinct," I will query various scholarly interpretations of the extinction of animals and the relationships between Native peoples and animals, inserting into this discussion the heterogeneous experiences, opinions, and analyses of Native people with whom I have been talking about abalone. In so doing, I aim to complicate and enrich one-dimensional invocations of "Native voice" found in some anthropological work. This analysis aims to confound the paradigm of natural history, underscoring what has already been substantiated in previous chapters: that abalone has been and remains a cultural being for California Indians in every sense of that term, even as this animal has entered the new century as an increasingly standardized, bio-engineered commodity.

Natural and Native:
Tropes of Extinction, Ideas of the Pristine

Stephen Asma (2001) and Donna Haraway (1989) have critiqued the natural-history paradigm.[1] The placement of Native peoples in the exhibit halls of natural-history museums is mirrored by the circulation of extinction tropes in contemporary environmental, cultural, and linguistic conservationism. The discourses of biological, ecological, cultural, and linguistic extinctions all seem to have converged in the 1990s and into the early twenty-first century as various nongovernmental organizations created to lobby and legislate for indigenous and minority peoples—and frequently academics, as well—deploy the language of extinction to arouse public concern, interest, and support. The link between Native peoples and pristine ecologies is not a new one, and the portrayal of Indian peoples in many museums throughout the United States within the context of "natural history," alongside exhibits of native flora and fauna, underscores this. That conjoining within public discourses of California's history reflects deeply held foundational narratives about Indians and nature that are made ever more normal and, indeed, natural.

Mike Davis (1998) has recently described the war against native Californian ecologies and animal life waged by Anglo-Americans since they took California from Mexico—itself the inheritor of a large chunk of the old Spanish imperium—a century and a half ago. Refusing to reproduce the Western idyll of wilderness and its dualistic opposition with urbanity, Davis's analysis moves the understanding of ecological histories far along. He reminds us to be aware that the terms of analysis used to understand pre-contact Native peoples are projections of capitalist society's anxieties about resources as refracted through race and class. But still lurking in his work are the dangers of "the pristine pre-contact moment" and what is obscured, perhaps unknowable, about pre-contact resource management.

Leading a wave of revised thinking about how California Indians lived in their manifold, ecologically rich environments before Europeans arrived was Lowell Bean and Thomas Blackburn's enormously influential edited volume *Native Californians: A Theoretical Retrospective* (1976), which included a number of older articles that had informed the work of the two editors. Bean summed up the volume's central theme:

The population density, extensive social scale, and societal complexity that developed in California were not just the consequence of efficient technology (e.g. proto-agricultural techniques) and a fortunate environment (e.g. acorns, salmon) which provided an extraordinary amount of energy potential; they were also the consequence of specific social institutions which served to increase productive resources and redistributed energy in such a way that the resultant sociocultural complexity was truly analogous to that customarily found in horticultural and agricultural societies. (Bean and Blackburn 1976: 119)

Contributors to the volume substantiated this theme in several ways. First, authors reiterate that the use of controlled burns by California Indians constituted a conscious strategy for creating environments favorable to vegetation that would attract wildlife or provide vegetable foods for humans. Second, they seem to agree that shamans regulated the harvest of staple foods, particularly acorns and salmon, which allocated labor in ways that maximized food production. Third, authors argue that trading relationships, marriage exchanges, and ritual performances shared among and between villages and larger groups acted to integrate large numbers of people and broad regions into social, cultural, political, and economic systems that increased their overall productivity.

Certainly, Bean and Blackburn were primarily concerned about dispelling the hegemonic characterization of California Indian societies as primitive and helping to change the way anthropologists have generally conceived of foraging peoples. Anthropology in the twenty-first century, particularly in its undergraduate pedagogical manifestations, still represents all foraging peoples as living in nomadic bands in the most biotically marginal habitats on earth. The examples of foraging peoples who lived in biotically rich habitats, such as those of the Pacific Northwest and California, whose social structure and economic systems sharply diverged from those of nomadic foragers such as the archetypal !Kung are usually treated as "exceptions that prove the rule." This maddening tendency, apparently entrenched in undergraduate textbooks, belies the realization that foragers, given a chance, would always choose to live in biotically rich habitats. An important upshot of the Bean and Blackburn book was to portray California Indians as environmentally conscious resource managers in a biotically super-rich habitat who had not only sustained but increased their food resources, notwithstanding the relatively large populations that had lived in pre-contact California (see Cook 1976).

Sean Sweezy refined that focus further, stating: "The large volume of ethnographic information does provide evidence that various aspects of world-view and ritual behavior functioned to organize and adapt human cultures to the ecological permutations of subsistence in California" (Sweezy 1975: 6). Cultural values common among pre-contact California Indians, he argues, accepted a natural world in which spirit beings controlled the environment, a world in which people formed an integral and inseparable part and in which they would be held accountable for their actions. In such a world, shamans could influence the spirit beings to the benefit of humans. Contending that shamanic ritual therefore served to manage food harvests in an apparently rational manner, Sweezy found that "the regulation of harvest procedures for essential resources may have assumed a distinct conservation and management orientation, with ritual specialists serving as short-term 'environmental managers'" (Sweezy 1975: 40). The slippery slope between sustainable outcomes and consciously conservationist intentions in the work of Sweezy and others in effect erases the boundary between Native knowledge systems and their practices, on the one hand, and Western biological science, on the other.

That slippage increases in later work, without, I would agree, necessarily misrepresenting what anthropologists and other scholars know about the various states of affairs extant in pre-contact California. At least some human interventions by Indians *did* appear to maintain and regenerate important sources of food. Moreover, pre-contact Native belief systems, insofar as they can be known a century and a half after the genocidal campaigns waged against California Indians by the Spaniards and Americans, also hinged on "the idea that human use *ensures* an abundance of plant and animal life" (Blackburn and Anderson 1993: 19). Yet Anderson's codification of practices California Indians used into "Indigenous Conservation Tenets" (Anderson 1991: 170), notwithstanding her own caveats about making such an argument, is misleading to the extent that "conservation" is a term loaded with cultural and political connotations at this historical moment in U.S. society. Even though Anderson admits that her "conservation tenets" are expressed "in Western terms," she nevertheless argues her case as if these tenets suffused indigenous practices as such.

Florence Shipek (1989) and Helen McCarthy, David Peri and Scott Patterson, and Sean Sweezy and Robert Heizer (all in Blackburn and Anderson 1993) take a more measured, nuanced approach to characterizing the sustainable outcomes of ritualized management of acorn and salmon resources, respectively, as conservationist. Interestingly, McCarthy in particular relies on the testimony and analysis of Native informants. M. Kat Anderson and colleagues (1998) again advance a position in which Native belief systems not only might be equated with a science of ecology and environmental planning but also arguably could be considered to offer techniques and practices better than whatever Western science can proffer. After reading these chapters many times, I was left wondering whether such authors consider Native American shamanic knowledge systems and ritualized harvests basically an odd, unfamiliar, but ultimately more advanced form of natural science.

One answer to such a query, an emphatic "no," derives from an opposing perspective that has unfortunately been caricatured even by its own proponents. The extreme forms of "extinction revisionism" represented by Paul Martin (Martin and Wright 1967), and the imagery of a Paleo-Indian "blitzkrieg" against Pleistocene mega-fauna, understandably result in hostility from Native intellectuals (see Deloria 1997), thereby poisoning the possibility of non-Native scholars' engaging their Indian counterparts. The popular media is always hungry for the most extreme and simplistic versions of controversial science (*New York Times* 1999, 2000), and as extinction-hyped scholars have turned their sights on much more recent species declines—buffalo, beaver, and other fur-bearing animals—Native intellectuals may rightly suspect a hidden agenda. It is not hard to imagine the consequences of painting Native peoples as just as ecologically dangerous, not to mention rapacious, as the white man. The negative outcomes would no doubt be directed toward the always very partial measures taken by federal and local authorities to respect, restore, or otherwise recognize the initially limited, subsequently abridged, and frequently terminated sovereignty rights that treaties specified in exchange for the cession of the territory that is now the United States. By the same token, there is much more narrowly focused, non-sensationalized work in this vein that is worth considering.

For example, Charles Simenstad and colleagues (1978) have shown that pre-contact Aleuts drastically reduced sea-otter populations in certain areas, which resulted in reconfigured coastal ecologies and food availability in specific areas of the Aleutian Islands. The debates between R. Lee Lyman (1995) and Terry Jones and William Hildebrand (1995) underscore the difficulties in actually substantiating the role Native peoples may have played on the Oregon and Northern California coast in the destruction of seal and sea-lion rookeries on the mainland.

In a much broader assessment of the so-called ecological Indian, Shepard Krech (1999) happily dispenses with the Paleo-Indian blitzkrieg. In general, Krech argues that sustainable practices do not equal conservation and that low population densities among pre-contact Native peoples were a likely factor in the sustainability of their harvest of animal species. He sees more evidence for Native peoples' conscious manipulation of vegetation—through fire, for example—to perpetuate and increase useful species than there is for such management of animal species. His chapter on the uses of fire may be his most evenhanded, stressing both the ways long-term utilization of controlled burns enhanced food resources and that there were limits to how much Native peoples could control the fires they set (see Lewis 1973). Krech stresses that there is no isomorphism between indigenous knowledge systems and practices, on the one hand, and natural science, on the other. During his own fieldwork in Gwich'in communities in northern Canada, he learned in detail the enormous differences between how indigenous and Western scientific knowledge systems explain animal behavior, abundance, reproduction, and the human role in all of these phenomena. Such differences, Krech maintains, may in particular situations have made it likely that Indian peoples harvested animal populations in biologically *unsustainable* ways.

Krech is not the only one to take such a position. More recently, Hildebrandt and Jones (2002) have argued that California Indians likely overexploited marine pinniped populations to such an extent that rookeries on many areas of the coast would have disappeared. But I think Krech's overall insight may be somewhat undermined in that he illustrates these general points by focusing only on the cases of three particular animals' natural histories: buffalo, deer, and beaver. Certainly, the trade in these animals quickly became integral to the incorporation of

Indian peoples into a colonial mercantilist and, later, an increasingly capitalist global economy. Moreover, in his and others' studies of these histories (Flores 1991; Isenberg 2000), important evidence is available that specifically undermines the characterization of Indian peoples as never harvesting more than they need to sustain animal populations. It might have made a more nuanced argument to develop a counter-example, such as salmon, where there is far more evidence for sustainable harvesting practices even long after colonial regimes successfully dominated Native territories. In any event, there is a notable silence in Krech's book concerning Native intellectuals' analysis of ecological histories, and I read this silence as implying (on Krech's part) that Native intellectuals in general would tend to defend the romantic character of the "ecological Indian."

In a sharply written evaluative analysis of conservation and sustainability among a broad range of foraging and horticultural societies, Eric Smith and Mark Wishnie (2000) agree that "ecosystem engineering" characterizes foragers such as the Indians of California. They stress that "small-scale societies have developed many practices designed to enhance livelihood for which habitat or biodiversity conservation is a by-product" (Smith and Wishnie 2000: 15). Such practices include matching harvests to needs, regulating the onset and duration of harvests, switching areas of harvest to regulate overall returns, and practices that result in the creation of habitat mosaics. Smith and Wishnie find that restraint in harvesting is rare among foragers, although a lack of restraint is not necessarily synonymous with depletion. Like Krech, they argue that the propagation of plant resources occurred more regularly than that of animal species. In a mirrored opposition to the ways that some analysts conflate Native knowledge systems and Western natural science, Smith and Wishnie reify the dualism between the two. If Native peoples avoid the harmful modification of biological habitats for "religious reasons," Smith and Wishnie seem to find the conservation outcomes even more epiphenomenal. I would argue that it is possible, however, that within Native knowledge systems certain outcomes *are* expected, even if they are not definable as "conservationist." Given the culturally specific meaning of "conservation" in our own society, it is incumbent on us not to discount the outcomes of Native practices as simply unforeseen or unintended but to inquire *within the terms of those knowledge systems what the expected or intended outcomes were* (see also White 1997). To make such inquiries, we must rely on the difficult, long-term, and necessarily collaborative project of ethnography, which, as Judith Berman (1996) showed with the Boas–Hunt partnership, is inevitably saturated by many kinds of ambiguity from the beginning, and perhaps even more so when the research questions are posed in terms so particular to the societies from which anthropologists themselves originate.

A review of Michael Alvard's intelligent, careful analysis of Amazonian hunters' practices also leads me to these conclusions. Alvard argues that "low population densities, lack of markets, and limited technology more parsimoniously explain the equilibrium enjoyed by native groups than does a putative harmonious relationship with nature" (Alvard 1994: 147). Conservation of animal resources, Alvard concludes, is epiphenomenal. While it is true that the Amazonian hunters he followed do seem to balance calculations of short-term costs with longer-term benefits, these calculations lead to behaviors that are the very opposite of conservation, such as increased hunting pressure on depleted species (Alvard 1993). So even when hunters harvest less than the maximum, which would dangerously deplete their resources, Alvard would insist that terming these outcomes "conservation" is inaccurate. I feel very comfortable with these conclusions, and not only because they are so well documented. Perhaps Alvard's work can convince anthropologists to stop posing or to greatly modify the terms of "the conservation question" in their work with indigenous peoples, since it is so clearly motivated by the environmental crisis of the West.

Arthur McEvoy, whose focus, most appropriately, is on the social history of Californian fisheries, has proposed that Native peoples in California learned over time how to manage their resources in a sustainable way, and that this process was "costly, time-consuming, and probably marked by expensive failure" (McEvoy 1986: 21). McEvoy does not discount the extent to which Native peoples' cultural modalities prior to contact with Europeans were tangential to contemporary understanding of "conservation." Nevertheless, he contends that California Indians "took steps to protect themselves from overexploiting [fisheries]" (McEvoy 1986: 26) by limiting their own populations, limiting the fishing they did by depending on multiple food resources, and regulating harvests via ritual. McEvoy introduces a clarifying sense of historical dynamic. Resource management by Native peoples changed over time and was not a solidified or static body of knowledge that was blown apart at contact. In this way, he refocuses the discussion away from conceptual incommensurabilities and toward a more continuous tracing of the relationships between various peoples and various animals. McEvoy argues that, because shellfish such as abalone are relatively slow reproducers and generally sensitive to environmental stress, "mollusks will bear only slight harvesting pressure" (McEvoy 1986: 23). More recently, William Preston's analysis supports McEvoy's contention that abalone could easily have been over-harvested (Preston 2002: 126). However, McEvoy reasons that California Indians must have learned over time to harvest "as much from their environment as it could predictably yield" (McEvoy 1986: 28). Such an argument might be developed as a dialectical intertwining between Western discourses of cultural and biological dynamism, on the one hand, and Native peoples' own practices and knowledge systems, on the other, insofar as these are accessible to one another.

Natural and Cultural Histories of Abalone and Company

Assessing the dynamic relationship between abalone and California Indians demands a confrontation with the impossibility of retrieving pre-contact practices and ideologies. At the same time, acknowledging that contemporary Indians necessarily must understand their ancestors' practices mainly through the complex and conjoined lenses of current ideas about ecology and conservation, as well as through their own families' memories and interpretations, marks a departure from the pitfalls of "the ecological Indian" and the pristine moment of contact. Indian management of the environment changed historically, but so did Natives' own understandings of that management in the past and the present, and both of these realizations are integral to this analysis. Such a historicizing of historicism may help us to avoid the "flora, fauna, and Indians" sort of natural history, while permitting us to emplace human activities in specific ecological and environmental transformations. While that is a step forward, there are nevertheless overarching problems associated with focusing in on any one animal–human relationship, when both contemporary ecological science and Native narrative seldom legitimize such a move. Predictably, there are consequences from that kind of focus.

One way to set the stage for these analytic moves takes stock of recent archaeological work, which indicates important shifts in Native utilization of abalone in response to climate changes. These changes and shifts took place so long ago that they are not a part of the cultural memory of contemporary Indians. But this work indicates what kinds of factors have been, and still are, shaping resource availability along the California coast, factors over which neither indigenous knowledge systems nor Western biological science have control in either tangible or conceptual ways, but to which Native management systems would have had to respond—perhaps, as McEvoy contends, making some mistakes along the way. In an early work dealing with these issues, Louis James Tartaglia (1976) relates environmental and cultural factors shaping pre-contact Southern California Indian abalone harvests. The two most common (and widely eaten) abalone species (historically) are restricted by water temperature. Black abalone (*Haliotis cracherodii*) favor warm intertidal waters, while red abalone (*Haliotis rufescens*) is a cool-water intertidal creature. The presence and absence of these species in shell middens over time indicates changes in oceanic temperatures but, more important for Tartaglia, also changes in diet and strategies for procuring food. Tartaglia argues that California Indians' utilization of diverse sources of food was also related to their tendency to exploit the most readily available, highest-yielding sources. With respect to shellfish, this meant that Indians harvested mussel beds until they were exhausted and took the biggest abalones they could find until they were gone, too. He finds evidence that as the biggest abalones were eaten up, the average size of shells decreased and decreased. As people ate more of the sexually immature individuals (under 10 centimeters in diameter), Tartaglia contends, human predation of abalone deeply affected populations that, in specific locations, forced pre-contact peoples to seek other food sources.

In the past two decades, some archaeologists have emphasized the role of climate changes in fluctuations in abalone populations. Michael Glassow (1996) reports that changes in ocean temperatures associated with El Niño events during several pre-contact periods up to 9,000 years ago expanded habitat zones for red abalone and therefore made certain areas far more attractive for human settlement. This argument is further elaborated in Glassow and colleagues (1994), which relates the exploitation of shellfish exclusively to changes in ocean temperatures in the past 7,000 years or so. By contrast, L. Mark Raab (1992), using optimal foraging analysis, reasserts the role played by pre-contact peoples in the Channel Islands (off the Southern California coast) in depleting black abalone populations. That depletion forced these populations to forage for other kinds of shellfish that provided less food value per unit of time spent collecting than abalone did (see also Raab and Yatsko 1992).[2] Given these disputes, how can one evaluate either the possibility that pre-contact peoples played a role in destroying abalone populations or the significance of climate change?

Pete Haaker, a biologist with the California Department of Fish and Game, argues (as Alvard does) that technical considerations limited how much pre-contact peoples could affect abalone populations (Haaker, personal communication 2000). Red abalone can live in the intertidal zone, where at low tide they can be rather easily harvested from land without diving. However, the species also maintains refugia fifty feet below the surface, where the water is very cold—too cold, Haaker insists, for the unprotected, technologically unassisted divers of pre-contact times. The Indians of the Humboldt Bay area, he relates, could harvest a cove—clean it out, if you will—and come back the next year to find abalone again, because the individuals from the refugia would re-colonize the zone above fifty feet up to the tidal area during those months. The refugia maintained healthy genetic populations, particularly since the largest (and oldest) specimens survived in the deeper waters to reproduce repeatedly. These characteristics of both the abalone's habitat and Native harvesting practices contributed to the Native peoples' ability to sustain their use of abalone resources from year to year—that is, in the absence of climate changes that might affect abalone populations beyond the control of *any* human intervention.

Given Haaker's argument, it makes sense to reintroduce features of Native harvest regulation described in the last section that also cast doubt on the "pre-contact Indians depleted abalone" argument. Whereas Tartaglia argued that a diverse resource base conditioned overexploitation of particular resources, most anthropologists have argued the opposite. Robert Greengo (1952) describes shellfish harvests as part of a "seasonal round" in which Indian peoples maximized their food stocks by consciously minimizing the negative impact on any one food source. The desire to minimize over-exploitation would have been particularly acute with reference to abalone, which Greengo agrees was the most valuable shellfish of all, given the sizable chunk of nutritious, high-quality meat it provided. Many groups among the coastal Yuki, Pomo, and Miwok on the Sonoma and Mendocino coasts and among the Chumash and Gabrielino on the Santa Barbara and Los Angeles coastlines may have depended on shellfish during much of the year. Greg Sarris (personal communication 2000) told me that abalone harvests, like the harvests of acorns and salmon, were regulated through song and ritual:

> Grandpa Tom Smith sang songs before he went out to harvest abalone. You had to have the songs, know when and how and where to perform them. And these songs and how to do them were the property of certain families. In our culture no one knew everything—knowledge was the property of different families, and each individual was left with a sense of wonder because of all the things you couldn't ever know—everyone's knowledge was by definition incomplete. . . . You had to know the abalone songs and perform them correctly, otherwise the tide would get you. You'd be swept away by the tide, and brought to the underwater world where you would have to live like the abalones.

Some readers of Sarris's work might question his access to this sort of information, given his experiences in childhood and early adulthood (described in Sarris 1994). But I would argue that his discourse is no more or less filtered than any contemporary Native person's perception of the practices of ancestors two or three generations back. What Sarris's comments clarify is one facet of the indigenous worldview—knowledge about harvesting particular foods as property—that created barriers to the over-harvesting of those foods. Even the smallest insights into those worldviews—and Sarris's was not a small one—might help to loosen the stranglehold of the conservationist paradigm so pervasive in the study of indigenous resource management.

Another facet of the nature of abalone in at least one indigenous worldview is found in this short tale recorded by John P. Harrington in the 1930s among lineages that lived in the coastal borderlands of the Esselen and Salinan peoples. Most likely, because of the loss of cultural knowledge afflicting Native peoples such as the Ohlone and the peoples of this coastline, this tale has not been told for many decades. In it, kinship orders the relations among supernatural entities, including abalone:

> Thunder lived in the west where the sun sets. Thunder stole Blue Hawk's wife. Hawk and Crow went to get the wife. They reached there and put the wife, who was a red dove, inside his flute. Hawk fled, passing Maneka Mountain on the way, and reached Morro Rock. Red Abalone was Hawk's uncle and Hawk begged his uncle to open, and he did and he was saved. Thunder hit Morro Rock and it went all to pieces. (Harrington 1931: reel 88, p. 439)[3]

In a short article characteristic of the insider reporting found in *News from Native California*, Rob Baker (1992) describes the practice among Coast Miwok of taking care of shellfish precisely by harvesting them. Like Sarris, Baker cites "Grandpa Tom Smith," lead informant for Isabel Kelly's exhaustive, encyclopedic survey of Coast Miwok culture, society, and history (Collier and Thalman 1996). Baker also spoke to contemporary Coast Miwoks, such as Sam Carrio, Elizabeth Campigli, and Virginia Jensen, about harvesting clams on the coast. Clam beds in Tomales Bay, he writes, were "a garden, a human creation, cultivated and kept healthy by the knowledgeable activities of those who know the land best." By repeatedly culling the larger clams from the beds, Coast Miwoks made sure that young clams had sufficient space to grow. But cultivating and harvesting a "clam garden" formed part of much larger systems of classification and harvesting of marine foods and of assigning and using tribal property (see Collier and Thalmon 1996: 125–28).

Once again, it is important to gauge these assessments of Native practices carefully for three reasons (at least). First, recall that ethnographically reported practices probably do not represent the practices of thousands of years ago about which archaeologists want to know. Second, contemporary Native peoples' testimonies are necessarily shaped by the contemporary discourses of conservation, ecology, and environment that they, like everyone else, must navigate. And last, the "mistakes" that McEvoy contends were part of the ecological history of Native practices are likely not reflected in ethnographic testimony, either. Abalone itself presents unique characteristics as an entity distinct from other "food resources," for abalone, as many Native people who have spoken in this book document, is more than a food. Its magnificent shell is also an integral part of its value, complicating the analysis of the harvest of this animal and its cultural significance. The trade in abalone shell, used to make regalia and various sacred and quotidian forms of ornamentation (cf. Lang 1993–94; Margolin 1993–94), extended far inland, as far as contemporary Arizona and New Mexico, as described by Charles Hanson (1973), as well as up the coast of California north of Mendocino, where abalone populations petered out entirely. Robert Heizer (1965) described the trade into the Pacific Northwest in the early colonial period. Norm Sloan (2003), a marine ecologist who works for and with the Haida in Gwaii Haanas National Park Reserve/Haida Heritage Site, has recently shown the distant northern reach of both pre- and post-Columbian trade in California red abalone, which stretched all the way to Haida Gwaii (the Queen Charlotte Islands) off the British Columbia coast.

Evaluations of the high value of abalone shell were found in narratives up and down the coast. Grandpa Tom Smith told Kelly: "The hoipu (local chief) is a boss. He has lots of beads and abalone shell; he doesn't give that abalone shell for nothing. It is worth more than clam money. Some hoipus pretty rich" (Collier and Thalman 1996: 343).

Predictably, the Yurok, whom Kroeber (1976 [1925]) considered obsessed with matters of wealth and value, ranked abalone within a larger hierarchy of treasured objects and materials. In the conclusion of this volume, I recount the classic story told by Robert Spott to Kroeber in which the value of different shells is explained. In that story, it is clear that while abalone is quite valuable, its worth cannot compare with that of dentalia shells of various sizes. In another tale, told to Kroeber by a man named Tskerkr from the coastal village of Espeu, the value of abalone can be seen to derive in part from marriage. A spirit person, Goose, was known as Great Money. The many children of Great Money were also geese. The action of the story, such as it is, involves the migration southward of the geese children to another place, Perwerhkuk. In that place, the children can eat and grow fat, and that place is also the home of Great Money's wife, Abalone (Kroeber 1976).

Themes from the two Yurok stories I have cited reprise the numerous variations of the story of Abalone Woman told by Yuroks, Hupas, Tolowas, Wiyots, Karuks, and the peoples of the Sinkyone coast. As we have seen, the story in its numerous forms relates the origin of abalone and why abalone is found only in certain very specific areas of this coast. It is above all a profoundly gendered narrative: Abalone is always a woman who is involved in a deeply problematic relationship with a man. That man in some versions is just a man—called Northwest-Young-Man in a Wiyot version recorded by Gladys Reichard (1925) or an unspecified man among the Bear River Mattole (in Nomland 1938). He is a wealthy man in Callie Lara's version and Dentalium Man among the Wiyot (in Teeter and Nichols 1993). In one Yurok version, he is Goose (Bell 1992), and in Vivien Hailstone's story, he is Crane. In some versions, the man marries Abalone Woman. In other versions, he does not. They have children in some versions but not in others. She leaves him in one telling; in another, he jilts her before they ever marry. In some versions, their breakup is violent and is complicated by wider conflict between neighboring peoples. In other versions, the parting is decisive yet pacific. Many, if not most, of the stories refer to the importance of place. Abalone Woman comes from the south; her journeys lead her to the south, where the first abalones were created and where abalone can still be found. Patrick's Point and Shelter Cove are frequently named as the northernmost points in abalone's range. In all of the versions of the story, something of great beauty—the abalone shell—is created by a conflict between male and female.[4]

Among the stories told, some abalone narratives are linked to specific harvesting practices in coastal regions, where the animal was extensively fished. One such region comprises the homelands of Coastal Pomo peoples along the Mendocino and Sonoma coasts. Ethnographic literature describes both the Kashaya and the Point Arena Pomo fishing and eating abalone along this stretch of coast (cf. Barrett 1933; Loeb 1926; Oswalt 1964; Sarris 1993, 1994), substantiated by my own fieldwork in Point Arena, working with Florence Silva. Robert Oswalt's narratives record that for the Kashaya, abalone was considered the first shellfish to live along the shore, confirmed in the Point Arena narrative by Florence. The high status that abalone boasted, as both a food and an active sentient being who sings and gambles with other creatures, is elaborated in other ways. Kashaya and Point Arena narratives make clear that both men and women gathered and processed abalone, which contrasts sharply with Pacific Northwest societies, where only women gathered shellfish, and this job was considered low status (cf. Claasen 1991; Moss

1993). In Point Arena, Florence remembered Boston's practices that "cultivated" the abalone along the coastlines to the south of the Point Arena lighthouse. He would search out abalone along the rocky shore and rub the bigger ones with a special stick he had made, causing them to spawn. During certain times of the year, he would sit on the beach, listening for the sound of the sea urchins spawning, and then systematically smash the urchins he found. Urchins, after all, like abalone, graze the kelp forest, and are thus abalone's primary ecological competitor.

Boston's understandings of coastal ecology and the huge abalone populations he and others of his and the next several generations helped to harvest, as reported by Florence and other Native people living along this coast (Sarris, personal communication 2000; Smith 1990; Sherrie Smith-Ferri, personal communication 2000) intersect in complex and profound ways with the thinking of some marine biologists. There are also interesting implications from the thinking of both Native people and the marine biologists for assessing the catastrophic decline of abalone. In "Abalone Population Declines and Fishery Management in Southern California" (Davis et al. 1992) and through my personal communication with Frank Shaughnessy, a marine biologist at Humboldt State University, I have learned that the abalone populations in the middle to late nineteenth century, which lasted until the late twentieth century, must be understood in the context of lethal hunting of sea otters by the Russians, Spanish, and Americans, which went on until the otter had been exterminated in most of its range. Without the otter, whose diet is composed mainly of shellfish, the coastal ecology changed substantially: Urchins and abalone competed for kelp, with urchins able to reproduce faster and live in many more types of micro-habitat than abalone. Abalone seems to have dominated in site-specific habitats, and the activities of knowledgeable people such as Boston may indeed have had a positive impact on their ability to expand their habitat. Shaughnessy is not so sure that the eradication of the otter necessarily increased abalone populations dramatically, but Natives and non-Natives alike report a super-abundance of abalone well into the twentieth century along the San Diego, Santa Barbara, Moro Bay, Monterey, and Mendocino coastlines. If this is even partly true, then the stupendous abalone fisheries of the twentieth century may have been the consequence of a very brief human-induced distortion of the coastal ecosystem.

A. L. Lundy's (1997) history of the late-nineteenth-century and twentieth-century abalone industry comes out of his own insider's perspective as a Euro-American and a fisherman. Although not as well known as I think it ought to be, his history of the industry is neither inaccessible nor esoteric and is particularly valuable, first, for the ethnic succession in the abalone industry that he recounts. After the Americans took control of California in 1850, Lundy acknowledges, Native American access to coastlines south of San Francisco Bay was all but eliminated. Chinese immigrants, who had eaten abalone back home, monopolized the fishery in Monterey, Santa Barbara, and especially San Diego until 1900, when a racist campaign that pathologized Chinese people and their fishing practices resulted in drastic curtailing of Chinese immigration and of their access to fisheries. Japanese immigrants, with considerably more advanced technology, fished abalone much more extensively until the 1940s, when they, too, were ethnically cleansed from the coastline. Anglo fisherman dominated the fishery for the rest of the century, during which the fabulous expansion of the abalone catch (1950–80), as well as the dramatic, disastrous decline (1980–present) occurred, which Lundy also richly documents. Most important still, Lundy crystallizes the fisherman's point of view regarding the relationship between this decline and the post-1970s reintroduction of the sea otter to particular stretches of the California coast. "Shellfish, not just abalone," writes Lundy (1997: 201), "cannot exist in any meaningful numbers with sea otters present in the same area." Elaborating, he writes,

> If the otter is allowed to spread to the southern islands and coastal areas, over time the stocks of lobster, crabs, abalone, sea urchins, plus many other species, will be devastated. If the sea otter is allowed to move northward to Sonoma and Mendocino counties, the last large population of red abalone in the state will be severely impacted. (Lundy 1997: 203)

While Lundy also attributes declines to the constant and ever more efficient harvesting of abalone by the Anglo fishermen, as well as to poachers who have evaded restrictions imposed since the onset of the declines, the role of the otter in his analysis figures prominently. Such a view also characterizes my conversations with a widely recognized expert on abalone who is also an Anglo fisherman, Buzz Owen (personal communication 2000). He argues that before contact, Native people knew about the relationship between otters and abalones, so they specifically hunted otters to maintain abalone populations. He, too, specifies the role of overfishing by the abalone industry as well as poaching in the overall decline of the fishery. Such fishermen, however, tend to focus on the effects of the reintroduction of the otter within their own career life spans.

Between archaeologists who have drawn attention to the dynamic and longstanding influences of climate on abalone populations and the marine biologists and fisherman who have focused on abalone-population fluctuations as a function of the presence and absence of sea otters, the notion of "a pristine moment" for abalone on the California coast becomes completely untenable. Likewise, the "ecological Indian" vanishes, replaced by an increased understanding of Native populations that have responded to changes they often cannot control, and whose practices in each dynamic circumstance have adapted both to maintain abalone as a food and to relate to abalone as a sentient being. Keeping in mind that the tribes were largely evacuated from coastal areas after the Americans took over California, and that restrictions on harvest and soaring retail prices also tended to exclude Native access, many of the Native individuals with whom I have spoken about abalone have not had the opportunity to fish or even eat abalone since the 1960s. This is true not only among the Ohlone and other unrecognized coastal tribes, but also among the many people who still tell abalone narratives and use the shell to make regalia.

Among the minority of Chumash, Pomo, Wiyot, and Yurok who still fish and eat abalone, it would be incorrect to assume that a "Native point of view" exists in isolation from the discourses of biologists, fishermen, and other involved non-Indian parties. But in distinction to the Anglo fisherman, these Native individuals stress site-specific sources of pollution, as well as overfishing, as the proximate causes for the decline and even possible extinction of some abalone species. Rudy Rosales, former chair of the Esselen Nation, blames overfishing and overpopulation in the Monterey Bay area. Florence contends that poaching is finishing off the red abalone populations on the Mendocino coast, which are suffering from the effects of agricultural runoff and stream turbidity caused by clear-cut logging inland. Tharon Weighill and his family explain the decline of abalone on the Santa Barbara coast as almost exclusively the effect of sustained, unrestrained, and industrialized overfishing. In a meeting of the Yurok Cultural Committee in 2000, Walt Lara Sr. (Callie Lara's husband) and other Yurok who know the rivers and coastline of their tribe theorized about the effects of logging and pulp mills on marine life, attributing the disappearance of abalone at Patrick's Point to both. Merv George at Hoopa Valley agrees. The demise of populations south of Humboldt Bay, where abalone was most abundant, Merv argues, was caused by the massive pulp mills of Eureka and the toxic pollution they pumped into the ocean for decades. Their analysis resonates with recent ecological and environmental critiques by Native intellectuals such as Winona LaDuke (1999).

The California Department of Fish and Game (2001), which in its own published materials traces abalone's decline mostly to human agency without neglecting to mention the role of otters, continues to restrict harvests. South of San Francisco, abalone fisheries are closed indefinitely. On the coast north of the San Francisco Bay Area before 2000, four abalone could be taken per day during season, and a total of one hundred was the maximum take per calendar year. Harvested abalone could not be sold or transported. In the wake of even faster declines in red abalone populations on the northern coast, the annual take has been reduced to a mere twenty-four, and only three may be taken daily. Under such circumstances, poaching continues to expand, and newspaper reporting makes sure to note the predominantly Asian surnames of the poachers who are apprehended (see, e.g., *San Jose Mercury News* 1999b), reifying the historically racialized character of animal–human relations in California.

Given the connection between soaring prices, increased rarity, criminal activity, and luxury, the commodification of abalone has proceeded apace, and the animal is now mass-produced in four farms located along the length of the coastline. In an increasingly common twist in this era of capitalist development, the production of commodified animals such as farmed abalone in "controlled" environments has exacerbated the threat to wild populations (see ABNET 1999). I learned much about these farms from those who own and operate them, people who surely never intended to behave as environmental criminals. The Monterey Abalone Company, for example, where I purchased abalone for the Ohlone Abalone Feast of 2000, grows abalone in the water beneath the public pier in

Monterey. Its abalone are fed kelp rather than synthetic food, and they live a more or less normal existence—for abalone, that is. The owners are quite open about their criticisms of the farming industry and its mistakes; they are also supportive of local Indian peoples. Like the marine biologists working for the California Department of Fish and Game and for local and international universities, farmers admit that at least one devastating disease, and likely two, was introduced into the marine environment by abalone farms. This occurred when the farms imported abalone eggs and sperm from other areas of the world: The gametes brought pathogens with them, and when the farmers selectively bred hybrids to develop fast-growing varieties, these new varieties were more vulnerable to infections. The diseases, as biologists, Anglo fishermen, and coastal Indians all recognize, have leveled possibly the lethal blow to wild abalone populations. The discourse of climate change hangs over all of these discussions as well, as the detrimental effects of warming ocean waters on kelp forests, which form the ecological base of the entire system, become much clearer.

Thus, natural and cultural—and economic and political—histories intertwine once again. In such circumstances, it may not be pessimistic to conclude that Native practices and knowledge, as well as the knowledge and practices of Anglo fishermen, have all become largely irrelevant to new ecological configurations that in every sense are now shaped by global economic and environmental processes. The seductive lure of a pristine moment perhaps increases as such processes rework coastal environments, but the natural and cultural history of abalone reminds us that such reworkings are not new. The Native peoples in California have not disappeared as a result of these transformations, and I wonder whether abalone populations, for all the distress they are experiencing, may not also weather these storms, although, as always, transformed.

Concluding Thoughts

There is no single, unified California Indian voice about past or present environmental issues, such as the extinction of the abalone. Such a unified or one-dimensional Native voice is no more a reality than the "ecological Indians" or "blitzkrieg Indians" I have critically considered in this chapter. I propose that an antidote to the imaginary unified "Native voice" would not itself be singular in nature but, instead, would originate in the work of diverse and distinct Native scholars. Their analyses of these social and environmental histories, of Native hunting and foraging practices, and of past scholarly treatments of these histories and practices will greatly enrich fields of inquiry that have not trained Native scholars in the past. Anthropology, for example, changed substantially as a result of the work of Native scholars such as Edward Dozier (Santa Clara Pueblo), Alfonso Ortiz (San Juan Pueblo), and Edmund Ladd (Zuni), and both anthropological and archaeological inquiry is changing in important ways now with the scholarship of Joe Watkins (Choctaw; see Watkins 2000), Winona LaDuke (Anishinabe; see LaDuke 1999), and others. In the case of California Native histories, colonialism and capitalist development removed Indian peoples from coastal ecologies more effectively, perhaps, than from any other ecological zone in the state. Native analyses of these particular histories are predicated on a shift in power relations in this state. Such a shift would afford both real and analytic access to the coast once again, as well as make possible a growing corps of Native scholarship.

If I could predict the epistemological character of that shift, I would imagine that it would involve a divorce of Native history from natural history as that marriage (in the form of the "flora, fauna, and Indians" approach) has thus far been represented in natural-history museums, textbooks, and classrooms. Simultaneously, a remarriage between broad social and ecological histories, on the one hand, and Native histories, on the other, needs to be arranged, but the contract would have to be written up by the Native partner. The contract, to extend the metaphor, would value the historic concerns, goals, and narratives of Native communities and hinge on developing Native knowledge systems and ways of getting knowledge. This is the way, I would argue, to stop perpetually posing questions about Native histories and Native relationships to the natural world based on non-Native obsessions. Those obsessions, as we have seen, frequently stem from contemporary environmental crises such as the conservation of resources. In the expanding environmental crisis of the twenty-first century, scholars need to become especially aware of such distinctions.

As Florence Silva demonstrated during her tenure as tribal chair in Point Arena, Native peoples with access to the coast are likely to get involved in environmental- and species-restoration projects. The value placed on abalone as food, the need for access to abalone shell to manufacture the regalia used in a number of Native religions, and the continuing, even increasing, significance of abalone narratives for many peoples mean that, among the many endangered animal populations of California that Native peoples in the state would want to restore, abalone will figure importantly. I would argue that Native sovereignty along the California coast, for both recognized tribes and those tribes still struggling for recognition, is the condition for increasing involvement by Native peoples in the fate of marine creatures such as abalone.

In the conclusion, I will return to the northern shores, where the Yurok people maintain more sovereignty over coastal territory than any other Indian people in the state. All of the themes explored in previous chapters are brought into high relief for a final consideration of the intertwining of sovereignty and identity in Native California.

Conclusion

Horizons of Collaborative Research

On the Yurok Coast

The Yurok Tribe, who live in Humboldt County north of the Hupa and west of the Karuk, maintain a foothold of sovereign control over their aboriginal coastline, where Yurok people continue to use marine resources and inhabit the territorial space of their cultural narratives and ceremonial life. Among the many Indian peoples in California, the Yurok maintain at least as strong a connection to their cultural identity and their sovereign territory as any other tribe. Thus, in closing this book, I pause on the Yurok coast to reflect on my original questions about abalone as a complex cultural symbol. Through this final consideration, I reflect also on horizons of future research and analysis.

A conclusion should provide a summation of what a book has been about or has been able to accomplish. But this conclusion also acknowledges the limitations the book encountered, thereby recognizing questions research did not address that are, and will remain, of great importance to the cultural work of Native intellectuals and leaders and the anthropologists with whom they may collaborate in the future. In this conclusion, I provide one final ethnographic scenario that encapsulates the range of topics others and I have explored and analyzed in this book. That scenario leads to a discussion of additional factors and contexts that need to be further researched. This chapter also offers one last opportunity to look in on the work of the individuals from several Native communities who collaborated in this volume.

In July 2003, Vernon Lewis, a Yurok man whose family comes from inland and upriver, set up an A-frame net on a beach north of Trinidad. This same kind of net was described by Alfred Kroeber in the *Handbook of the Indians of California* (1976 [1925]). With his two young sons, Vernon waded out into the shallow water, looking for schools of surf fish to skim his net through in order to catch them. Vernon had bought his net from an older Yurok fisherman who no longer went out, and he showed curious onlookers, including me and my family, how the traditional net worked as he rapidly accumulated a growing pile of the small fish. Watching him fish then, and reflecting on what I saw later, I realized that here on the Yurok coast every aspect of abalone's importance to Native California peoples converges, rendering issues of sovereignty inseparable from considerations of identity, making clear once again that thinking about marine-resource utilization also always entails understanding the meaning of narratives and of regalia. Moreover, here among the Yurok, the plurality of voices and interpretations remains strong and can never be downplayed.

Although often considered a riverine people, whose reservation, after all, does follow the course of the Klamath River to its intersection with the Trinity River, the Yurok also lived in large and important villages along the coastline of contemporary Humboldt and Del Norte counties. To this day, several rancherias within historical Yurok territory inhabited by many Yurok but not geographically contiguous with the main Yurok reservation hug the coastline. The word "Yurok" means "downriver" in the language of the neighboring Karuk ("upriver") people, but that orientation extended to the mouth of the Klamath and southward toward Trinidad Head.[1] Along the Yurok Coast, the largest and most important villages included Rek woi (located downriver from the white town of Requa at the mouth of the Klamath), Tsurai (in the sheltered cove near Trinidad Head, or Tsuräu), Opuywa (at the south end of Big Lagoon), Tsahpek (located at the south end of the Stone Lagoon sand spit), Orek (south of the white town of Orick), Welkwar, Espau (at the south end of Gold Bluff), and Omen. Sumeg at Patrick's Point, now a reconstructed Yurok village, was previously covered by seasonal marine-resource harvest sites. Among these sites, one, called O lem by the

Yurok, is also currently known as Abalone Point. The area was not permanently inhabited probably because of severe winter weather. The Yurok *woge* (Immortals) such as Porpoise, Thunder, Earthquake, and Abalone all maintained houses here.

According to Kroeber, the woge were "the institutors of the world" (1976: vi). They are, for Yurok, an older race, more powerful and far wiser than human beings, and were implicated in the processes of creating the world and everything in it. Thomas Buckley (2002: 7, 282, n. 4) writes that the word literally means "ancient or holy ones" and also uses the term "Spirit People or First People." Many Yurok refer to them as "the Immortals," which corresponds to one translation of the Hupa Kehenni, also considered spirit beings. The woge established the world and all of its creatures and parameters before human beings arrived. After the human beings came on the scene, the woge departed, but they continue to exist in a parallel dimension, from which they can occasionally be seen or heard by human beings. This is particularly possible during the annual sacred dance cycles, which in their totality are sometimes referred to as the World Renewal religion, shared among and yet distinctive for the Yurok, Hupa, Karuk, Tolowa, and Wiyot peoples. During the Yurok enactment of the dances, an area is set aside for the woge and ancestral spirits, from which they can witness the performance and where humans can sometimes glimpse them.

Kroeber (1976 [1925]) frequently referred to the people living in the coastal villages previously mentioned and the smaller ones between them as "Coast Yurok," or Ner er ner in the Yurok language. Kroeber (1976) made it clear that a distinctive dialect of the Yurok language was spoken among the Coast Yurok.[2] Robert Heizer, a distinguished student of Kroeber, wrote a "documentary history" of Tsurai, the coastal village near Trinidad Head, tracing continuities and disjunctures from precontact times through the early period of European exploration, into the period of extensive trade, and finally into the American period, ending in the early twentieth century (see Heizer and Mills 1952).

There can be no doubt that coastal geographies, fauna, and characters play essential roles in the larger opus of Yurok history, narrative and tale. Wohpekumeu, one of the several great personalities of Yurok narrative, is "the widower from across the ocean" (the same spirit is named "Across-the-Water-Widower" in Karuk, according to Julian Lang). There is "the inland whale," the main character of perhaps the most widely known Yurok mythic narrative thanks to Theodora Kroeber (1964), the famous anthropologist's spouse. Rekwoi embodied the meeting of the river and ocean worlds and was formerly a center of ceremony and ritual, although Weitchpec and Pecwan are currently more important for contemporary Yurok ceremonial revivalism. But where does abalone fit into the cultural worldview of the Coast Yurok and the Yurok in general? Abalone Woman stories are told among many Yurok families and lineages, but Abalone figures in other tales, as well. Contemporary Yurok stressed to me that each of the narratives can be told in multiple ways, with a plurality of meanings and implications, and that there is no single "correct way" to either tell or interpret these stories.

In one tale recorded by Kroeber and Robert Spott, Yurok notions of value are expressed through a hierarchy of seashells, among which abalone (Haliotis spp.) figures importantly. Interestingly, in the tale, marine shells would seem to have originated in the river:

> In woge times every kind of shell went into the ocean from inland. That is why the upriver people and the inlanders use dentalia, clamshells, and other kinds: because formerly these all lived upriver. When they were about to undergo the change, they said they wanted to live in the ocean hereafter, but that they did want to come back inland sometimes; "that is why they will use my shells sometimes." (Kroeber and Spott 1997 [1942]: 249)

The shells crowd into a boat procession, and as they sing and dance, they are arranged thus:

> In front went dentalia (tsík). Next were the small dentalia (tseikheni tsík); then the dentalium beads (terkutem). Behind these were the haliotis (yer'erner), and then the little clamshells (sekse) which are sewn on women's dresses. Behind them were the kererts wino'os, the thimble-like shells which suck fast on the rocks, and then the little dark-colored snails, both of which hang on women's dresses. After them came the olivellas (turukr); then the smoothed mussel shells such as are used for spoons. Which we call roptei, or as the people farther up the river say hegwon. Last of all were the plain mussel shells (pi'i uwerser). (Kroeber and Spott 1997 [1942]: 249–50)

As the boats float downriver, the procession separates, and some shells, such as dentalia, go northward. But abalone goes south, singing: "Haliotis, dancing in a boat, south I go to capsize" (Kroeber and Spott 1997

[1942]: 250) into the marine habitat that becomes its home. And indeed, abalone still lives, albeit in much reduced numbers, at the very southern edge of the Yurok coast. Although in this story the valuable shells come down the river to the coast, in another story, titled "Tsuräu Young Man" (Kroeber 1976), regalia made of enormously valuable woodpecker crests as well as ceremonial deerskins move on boats from the coast to the river and then upriver. Clearly, there are complex and many layered relationships between coast and river with respect to valuable materials. An alternative telling of the story in Kroeber and Spott that I heard views the boat procession as part of a marriage entourage. Abalone (Yer'erner) was the bride, and she was told not to look back at her people or she would be hit with an oar. She ignored the warnings and was indeed slapped and suffered injury. To recompense her for her injuries, she was rewarded by becoming the shell that lives in the deepest part of the ocean; but the outside of this shell remained forever red from the blood she had shed. This telling resonates with the story of gendered violence that Callie Lara and others see as integral to Abalone Woman's travails and the significance of her story for contemporary Native peoples.

In Yurok tales and among contemporary Yurok, abalone is associated with the south and with certain places. The Yurok variations on the Abalone Woman narrative inevitably situate themselves geographically. Ella Norris's version, told to Buckley (2002) in 1976, locates the tears of Abalone Woman that turned into shells at Pebble Beach, just south of another place where abalone was historically harvested, while her husband ends up at Shelter Cove, 120 miles to the south in Sinkyone territory. The geography of this story suggests that Norris may have been telling a Tolowa or Tolowa-derived version of the story, since Pebble Beach is located north of the Klamath River and the Yurok coastal lands.[3] In a collection of "ancient legends" collected among unnamed Yurok by Fay G. Aldrich and Ida McBride (two Yurok sisters who were the nieces of Fannie Flounder, an important informant of Kroeber) in 1939, Abalone Woman also travels:

Ages ago when animals, birds and fishes had the forms of men and women, Ka-Luck [Kay luck], wild goose of the North, married Yer-ner [sic], the abalone of southern rocky shores, and took her to his northern home.

They were very happy, gentle Yer-ner thinking only of the comfort of Ka-Luck and their many children.

Ka-Luck became troubled as he thought that during their many years together he had never seen Yer-ner partake of even a single morsel of food, though acorns, dried salmon, seaweed and all other kinds of Indian foods did thrifty Yer-ner prepare.

He watched her until one day he saw Yer-ner broil a piece of kelp on the coals. This she ate with much relish. That Yer-ner would scorn good food that he provided for common sea kelp so angered him that he leaped from his hiding place and severely beat her. Heard her crying but he did not go to her although in his heart was only sorrow for what he ha[d] done.

In the morning she was gone, with only her footprints fading away toward the South. Though he followed rapidly he could not overtake her until Patrick's Point. As he came near, he saw that she was weeping and that the tears were filling to overflowing her little cup which she carried in her hands. (Bell 1992: 87)

Patrick's Point, the site of many seasonal camps where various marine resources were procured, is located north of Tsurai and is frequently mentioned as a place along the Yurok coast where abalone could be found, both in the literature and among older people who in their lifetimes intensively harvested marine resources. The midden that remains from the largest seasonal camp on Patrick's Point is the previously mentioned Abalone Point, where excavations in the early 1970s uncovered substantial quantities of abalone shell. Chuck Williams, a man who spent his life fishing on the north coast and whom I interviewed in Crescent City in 2002, recalled the salmon run at Rek woi. He also spoke of an episode in which his grandmother and great-aunt calmed a storm with large swells at the very mouth of the Klamath by singing three songs. He remembered the abalone that family members harvested at Patrick's Point even through the 1940s. Tom Williams (unrelated to Chuck), a man who all his life efficiently harvested and subsisted on coastal resources in and around the Big Lagoon rancheria where he lived, recalled the abalone of Patrick's Point, as well. He also mentioned other particular places where abalone had once been available on the Yurok Coast. Like Walt Lara Sr., quoted in chapter 6, Tom Williams thought that the pollution from paper mills had been largely to blame for the decline of abalone populations. Younger tribal members, born after the exhaustion of abalone resources in Yurok territory, identify existing abalone fisheries well to the south, along the Mendocino coast. One very popular place is Shelter Cove, the destination of "Dirt-Boy," whom, interestingly enough, Ella Norris considered Abalone Woman's son but whom Julian Lang identified as Abalone Woman's husband.

The importance of abalone in Yurok dance regalia has remained undiminished, notwithstanding the virtual extinction of this animal along the tribe's coast. Yurok Brush Dances have been held continuously and with regularity through the decades, nowadays at Sumeg, as well, and in this ritual abalone shell is used abundantly in women's regalia, particularly dresses, and in men's necklaces. The Pekwan Jump Dance was revived in the 1980s, and since 2000, the Deerskin Dance has been held once again at the ancient dance grounds at Weitchpec, where the Trinity flows into the Klamath. During this ritual, the most important of all, abalone regalia figures quite importantly. Those dance families who "hold" old heirloom regalia, each piece of which is a living, sentient being, as well as those who manufacture new regalia find these materials in increasing demand as the ritual cycles revive and renew across Yurok country and the lands of nearby tribes. Holders of regalia do not own or possess these items; they are instead responsible for their care and repair, as well as for taking them to the appropriate rituals when and where they are needed.[4]

The sentient agency of abalone regalia, and the continuing significance of narratives about a powerful spirit being named Abalone Woman, mean that even though abalone itself has become scarce in the waters of the Yurok coast, there is no possibility that this creature is now becoming extinct for the Yurok or will do so for the foreseeable future. The multivalent significance of abalone, and of Abalone as woge, is far more powerful here than the deadly mark of extinction.

Identity under the Sign of Sovereignty

Abalone as food, regalia, narrative, and spirit person is still relevant to many Native California peoples, as I, and others in this volume, have shown. Is it an encompassing, complex cultural symbol, as I wondered at the beginning of this volume? I do not any longer think that question can be answered in a definitive or categorical fashion. The answer(s) to the question depend on who is asking it and why, and by this I do not mean to imply that only Native people can address such questions while non-Native anthropologists cannot. It is a question whose answer must emerge out of particular experiences and relationships to ritual and daily life. In different ways, for John Boston in the past and for Julian Lang in the present, abalone did and does encompass an expansive and complexly meaningful symbolic realm. For the Ohlones and the Wiyot, the possibility that abalone might become such a symbol is emerging in the ongoing processes of cultural revivification that may in the end demand a host of symbolic mediations beyond the stretch of abalone narratives and regalia. The value and meaning of abalone is therefore tied to tribal, community, and individual histories that are always dynamic. Notwithstanding the important differences between tribes struggling with legacies of genocide and erasure, and those which are less burdened in that regard, each person with whom I collaborated in this book repeatedly stressed that tribal sovereignty was inseparably linked to issues of cultural identity and revivification. Sovereignty, they made clear, sustains the territories where Native people enact and revive their cultural identities, creating and re-creating symbolic realms.

Such a formulation corresponds to the discussion in this book's introduction; but what are the limits and paradoxes inhering in the sovereignty of Indian tribes on their reservations? As I have noted elsewhere (Field 2008), nowhere in the Western Hemisphere can indigenous movements be characterized as separatist or secessionist. There are no indigenous leaders calling for the establishment of new nation-states; their call is always, instead, for the reconfiguration of the existing nation-states in such a manner as to recognize and affirm indigenous cultural identities and their sovereign status. Many of the possible expressions of such sovereign status are unattractive, to say the least. In the United States, until the casino era, what was left of Indian sovereignty after the allotment of Indian lands in the late nineteenth century and the termination policies of the mid-twentieth century was extremely constrained in the face of economic strangulation that had rendered most reservations rural ghettos. In the Bantustans of apartheid-era South Africa, modeled on the reservation system of the United States, the white-supremacist regime tried to use a sovereignty model to isolate Native peoples in impoverished rural zones, eliminate state responsibility for their welfare, and thus create conditions whereby these populations were concentrated and maximally exploitable. The autonomous Palestinian areas also concentrate a large population into small, densely packed zones. Israeli governments have demanded that the "sovereign" Palestinian Authority police its people in such a manner as to relieve the Israeli Army of at least some of the burden of controlling that population.

By contrast, since the 1990s the sovereignty of minority peoples and their home territories in the European Union presents a different picture. The European Union has promoted the languages and cultures of distinctive regions within nation-states—Wales and Scotland, Brittany and Occitania, the Basque Country and Catalunya, to name several—linked to a simultaneous process of promoting the political autonomy of such regions and the decreasing importance of national borders. The emergence of a federal Europe composed of distinct cultural and linguistic regions, as Tom Nairn (2003 [1977]) predicted three decades ago, may presage the break-up of some historic nation-states and the re-emergence of the sovereignty of subjugated nations. A united Europe may just be big enough and federal enough to provide space for the sovereignty of formerly subjugated nations.

Between the nightmarish prospect of the Bantustans, on the one hand, and the promise of a "Europe of regions," on the other, the survival of indigenous peoples in the United States derives from another history altogether, and the resurgence of those Native peoples presents a different story. Certainly, the infusion of capital into reservation economies by the advent of the casino age—whatever its many problems and drawbacks—has expanded the discourse of sovereignty on reservations, none of it separatist, secessionist, or Balkanizing. This capital is fueling a surge in language preservation and revitalization programs and other forms of cultural revival referred to in this book. In California, tribes with casinos hosted the California Indian Basketweavers' Association conference in 2005, at which Native foods and cuisine were also prominently featured, and the trope of abalone as food, regalia, and narrative was topical. Just as riverine tribes in Northern California, Oregon, and Washington address and now fund salmon-conservation projects, it is only a matter of time before tribes with capital seek to invest in marine enterprises and environmental restoration of marine habitats, as Florence Silva tried to do many years ago.

Thus, this book leads me, and perhaps others, to a focus on changing reservation economies, especially as transformed by casinos but also by the expansion of tourism. In both cases, some researchers will ask whether the economic space provided by these industries not only makes it possible to fund projects of cultural revivification on Native territory but may also, by advancing the capitalist penetration of reservation economies and social structure, undermine tribal values, rituals, and narratives or strip them of their complex meanings. That is an anxiety that has haunted the interactions between Natives and non-Natives since Europeans first arrived on these shores and some among them began to tell their own stories about "the vanishing Indian." Only profoundly collaborative research between Native leaders and intellectuals, on the one hand, and non-Native social scientists, on the other, can avoid the pitfalls of that old story and pose more trenchant research questions about the relationship between changing reservation economies and social structure and the progress toward cultural revivification. As James Clifford (2004: 6) has written, there is real "potential for alliances when they are based on shared resources, repositioned indigenous and academic authorities, and relations of genuine respect."

Given that my first decade of work with California Indians focused on the struggles of unrecognized tribes, such as the Muwekma Ohlone, to achieve federal recognition, I am also very aware that the concept and practice of Native sovereignty is still under attack in the United States. In mid-2005, the *Albuquerque Journal*, daily newspaper of the largest city in a state where Native peoples are both more numerous and more visible than practically any other in the country, ran an editorial from a "well-respected" retired journalist titled "Indian Sovereignty Has Outlived Its Practicality."[5] Among his many statements, the author (in 2006, the Republican candidate for governor) professed that "the overwhelming list of evidence that the Indians' status as wards of the federal government but 'sovereign' as against the states, is not in anyone's best interests. . . . This is the time for making rational what it means to be American, not playing footsie with those who seek national weakness through divisive schemes leading straight toward Balkanization. . . . An earnest discussion [is needed] as to how we achieve equal standing among all American citizens, none superior, none inferior, and all celebrated as individuals" (Dendahl in *Albuquerque Journal*, 9 September 2005). Such views neatly dovetail with positions historically taken by both the BIA and the BAR, which in the former case have for the past century undermined Indian control over the resources found on their territories, and in the latter case have consistently blocked the fair application of regulations for recognizing unacknowledged tribes.

Both the enemies and defenders of Native sovereignty in the United States would agree that it has been sovereignty that has prevented Native Americans from being absorbed into the population as just one more ethnic minority, under the ideological aegis of American individualism. That insight, from both the allies and the enemies of native sovereignty, resonates with John and Jean Comaroff's (1992) definition of ethnicity as a marked subaltern identity assumed by subjugated peoples who find themselves living within the polities of the peoples who subjugated them. Likewise, the Miskitu leader who proclaimed during the Nicaraguan Contra wars of the 1980s that "ethnic groups run restaurants. . . . We are a people. . . . We want self-determination," (Hale 1994:214) succinctly recognized that, for indigenous peoples, becoming an ethnic group would signify the loss of the sovereign status that creates space for the reproduction of Native cultural identities. The ultimate cultural assimilation of indigenous peoples into the nation-states where their populations are located thus hinges on the loss of sovereign status. This is an arena in which social scientists working in collaboration with Native peoples still have a great deal to contribute, certainly by unmasking the chimera of Balkanization but also by elaborating the complex meaning and significance of Native sovereignty, as this volume has done.

Meanwhile, the Ohlone acknowledgment struggle continues as the tribe explores judicial and legislative strategies for achieving recognition. It is not at all impossible that a positive resolution of their longstanding struggle will occur. The Wiyot are cleaning up Indian Island and advancing the process of recovering their cultural patrimony. Cheryl Seidner and Leona Wilkinson talk increasingly of holding World Renewal ceremonies, the first among the Wiyot in many decades, on Indian Island. Bradley Marshall continues to make extremely fine and highly regarded abalone regalia, for which there will be increasing demand among many Native peoples in the state. Florence Silva tells me that she continues to teach her language to her family members, to take care of the lands around the Garcia River, sun-drying abalone in the summers. She stresses the teaching of courtesy and respect for all beings. Julian Lang will be involved in rebuilding the ceremonial house of the Karuk tribe, tragically destroyed in the summer of 2006, and in other language and cultural projects. He and I will continue to work on re-creating his Abalone Woman installation in the coming years.

Notes

1. Muwekma Ohlone Cultural Patrimony

1. Ishi was the subject of a famous book by Theodora Kroeber, Alfred's wife, and Ishi's story as told by her composes what most people in the United States "know" about Ishi. Following the rediscovery of Ishi's brain in the Smithsonian Institution and its repatriation to California Indians thereafter, many social scientists renewed their interest in the Ishi affair. Two important books on the subject are critically appraised in Field 2005.

2. The owners of this particular abalone farm had expressed their support of both local Indian peoples and of environmentally conscious farming methods, but I later learned how implicated the production of bioengineered, domesticated abalone was in the problems of the wild populations (see chapter 6).

3. Other materials that I have written for the Muwekma Ohlone, mostly in collaboration with Alan Leventhal, that respond to BAR/BIA determinations, and are designed to refute them point by point, by necessity remain unpublished and basically inaccessible.

4. A very old basket in the collection at the University of California, Davis, is attributed to the Ohlones of Mission San Jose and is said to have once belonged to the Spanish colonial governor of Alta California.

5. I visited museums in Munich, Frankfurt, Heidelberg, Copenhagen, and Stockholm in search of Ohlone material culture from the nineteenth century. I was received warmly everywhere I went and was tremendously aided by curators in each museum. However, I was also led to understand that there was no possibility that my research could be linked to a process of repatriation of the artifacts I was inspecting back to the Native peoples who had made them. This reality was made most explicit in the museums in Stockholm and Copenhagen, which had in fact recently repatriated large collections to indigenous peoples in their own colonial spheres—to the Sami in Sweden and to Greenland Inuit in the

case of Denmark. In both cases, brand-new museums under the control of these Native peoples had recently been established. But the issue was also certainly a factor in Germany, although perhaps in a mirror-image fashion. German curators wanted to see collections repatriated to Germany from Russian museums where they had been taken after World War Two. In any case, repatriation was in the air, as just around the time of my museum tour, Greece had once again raised the issue of the Elgin marbles with the British Museum, reminding everyone in the museum world precisely how grand the stakes were in setting any precedents.

6. Another axis of the BAR's strategy has been to undermine the substantiation of Muwekma sociocultural continuity by relying on a narrow, and ultimately ahistorical, conceptualization of the term "tribe" and ancillary terms such as "Indian entity" and "band."

7. Identifying and understanding the Joe Miller necklace could never have occurred without the help of Craig Bates.

3. Florence Silva

1. Florence and I considered three other ethnographic descriptions about her family, specifically about her grandfather and mother, found in Edwin Loeb's *Pomo Folkways* (1926) and especially in Cora Du Bois's *The 1870 Ghost Dance* (1939). We also read several stories out of Samuel Barrett's *Pomo Myths* (1933) together during the period we were actively discussing the three ethnographic texts. Dorothea Theodoratus's 1971 ethnography of the Point Arena and Manchester rancherias also became important in what unfolded in the relationship between Florence and me and the work we did. Birbeck Wilson's *Ukiah Valley Pomo Religious Life, Supernatural Doctoring, and Beliefs* (1968) had much more limited relevance to the topics Florence and I discussed but was still not completely irrelevant.

2. Pomo, and Pomoan, like many ethnonyms, is a contrived term. Victoria Patterson provides the following description of their derivation:

"Pomo" was actually the name of a village in a small valley in Mendocino County; it means "at the red earth hole." It has come to be the designation for a group of federally recognized tribes from Mendocino, Lake, and Sonoma counties. The tribes were grouped by the Bureau of Indian Affairs on the basis of linguistic research that linked the seven distinct languages spoken by Native peoples of this region into a language family known as Pomoan. The seven languages are believed to have derived from a single precursor—Proto-Pomoan—whose speakers spread out from the shores of Clear Lake. (Patterson 1998: 5)

I was to learn that Florence very seldom used the word "Pomo" to describe her Point Arena people or her religion and thought the term a strange and misleading one. I follow her lead in this text by trying to use specific terminologies as much as possible and avoiding the pitfalls of ethnonyms such as "Pomo" that gloss over so many historical and cultural realities.

3. My reading of Du Bois suggests that she coined the term "Bole Maru" from two words—"Bole" from the Patwin language, and "Maru" from Pomoan languages—both of which mean "dreamer." It is not clear from her ethnographic data that any of her informants actually used this term. In Sarris's biography of Mabel McKay, McKay did not use the term but instead referred to that tradition as "the Dreamer religion." Florence used neither term, but I prefer the term McKay apparently used instead of one that likely had little or no actual use.

4. My sense of how to go about doing fieldwork in Pomo country has in large part been guided by the work of Greg Sarris (1993, 1994), with whom I have spoken in depth about this project, and many issues in the anthropological literature about Pomoan peoples over the past three years. Sarris's work diverges from other important interpretive advances because he is interested in a Native critique of anthropological texts (see Trafzer 1993 for a different strategy and Danker 1993 for a somewhat resonant one). For anthropologists, Sarris's work is situated within the arc of the "literary turn" in anthropology: the postmodern critique of ethnographic writing; the specification of positioning and of limited objectivities; and the dialogic, polyvocal nature of anthropological fieldwork. Simultaneously, Sarris's work is made historically possible by the phenomenon of postcoloniality in anthropology, which has meant, among other things, the increased presence of scholars hailing from areas of the world and ethnic and racial groups that historically have constituted the object of anthropological research. Postmodernism in the hands and minds of postcolonial scholars has changed anthropology, and Sarris's work is exemplary in this regard. He is Coast Miwok and Kashaya Pomo, and he has analyzed the anthropological literature about the Pomo peoples and Pomo country extensively. In *Keeping Slug Woman Alive*, Sarris's multifaceted exegesis of Elizabeth Colson's edited volume *Autobiographies of Three Pomo Women* (1974), he outlines several important criteria.

There is also a broad feminist literature that explicitly addresses the exploitative nature of participant observation in ethnographic fieldwork and the ways that ethnography leads to betrayal (see, e.g., Stacey 1988). Steven Rubinstein's recent article (Rubinstein 2004) provides an excellent review of that literature and his understandings of the roles played by desire, exchange, friendship, and sexuality in the fieldwork encounter.

5. Meighan and Riddell (1972: 117) state that the abalone pectorals used by those dancing the Abalone Dance at Kashaya "are said to signify righteousness."

6. Smith-Ferri emphasized that so-called uncooperative informants might well be resisting the conditions and terms around which interviewing was taking place.

7. Du Bois used the surname "Bijola" for Florence's mother, a fact that still irritates Florence considerably. Her actual surname was the Sicilian name "Bigioli."

8. The primacy of the visual in ethnographic research and anthropological literature is by now well known and was best described by Paul Stoller (1989). I had never confronted that primacy so clearly until I came to understood how much my assumptions about the use of abalone in regalia hinged on its presumption.

9. Barrett published "Pomo Myths" as curator of anthropology at the Milwaukee Public Museum, which also published the work. The volume is clearly based on many years of recording narratives with individuals from many different Pomo groups.

5. Cultural Revivification

1. One well-known artist in the Hoopa Valley has only danced once, he told us. That was at the Deerskin Dance. But the rest of the time he goes and is present at the rituals, even if he does not dance. He says that the Indian religion "gleans" spirit, while the Shaker way (his brand of Christianity) goes right to the source. A Hupa woman who is a well-known storyteller, by contrast, does not really seem to struggle much about being a Presbyterian and also participating in the Indian religion. She was proud to tell us about that all of her grandchildren go to church and also participate in the dances.

6. Extinction Narratives

1. Stephen Asma (2001) has written cogently about taxidermy, extinction, and the creation of the natural-history museum. In contrast, James Clifford (1997) has argued that the museum at Fort Ross actually provides a forum for Native agency and voice, both historically and currently. My own impression of that museum, after many visits and conversations with museum staff, is that it offers a number of layers of interpretation that have developed during the years of its existence. It really is a colonial reconstruction, which cannot help but focus on the Russian venture and its fortunes. In recent years, increased input from the Kashaya Pomo has added supplementary interpretive text and perspective. But the manifestations of those supplements are still to a certain extent at the periphery of the "main" story of the Russian colony.

2. There has been a spate of excellent recent scholarship about foraging peoples in biotically rich habitats (such as California) and useful theorizing concerning the processes that intensify social stratification, economic diversification, the development of complex polities under such conditions (see, e.g., Ames 1994; Holly 2005). Writing about such processes in pre-contact California, the archaeologists Mark Raab and Terry Jones offer insights that resonate with my own analysis of the more recent ethnographic past:

Research shows that California's ancient peoples played an appreciable role in shaping their host ecosystems. We cannot conclude, however, that these influences resulted in the timeless and wholly benign cultural-environmental regimes envisioned by ecofunctionalism," which is their shorthand for portraying California Indians as environmentally conscious resource managers in a biotically super-rich habitat.

Evidence . . . suggests a far more dynamic prehistoric world in which the efficiency of prehistoric foraging practices varied greatly across time with regard to both plant and animal food resources. Moreover, these data indicate that human adaptive responses probably were never able to achieve an ultimate-cultural-environmental equilibrium, owing to the influences of climactic stresses, demographic pressures, resource intensification, and other forces. (Raab and Jones 2004: 205)

3. The original excerpt from Harrington was partly in Californio Spanish, which I have translated. I have added a few extra pronouns and prepositions, as well, for better readability. The name of the mountain in the story was from an indigenous language and in the manuscript was written with some of Harrington's idiosyncratic and difficult-to-reproduce diacritical marks.

4. For comparative work on the ways animal–human relationships are understood, narrated, and acted on among other hunting and gathering peoples, see, among others, Bird-Davis 1993, 1999; Brightman 1993; Ingold 1995, 1996; Tanner 1979.

Conclusion

The first part of this conclusion, which discusses abalone narratives, marine resources, and cultural identity along the Yurok coast, was written in collaboration with the Yurok Tribe's Culture Committee.

1. Because the predominant river current continues into the ocean in a northerly direction, north along the coast toward Crescent City was called "downriver," while south along the coast was called "upriver." The Yurok did not have four cardinal directions. Instead, there were three directions: *pechik* (upriver); *pulik* (downriver); and *health kau* (away from the river).

2. As I already explored in chapters 3 and 5 with reference to "Ohlone" and "Pomo," respectively, ethnonyms are always and unavoidably controversial. In Indian Country, the controversies revolve around the intersections and tangents among, first, pre-contact terminologies, categories, and conceptualizations; second, anthropologists' categories and naming systems, themselves subject to change over time; and third, the tribal names established and made official by the U.S. government through the BIA. The Yurok Culture Committee points out that

> "Puliklah" or "poliklah," which translates as "down river people," was introduced in the 1950s, was brought back in the 1970s and again was brought back in the 1990s when the Yurok Tribe was being reorganized. It seems as though the terms are seldom used anymore due to the tribal government's selection of the word "Yurok" to name the tribe.

"Ner er ner" is historically the denomination for the coastal people from Orek south to Little River (or "Sre por" in Yurok).

3. This is one possible analysis of the Norris story. Both Pebble Beach and Shelter Cove were abalone-harvest areas in pre-contact times.

4. Frank Gist, one holder of regalia, stressed these duties and responsibilities to me in 2000.

5. Thanks to my colleague Beverly Singer for bringing this editorial to my attention.

References

ABNET (Abalone Network). 1999. E-mail exchanges. Http://web.uct.ac.za/depts/zoology/abnet/ (accessed December 5–8, 2000).

Alvard, Michael S. 1993. "Testing the 'Ecologically Noble Savage' Hypothesis: Interspecific Prey Choice by Piro Hunters of Amazonian Peru." *Human Ecology* 21(4): 355–87.

——. 1994. "Conservation by Native Peoples: Prey Choice in a Depleted Habitat." *Human Nature* 5(2): 127–54.

Ames, Kenneth M. 1994. "The Northwest Coast: Complex Hunter-Gatherers, Ecology, and Social Evolution." *Annual Review of Anthropology* 73: 209–29.

Anderson, Benedict. 1983. *Imagined Communities: Reflections of the Origin and Spread of Nationalism.* London: Verso.

Anderson, M. Kat. 1991. "Native Californians as Ancient and Contemporary Cultivators." Pp. 151–75 in *Before the Wilderness: Environmental Management by Native Californians,* ed. Thomas C. Blackburn and Kat Anderson. Menlo Park, Calif.: Ballena Press.

Anderson, M. Kat, Michael G. Barbour, and Valerie Whitworth. 1998. "A World of Balance and Plenty. Land, Plants, Animals, and Humans In Pre-European California." Pp. 12–47 in *Contested Eden: California before the Gold Rush,* ed. R. A. Gutiérrez and R. J. Orsi. Berkeley: University of California Press.

Asma, Stephen T. 2001. *Stuffed Animals and Pickled Heads: The Culture and Evolution of Natural History Museums.* Oxford: Oxford University Press.

Baker, Lee. 1998. *From Savage to Negro: Anthropology and the Construction of Race.* Berkeley: University of California Press.

Baker, Rob. 1992. "The Clam 'Gardens' of Tomales Bay." *News from Native California* 6(2): 28–29.

Barrett, Samuel A. 1933. "Pomo Myths." *Bulletin of the Public Museum of the City of Milwaukee* 15: 1–608.

——. 1996. *Pomo Indian Basketry*. With a new introduction by Sherrie Smith-Ferri. Berkeley, Calif.: Phoebe Hearst Museum of Anthropology.

Basso, Keith H. 1996. *Wisdom Sits in Places: Landscape and Language among the Western Apache*. Albuquerque: University of New Mexico Press.

Bates, Craig D. 1983. "The California Collection of J. G. Voznesenski." *American Indian Art Magazine* 8(3): 36–41.

——. N.d. "People from the Water." Unpublished ms. on file with the author.

Bean, Lowell J., and Thomas C. Blackburn, eds. 1976. *Native California: A Theoretical Retrospective*. Menlo Park, Calif.: Ballena Press.

Bell, Rosemary. 1992. *Yurok Tales*. Etna, Calif.: Bell Books.

Bennett, John. 1996. "Applied and Action Anthropology: Ideological and Conceptual Aspects." *Current Anthropology* 36: S23–S53.

Berman, Judith. 1996. " 'The Culture as It Appears to the Indian Himself': Boas, George Hunt, and the Methods of Ethnography." Pp. 215–56 in *Volksgeist as Method and Ethic: Essays on Boasian Ethnography and the German Anthropological Tradition*, ed. G. W. Stocking. Madison: University of Wisconsin Press.

Biolsi, Thomas. 2005. "Imagined Geographies: Sovereignty, Indigenous Space, and American Indian Struggle." *American Ethnologist* 32(2): 239–59.

Bird-Davis, Nurit. 1993. "Tribal Metaphorization of Human–Nature Relatedness: A Comparative Analysis." Pp. 112–26 in *Environmentalism: The View from Anthropology*, ed. K. Milton. London: Routledge.

——. 1999. " 'Animism' Revisited: Personhood, Environment, and Relational Epistemology." *Current Anthropology* 40 (supp.): 67–91.

Blackburn, Thomas C., and Kat Anderson. 1993. "Introduction: Managing the Domesticated Environment." Pp. 15–27 in *Before the Wilderness: Environmental Management by Native Californians*, ed. Thomas C. Blackburn and Kat Anderson. Menlo Park, Calif.: Ballena Press.

Blackburn, Thomas C., and Travis Hudson. 1990. *Time's Flotsam: Overseas Collections of California Indian Material Culture*. Menlo Park, Calif.: Ballena Press/Santa Barbara Museum of Natural History.

Brainerd, Molly. n.d. "Wiyot and Mattole." *Ethnographic Recordings at the Lowie Museum of Anthropology*. Volume 1: *Northwestern California*, Series No. 78. Berkeley: University of California.

Brightman, Robert. 1993. *Grateful Prey: Rock Cree Human–Animal Relationships*. Los Angeles: University of California Press.

Broughton, Jack M. 2002. "Pre-Columbian Human Impact on California Vertebrates: Evidence from Old Bones and Implications for Wilderness Policy." Pp. 44–71 in *Wilderness and Political Ecology: Aboriginal Influences and the Original State of Nature*, ed. Charles E. Kay and Randy T. Simmons. Salt Lake City: University of Utah Press.

Buckley, Thomas. 1996. " 'The Little History of Pitiful Events': The Epistemological and Moral Concerns of Kroeber's Californian Ethnology." Pp. 257–97 in *Volksgeist as Method and Ethic: Essays on Boasian Ethnography and the German Anthropological Tradition*, ed. G. W. Stocking. Madison: University of Wisconsin Press.

———. 2002. *Standing Ground: Yurok Indian Spirituality, 1850–1990*. Berkeley: University of California Press.

California Department of Fish and Game (CDFG). 2001. "Abalone Fishery." CDFG website. Www.dfg.ca.gov/marine/ab—workshop.asp (accessed December 15, 2001).

Cambra, Rosemary. 1989. "Control of Ancestral Remains." *News from Native California* 4(1): 15–17.

Campbell, Howard, Leigh Binford, Miguel Bartolomé, and Alicia Barabas. 1993. *Zapotec Struggles: Histories, Politics, and Representations from Juchitán, Oaxaca*. Washington, D.C.: Smithsonian Institution Press.

Castañeda, Quetzil. 1996. *In the Museum of Maya Culture: Touring Chichen Itza*. Minneapolis: University of Minnesota Press.

Castillo, Edward D. 1978. "The Impact of Euro-American Exploration and Settlement." Pp. 99–127 in *Handbook of North American Indians*, Volume 8: *California*, ed. Robert F. Heizer. Washington, D.C.: Smithsonian Institution Press.

———. 1989. "The Native Response to the Colonization of Alta California." Pp. 377–94 in *Columbian Consequences*, vol. 1, ed. David Hurst Thomas. Washington, D.C.: Smithsonian Institution Press.

Claasen, Cheryl P. 1991. "Gender, Shellfishing, and the Shell Mound Archaic." Pp. 276–300 in *Engendering Archaeology: Women and Prehistory*, ed. J. Gero and M. W. Conkey. Cambridge, Mass.: Basil Blackwell.

Clifford, James. 1986. *The Predicament of Culture: Twentieth Century Ethnography, Literature, and Art*. Cambridge, Mass.: Harvard University Press.

———. 1997. *Routes: Travel and Translation in the Late Twentieth Century*. Cambridge, Mass.: Harvard University Press.

———. 2004. "Looking Several Ways: Anthropology and Native Heritage in Alaska." *Current Anthropology* 45(1): 5–29.

Collier, Mary E. Trumbull, and Sylvia Barker Thalman, eds. 1996. *Interviews with Tom Smith and Maria Copa: Isabel Kelly's Ethnographic Notes on the Coast Miwok Indians of Marin and Southern Sonoma Counties, California*. MAPOM Occasional Papers, no. 6. San Rafael, Calif.: Miwok Archaeological Preserve of Marin.

Colson, Elizabeth, ed. 1974. *Autobiographies of Three Pomo Women*. Berkeley: Archaeological Research Facility, Department of Anthropology, University of California.

Comaroff, John, and Jean Comaroff. 1992. *Ethnography and the Historical Imagination*. Boulder, Colo.: Westview Press.

Cook, Samuel R. 2000. *Monacans and Miners: Native Americans and Coal Mining Communities in Appalachia*. Lincoln: University of Nebraska Press.

Cook, Sherburne F. 1976. *The Conflict between the California Indian and White Civilization*. Berkeley: University of California Press.

Cox, Keith W. 1962. "California Abalones, Family Haliotidae." *California Department of Fish and Game Fish Bulletin* 118: 1–133.

Crehan, Kate. 2002. *Gramsci, Culture and Anthropology*. Berkeley: University of California Press.

Cronon, William. 1983. *Changes in the Land: Indians, Colonists, and the Ecology of New England*. New York: Hill and Wang.

Danker, Kathleen A. 1993. "Because of This I Am Called the Foolish One: Felix White Sr.'s Interpretation of the Winnebago Trickster." Pp. 505–28 in *New Voices in Native American Literary Criticism*, ed. Arnold Krupat. Washington, D.C.: Smithsonian Institution Press.

Davis, Gary E., Daniel V. Richards, Peter Haaker, and Davis O. Parker. 1992. "Abalone Population Declines and Fishery Management in Southern California." Pp. 237–51 in *Abalone of the World*, ed. S. A. Shepherd, S. Gúzmán del Próo and M. J. Tegner. Oxford: Blackwell Scientific.

Davis, Mike. 1998. *Ecology of Fear: Los Angeles and the Imagination of Disaster*. New York: Vintage Books.

Deloria Jr., Vine. 1969. *Custer Died for Your Sins: An Indian Manifesto*. New York: Macmillan.

——. 1997. *Red Earth, White Lies: Native Americans and the Myth of Scientific Fact*. Golden, Colo.: Fulcrum Publishing.

Dendahl, John. 2005. "Indian Sovereignty Has Outlived Its Practicality." *Albuquerque Journal*. September 9.

Du Bois, Cora A. 1939. *The 1870 Ghost Dance*. Anthropological Records, vol. 3, no. 1. Berkeley: University of California Press.

Field, Les. 1999a. *The Grimace of Macho Ratón: Artisans, Identity and Nation in Late Twentieth Century Western Nicaragua*. Durham: Duke University Press.

——. 1999b. "Complicities and Collaborations: Anthropologists and the 'Unacknowledged Tribes' of California." *Current Anthropology* 40(2): 193–209.

——. 2002. "Blood and Traits: Preliminary Observations on the Analysis of Mestizo and Indigenous Identities in Latin vs. North America." *Journal of Latin American Anthropology* 7(1): 2–33.

——. 2003. "Dynamic Tensions in Indigenous Sovereignty and Representation: A Sampler." *American Ethnologist* 30(3): 447–53.

——. 2004. "From Applied Anthropology to Collaborative Applications of Anthropological Tools: Examples from Indian Country." Pp. 472–89 in *A Companion to the Anthropology of North American Indians*, ed. Thomas Biolsi. Malden, Mass.: Blackwell.

——. 2005. "Who Is This Really about Anyway? Ishi Kroeber and the Intertwining of California Indian and Anthropological Histories." *Journal of Anthropological Research* 61(1): 81–93.

——. 2008. "Global Indigenous Movements: Convergence and Differentiation in the Face of the Twenty-first Century State." In *Crossing Boundaries: Transnational Americanist Anthropology*, ed. K. Fine-Dare. Lincoln: University of Nebraska Press, in press.

——. Forthcoming. "Double Trouble: Implications of Historicizing Identity Discourses." In *Anthropology and the Politics of Representation*, ed. G. Vargas Cetina and S. Lathrap. Berkeley: University of California Press, volume under review.

Field, Les, and Richard G. Fox. 2007. *Anthropology Put to Work*. Oxford: Berg Publishers.

Field, Les, and Alan Leventhal. 2003. "'What Must It Have Been Like!' Critical Considerations of Precontact Ohlone Cosmology as Interpreted through Central California Ethnohistory." *Wicazo Sa Review* 18(2): 95–126.

Field, Les, Alan Leventhal, Dolores Sanchez, and Rosemary Cambra. 1992. "A Contemporary Ohlone Tribal Revitalization Movement: A Perspective from the Muwekma Costanoan/Ohlone Indians of the San Francisco Bay Area." *California History* 71(3): 412–31.

Field, Les, and Muwekma Ohlone Tribe. 2003. "Unacknowledged Tribes, Dangerous Knowledge: The Muwekma Ohlone and How Indian Identities Are 'Known.'" *Wicazo Sa Review* 18(2): 79–94.

Fitzhugh, William, and Chisato O. Dubreuil, eds. 1999. *Ainu: Spirit of a Northern People*. Seattle: University of Washington Press.

Flores, Dan. 1991. "Bison Ecology and Bison Diplomacy: The Southern Plains from 1800 to 1850." *Journal of American History* 78: 465–85.

Foley, Douglas. 1999. "The Fox Project: A Reappraisal." *Current Anthropology* 40: 193–209.

Forbes, Jack D. 1982. *Native Americans of California and Nevada*. Happy Camp, Calif.: Naturegraph.

Garroutte, Eva Marie. 2003. *Real Indians: Identity and Survival of Native America*. Berkeley: University of California Press.

Gifford, Edward W. 1926. "Miwok Cults." *University of California Publications in American Archaeology and Ethnology* 18: 392–408.

——. 1947. *California Shell Artifacts*. Anthropological Records, no. 9. Berkeley: University of California Press.

Glassow, Michael A. 1996. *Purisimeño Chumash Prehistory: Maritime Adap-*

tations along the Southern California Coast. New York: Harcourt Brace College.

Glassow, Michael A., Douglas J. Kennett, James P. Kennett, and Larry R. Wilcoxon. 1994. "Confirmation of Middle Holocene Ocean Cooling Inferred from Stable Isotopic Analysis of Prehistoric Shells from Santa Cruz Island, California." Pp. 223–32 in *The Fourth California Islands Symposium: Update on the Status of Resources,* ed. W. L. Halvorson and G. J. Maender. Santa Barbara, Calif.: Santa Barbara Museum of Natural History.

Goddard, Pliny Earle. 1903. *Life and Culture of the Hupa.* Berkeley: University of California Publications in American Archaeology and Anthropology, Vol. 1(1).

Greengo, Robert E. 1952. "Shellfish Foods of the California Indians." *Kroeber Anthropological Society Papers* 7: 63–114.

Haaker, Peter L. 1993. "Assessment of Abalone Resources at the Channel Islands." Pp. 84–95 in *The Fourth California Islands Symposium: Update on the Status of Resources,* ed. W. L. Halvorson and G. J. Maender. Santa Barbara, Calif.: Santa Barbara Museum of Natural History.

Haaker, Peter L., Kristine C. Henderson, and David O. Parker. 1986. *California Abalone.* California Department of Fish and Game, Marine Resources Leaflet 11, Sacramento.

Haas, Mary, collector. 1982. "Mattole (Catherine Rodriquez-Nieto)." Sound Recordings of Native American Languages. Berkeley: University of California, Berkeley Language Laboratory.

Hale, Charles R. 1994. *Resistance and Contradiction: Miskitu Indians and the Nicaraguan State, 1894–1987.* Palo Alto, Calif.: Stanford University Press.

———. 2006. *Más Que un Indio / More Than an Indian: Racial Ambivalence and Neoliberal Multiculturalism in Guatemala.* Santa Fe, N.M.: School of American Research Press.

Hanson Jr., Charles. 1973. "The Abalone Shell as a Trade Item." *Museum of the Fur Trade Quarterly* 9(3): 8–10.

Haraway, Donna. 1988. "Situated Knowledges: The Science Question on Feminism and the Privilege of Partial Perspective." *Feminist Studies* 14(3): 575–99.

———. 1989. "Teddy Bear Patriarchy: Taxidermy in the Garden of Eden, New York City, 1908–36." Pp. 26–58 in *Primate Visions: Gender, Race and Nature in the World of Modern Science,* ed. Donna Haraway. New York: Routledge.

Harrington, John Peabody. 1931. Notes on microfilm. Reel 88: 439. Library Collection, San Jose State University, San Jose, California.

Heizer, Robert F. 1965. "Indians and Abalone Shell." *California Monthly* 75(9): 12–15.

Heizer, Robert F., and Albert B. Elsasser. 1980. *The Natural World of the California Indians.* Berkeley: University of California Press.

Heizer, Robert F., and John E. Mills. 1952. *The Four Ages of Tsurai: A Documentary History of the Indian Village on Trinidad Bay*. Berkeley: University of California Press.

Hendrickson, Carol. 1995. *Weaving Identities: Construction of Dress and Self in a Highland Guatemala Town*. Austin: University of Texas Press.

Hildebrandt, William R., and Terry L. Jones. "Depletion of Prehistoric Pinniped Populations along the California and Oregon Coasts: Were Humans the Cause?" Pp. 72–110 in *Wilderness and Political Ecology: Aboriginal Influences and the Original State of Nature*, ed. Charles E. Kay and Randy T. Simmons. Salt Lake City: University of Utah Press.

Hinton, Alexander. 2005. *Why Did They Kill? Cambodia in the Shadow of Genocide*. Berkeley: University of California Press.

Holly Jr., Donald H. 2005. "The Place of 'Others' in Hunter-Gatherer Intensification." *American Anthropologist* 107(2): 207–21.

Hudson, John W. 1897. "Pomo Wampum Makers: An Aboriginal Double Standard." *Overland Monthly* 30(176): 102–8.

Hunn, Eugene. 1993. "What Is Traditional Ecological Knowledge?" Pp. 13–15 in *Traditional Ecological Knowledge: Wisdom for Sustainable Development*, ed. N. Williams and G. Baines. Canberra: Centre for Resource and Environmental Studies, Australian National University.

Hurtado, Albert. 1988. *Indian Survival on the California Frontier*. New Haven, Conn.: Yale University Press.

Ingold, Tim. 1995. "Building, Dwelling, Living: How Animals and People Make Themselves at Home in the World." Pp. 57–80 in *Shifting Contexts: Transformations in Anthropological Knowledge*, ed. Marilyn Strathern. London: Routledge.

——. 1996. "Hunting and Gathering as Ways of Perceiving the Environment." Pp. 117–36 in *Redefining Nature: Ecology, Culture, and Domestication*, ed. R. Ellen and K. Fukui. Oxford: Berg.

Isenberg, Andrew C. 2000. *The Destruction of the Bison: An Environmental History, 1750–1920*. Cambridge: Cambridge University Press.

Jackson, Robert H., and Edward Castillo. 1995. *Indians, Franciscans, and Spanish Colonization: The Impact of the Mission System on California Indians*. Albuquerque: University of New Mexico Press.

Jenkins, Richard, and Dorothy J. Theodoratus. 1989. "Update on Point Arena Roundhouse." *News from Native California* 3(1): 13.

Johnson, Ron, and Colleen Kelley Marks. 1997. *Her Mind Made Up: Weaving Caps the Indian Way*. Arcata, Calif.: Reese Bullen Gallery, Humboldt State University.

Jones, Terry L., and William R. Hildebrandt. 1995. "Reasserting a Prehistoric

Tragedy of the Commons: Reply to Lyman." *Journal of Anthropological Archaeology* 14: 78–98.

Kowinski, William S. 2004. "In 1860 Six Murderers Nearly Wiped Out the Wiyot Indian Tribe." *San Francisco Chronicle*, February 28, section D.

Krech, Shepard, III. 1999. *The Ecological Indian: Myth and History.* New York: W. W. Norton.

Kroeber, Alfred L. 1976 (1925). *Handbook of the Indians of California*, reprint. ed. New York: Dover Publications.

——. 1976. *Yurok Myths.* Berkeley: University of California Press.

Kroeber, Alfred L., and Robert Spott. 1997 (1942). *Yurok Narratives*, reprint. ed. Trinidad, Calif.: Trinidad Museum Society.

Kroeber, Theodora. 1964. *The Inland Whale.* Berkeley: University of California Press.

Krupat, Arnold. 1985. *For Those Who Come After.* Berkeley: University of California Press.

LaDuke, Winona. 1999. *All Our Relations: Native Struggles for Land and Life.* Cambridge, Mass.: South End Press.

Lang, Julian, ed. and trans. 1994. *Ararapíkva: Creation Stories of the People: Traditional Karuk Indian Literature from Northwestern California.* Berkeley: Heyday Books.

——. 1993–94. "The Embodiment of Wealth" and "The Dances and Regalia." *News from Native California* 7(4): 25–27, 34–41.

——. 1992. "Peethivthaaneen—The Earth." *News from Native California* 6(2): 17.

Lassiter, Luke Eric. 2005. *The Chicago Guide to Collaborative Ethnography.* Chicago: University of Chicago Press.

——. 1998. *The Power of Kiowa Song: A Collaborative Ethnography.* Tucson: University of Arizona Press.

Lassiter, Luke Eric, Clyde Ellis, and Ralph Kotay. 2002. *The Jesus Road: Kiowas, Christianity, and Indian Hymns.* Lincoln: University of Nebraska Press.

Leventhal, Alan, Les Field, Hank Alvarez, and Rosemary Cambra. 1994. "The Ohlone: Back from Extinction." Pp. 297–336 in *The Ohlone Past and Present: Native Americans of the San Francisco Bay Region*, ed. Lowell J. Bean. Menlo Park, Calif.: Ballena Press.

Levy, Richard. 1978. "Costanoan." Pp. 485–95 in *Handbook of North American Indians*, Volume 8: *California*, ed. Robert F. Heizer. Washington, D.C.: Smithsonian Institution Press.

Lewis, Henry T. 1973. "Patterns of Indian Burning in California: Ecology and Ethnohistory." Pp. 55–117 in *Before the Wilderness: Environmental Management by Native Californians*, ed. Thomas C. Blackburn and Kat Anderson. Menlo Park, Calif.: Ballena Press.

Li, Fang-kuei. 1930. *Mattole: An Athabaskan Language.* University of Chicago Publications in Anthropology. Chicago: University of Chicago Press.

Lightfoot, Kent G. 2005. *Indians, Missionaries, and Merchants: The Legacy of Colonial Encounters on the California Frontiers.* Berkeley: University of California Press.

Loeb, Edwin M. 1926. "Pomo Folkways" *University of California Publications in American Archaeology and Ethnology* 19(2): 149–409.

Lundy, A. L. 1997. *The California Abalone Industry: A Pictorial History.* Flagstaff, Ariz.: Best Publishing.

Lurie, Nancy O. 1973. "Action Anthropology and the American Indian." Pp. 4–22 in *Anthropology and the American Indian: A Symposium.* San Francisco: Indian Historical Press.

Lyman, R. Lee. 1995. "On the Evolution of Marine Mammal Hunting on the West Coast of North America." *Journal of Anthropological Archaeology* 14: 45–77.

Mannheim, Bruce, and Dennis Tedlock. 1995. *The Dialogic Emergence of Culture.* Urbana: University of Illinois Press.

Marcus, George E., and Michael M. J. Fischer. 1986. *Anthropology as Cultural Critique: An Experimental Moment in the Human Sciences.* Chicago: University of Chicago Press.

Margolin, Malcolm. 1978. *The Ohlone Way: Indian Life in the San Francisco–Monterey Bay Area.* Berkeley, Calif.: Heyday Books.

——. 1993–94. "Wealth and Spirit." *News from Native California* 7(4): 28–33.

Martin, Paul S., and Herbert E. Wright, eds. 1967. *Pleistocene Extinctions: The Search for a Cause.* New Haven, Conn.: Yale University Press.

McCarthy, Helen. 1991. "Managing Oaks and the Acorn Crop." Pp. 213–29 in *Before the Wilderness: Environmental Management by Native Californians,* ed. Thomas C. Blackburn and Kat Anderson. Menlo Park, Calif.: Ballena Press.

McEvoy, Arthur F. 1986. *The Fisherman's Problem: Ecology and Law in the California Fisheries, 1850–1980.* Cambridge: Cambridge University Press.

McLendon, Sally. 1998. "Pomo Basket Weavers in the University of Pennsylvania Museum Collection." *Expedition* 40(1): 34–45.

Meighan, C. W., and F. A. Riddell. 1972. *The Maru Cult of the Pomo Indians: A California Ghost Dance Survival.* Southwest Museum Paper, no. 23. Los Angeles: Southwest Museum.

Merrill, William L., Edmund J. Ladd, and T. J. Ferguson. 1993. "The Return of the Ahayuida: Lessons for Repatriation from Zuni Pueblo and the Smithsonian Institution." *Current Anthropology* 34: 523–67.

Milliken, Randall. 1995. *A Time of Little Choice: The Disintegration of Tribal*

Culture in the San Francisco Bay Area 1769–1810. Menlo Park, Calif.: Ballena Press.

Moss, Madonna L. 1993. "Shellfish, Gender, and Status on the Northwest Coast: Reconciling Archaeological, Ethnographic, and Ethnohistorical Records of the Tlingit." *American Anthropologist* 95(3): 631–52.

Nairn, Tom. 2003 (1977). *The Break-Up of Britain: Crisis and Neo-Nationalism*. Altona, Victoria: Common Ground Publishing.

Nelson, Byron, Jr. 1988. *Our Home Forever: The Hupa Indians of Northern California*. Salt Lake City: Howe Brothers.

Neumann, Thomas W. 2002. "The Role of Prehistoric Peoples in Shaping Ecosystems in the Eastern United States: Implications for Restoration Ecology and Wilderness Management." Pp. 141–78 in *Wilderness and Political Ecology: Aboriginal Influences and the Original State of Nature*, ed. Charles E. Kay and Randy T. Simmons. Salt Lake City: University of Utah Press.

New York Times. 2000. "Suspects in 'Blitzkrieg' Extinctions: Primitive Hunters." March 26.

——. 1999. "Historians Revisit Slaughter on the Plains." November 16.

Nomland, Gladys. 1938. *Bear River Ethnography*. Berkeley: University of California Press.

Nordstrom, Carolyn. 1997. *A Different Kind of War Story*. Philadelphia: University of Pennsylvania Press.

Norton, Jack. 1979/1997 reprint. *When Our Worlds Cried: Genocide in Northern California*. San Francisco: Indian Historian Press.

O'Neale, Lila M. 1932. *Yurok-Karok Basket Weavers*. Berkeley: University of California Press.

Ortner, Sherry. 1979. "On Key Symbols." Pp. 92–98 in *Reader in Comparative Religion: An Anthropological Analysis*, 4th ed., ed. W. A. Lessa and E. Z. Vogt. New York: HarperCollins.

Oswalt, Robert L. 1964. *Kashaya Texts*. Berkeley: University of California Press.

Patterson, Victoria. 1998. "Change and Continuity: Transformations of Pomo Life." *Expedition* 40(1): 3–14.

Peri, David W., and Scott M. Patterson. 1993. "'The Basket Is in the Roots, That's Where It Begins.'" Pp. 175–95 in *Before the Wilderness: Environmental Management by Native Californians*, ed. Thomas C. Blackburn and Kat Anderson. Menlo Park, Calif.: Ballena Press.

Phillips, George Harwood. 1997. *Indians and Indian Agents: The Origins of the Reservation System in California, 1849–1852*. Norman: University of Oklahoma Press.

Preston, William L. 2002. "Post-Columbian Wildlife Irruptions on California: Implications for Cultural and Environmental Understanding." Pp. 111–40 in

Wilderness and Political Ecology: Aboriginal Influences and the Original State of Nature, ed. Charles E. Kay and Randy T. Simmons. Salt Lake City: University of Utah Press.

Quilter, Jeffrey, and John W. Hoopes, eds. 2003. *Gold and Power in Ancient Costa Rica, Panama, and Colombia: A Symposium at Dumbarton Oaks, 9 and 10 October 1999*. Washington, D.C.: Dumbarton Oaks Research Library and Collections.

Raab, L. Mark. 1992. "An Optimal Foraging Analysis of Prehistoric Shellfish Collecting on San Clemente Island, California." *Journal of Ethnobiology* 12(1): 63–80.

Raab, L. Mark, and Terry L. Jones. 2004. "The Future of California Prehistory." Pp. 204–12 in *Prehistoric California: Archaeology and the Myth of Paradise*, ed. L. Mark Raab and Terry L. Jones. Salt Lake City: University of Utah Press.

Raab, L. Mark, and Andrew Yatsko. 1992. "Ancient Maritime Adaptations of the California Bight: A Perspective from San Clemente Island, California." Pp. 173–93. in *Essays on the Prehistory of Maritime California*, ed. Terry L. Jones, Davis, Calif.: Center for Archaeological Research, University of California.

Rappaport, Joanne. 2005. *Intercultural Utopias: Public Intellectuals and Cultural Innovation in the Colombian Indigenous Movement*. Durham: Duke University Press.

Rawls, James J. 1984. *Indians of California: The Changing Image*. Norman: University of Oklahoma Press.

Reichard, Gladys. 1925. "Wiyot Grammar and Texts." *University of California Publications in American Archaeology and Ethnology* 22(1): 1–215.

Reid, Martine. 2004. "The Body Transformed: Body Art and Adornment among the Prehistoric and Historic Northwest Coast People." Pp. 54–69 in *Totems to Turquoise: Native American Jewelry Arts of the Northwest and Southwest*, ed. Kari Chalker. New York: Harry N. Abrams/American Museum of Natural History.

Ridington, Robin, and Dennis Hastings. 1997. *Blessing for a Long Time: The Sacred Pole of the Omaha Tribe*. Lincoln: University of Nebraska Press.

Rubinstein, Steven L. 2004. "Fieldwork and the Erotic Economy on the Colonial Frontier." *Signs* 29(4): 1041–71.

Salvador, Mari Lyn, ed. 1997. *The Art of Being Kuna: Layers of Meaning among the Kuna of Panama*. Los Angeles: Fowler Museum of Cultural History, University of California, Los Angeles.

San Francisco Examiner. 2000. "Abalone Nearly Gone from State's Coast." July 2.

San Jose Mercury News. 1999a. "Abalone Most Rare." October 26.

——. 1999b. "Abalone Poaching Alleged." September 11.

Sandoz, Mari. 1992. *Cheyenne Autumn*. Lincoln: University of Nebraska Press.

Sarris, Greg. 1993. *Keeping Slug Woman Alive: A Holistic Approach to American Indian Texts*. Berkeley: University of California Press.

——. 1994. *Mabel McKay: Weaving the Dream*. Berkeley: University of California Press.

Shanks, Ralph. 2006. *Indian Baskets of Central California, Art, Culture and History: Native American Basketry from San Francisco Bay and Monterey Bay North to Mendocino and East to the Sierras*. Novato, Calif.: Miwok Archaeological Preserve of Marin.

Shipek, Florence C. 1989. "An Example of Intensive Plant Husbandry: The Kumeyaay of Southern California." Pp. 159–70 in *Foraging and Farming: The Evolution of Plant Exploitation*, ed. D. Harris and G. Hillman. London: Unwin Hyman.

Sider, Gerald. 2003. *Living Indian Histories: Lumbee and Tuscarora People in North Carolina*. Chapel Hill: University of North Carolina Press.

Simenstad, Charles A., James A. Estes, and Karl W. Kenyon. 1978. "Aleuts, Sea Otters, and Alternate Stable-State Communities." *Science* 200(28): 403–11.

Slagle, Allogan. 1989. "Unfinished Justice: Completing the Restoration and Acknowledgment of California Indian Tribes." *American Indian Quarterly* (13)4: 325–45.

Sloan, N. L. 2003. "Evidence of California-Area Abalone Shell in Haida Trade and Culture." *Canadian Journal of Archaeology* 27: 273–86.

Smith, Eric Alden, and Mark Wishnie. 2000. "Conservation and Subsistence in Small-Scale Societies." *Annual Review of Anthropology* 29: 493–524.

Smith, Kathleen. 1990. "Abalone: A Precious Gift." *News from Native California* 4(3): 14–15

Stacey, Judith. 1988. "Can There Be a Feminist Ethnography?" *Women's Studies International Forum* 11(1): 21–27.

Stoller, Paul. 1989. *The Taste of Ethnographic Things: The Senses in Anthropology*. Philadelphia: University of Pennsylvania Press.

Sturm, Circe. 2002. *Blood Politics: Race, Culture, and Identity in the Cherokee Nation of Oklahoma*. Berkeley: University of California Press.

Sweezy, Sean. 1975. "The Energetics of Subsistence-Assurance Ritual in Native California." *Contributions of the University of California Archaeological Research Facility* 23: 1–46.

Sweezy, Sean L., and Robert F. Heizer. 1993. "Ritual Management of Salmonid Fish Resources in California." Pp. 299–329 in *Before the Wilderness: Environmental Management by Native Californians*, ed. Thomas C. Blackburn and Kat Anderson. Menlo Park, Calif.: Ballena Press.

Tanner, Adrian. 1979. *Bringing Home Animals: Religious Ideology and Mode of Production of the Mistassini Cree*. London: E. Hurst.

Tapsell, Paul. 2000. *Pukaki: A Comet Returns*. Auckland: Reed Books.

Tartaglia, Louis James. 1976. "Prehistoric Maritime Adaptations in Southern California." Ph.D. diss., Department of Anthropology, University of California, Los Angeles.

Tedlock, Dennis. 1983. *The Spoken Word and the Work of Interpretation*. Philadelphia: University of Pennsylvania Press.

Tedlock, Dennis, and Bruce Mannheim, eds. 1995. *The Dialogic Emergence of Culture*. Urbana: University of Illinois Press.

Teeter, Karl. 1964. *The Wiyot Language*. University of California Publications in Linguistics, vol. 37. Berkeley: University of California Press.

Teeter, Karl, and John D. Nichols. 1993. *Wiyot Handbook II: Interlinear Translation and English Index*. Winnipeg: Algonquian and Iroquoian Linguistics.

Theodoratus, Dorothea J. 1971. "Identity Crises: Changes in Life Style of the Manchester Band of Pomo Indians." Ph.D. diss., Department of Anthropology, Syracuse University, Syracuse, New York.

——. 1987. "Preserving the Point Arena Roundhouse." *News from Native California* 1(4):4–5.

Thornton, Russell. 2000. Review of *Indians and Anthropologists: Vine Deloria, Jr., and the Critique of Anthropology* [ed. Thomas Biolsi and Larry J. Zimmerman]. *American Ethnologist* 27(3): 762–63.

Trafzer, Clifford E. 1993. "Grandmother, Grandfather, and the First History of the Americas." Pp. 474–87 in *New Voices in Native American Literary Criticism*, ed. Arnold Krupat. Washington, D.C.: Smithsonian Institution Press.

Turner, Victor. 1982. *Celebration: Studies in Festivity and Ritual*. Washington, D.C.: Smithsonian Institution Press.

Vogel, Meghan. 2004. "Portion of Indian Island Returned to Wiyot Tribe." *Times-Standard* [Eureka, Calif.]. May 20.

von Langsdorff, Georg Heinrich. 1993. *Remarks and Observations on a Voyage around the World from 1803 to 1807*, vol. 1. Kingston, Ont.: Limestone Press.

Watkins, Joe. 2000. *Indigenous Archaeology: American Indian Values and Scientific Practice*. Walnut Creek, Calif.: Altamira Press.

White, Richard. 1997. "Indian Peoples and the Natural World: Asking the Right Questions." Pp. 87–100 in *Rethinking American Indian History*, ed. R. Fixico. Albuquerque: University of New Mexico Press.

Wilson, Birbeck. 1968. *Ukiah Valley Pomo Religious Life, Supernatural Doctoring, and Beliefs: Observations of 1939–1941*. Berkeley: University of California Archaeological Survey.

Wolf, Eric R. 1982. *Europe and the People without History*. Berkeley: University of California Press.

——. 1999. *Envisioning Power: Ideologies of Dominance and Crisis*. Berkeley: University of California Press.

——. 2001. *Pathways of Power: Building an Anthropology of the Modern World*. Berkeley: University of California Press.

Index

Page numbers in italics refer to illustrations.

Abalone, 1–3, 59, 167–68; as animal, 15, 74–77, 117, 139, 147–55; as food, 3, 21–22, 74–75, 93–94, 147–55, 166; in narratives, 13, 14, 15, 52, 53–55, 98–102, *104*, *105*, *106*, 111, 112–15, 152–54, 164–66, 167; in necklaces and other ornaments, 17, 19, 22, 26, 37, 39–42, 43–44, 87, 122; in regalia, 14, 39–42, 43–44, 75–76, 87, 92, 111, 117, 122–29, 133, 135, 167, 178n4; as shell, 97–98, 117, 118–21, 151–52, 160, 164
Adelhauser Museum für Natur und Völkerkunde (Freiburg, Germany), 30, 31, *47*
Ainu (Japan), 38
Alvard, Michael, 146
Alvarez, Hank, 22, 44
American Indian Historical Society (AIHS), 29
American Indians: anthropologists and, 10–11, 16, 94, 135; identity of, 9–10; scholars/intellectuals, 159; sovereignty of, 8–9, 83, 168–71
Anderson, Benedict, 10

Anderson, M. Kat, 142, 143
Animals: extinction of, 139, 140, 143–45; as stories, 78; as symbols, 1, 11, 161, 167–68

Baker, Rob, 151
Barrett, Samuel, 78, 80, 174n1, 176n9
Basso, Keith, 38
Bates, Craig, 29–32, 174n7
Bean, Lowell and Thomas Blackburn, 140–42
Beechey, F. W., and A. F. Belcher, 33
Belcher, A. F., and F. W. Beechey, 33
Bibby, Brian, 30
Bigioli, Annie, 14, 64, 69, 71–72, 73, 76, 82, 176n7
Biolsi, Thomas, 9
Blackburn, Thomas, and Travis Hudson, 30
Boas, Franz, 60; George Hunt and, 8, 70, 146
Boston, John, 14, 39–40, 41, 49, 62, 64, 65–67, 69–72, 74–76, 81, 82, 154, 168
Buckley, Thomas, 64, 67, 165
Bureau of Indian Affairs/Branch of Acknowledgement Research (BAR/BIA), 27, 28, 174n6

California: American history of, 88–91, 140; Spanish history of, 4, 20, 25, 34; Russian history of, 25

Cambra, Rosemary, 18, 21, 24, 43, 44

Christianity: Bole Maru and, 68, 69, 71, 76–77; at Hoopa Valley reservation, 110, 119, 121, 130, 176n1 (chap. 5)

Chumash, 137, 150, 156

Clamshell beads, 30–31

Clarke Museum (Eureka, Calif.), 125, 127, 128

Clifford, James, 5–6, 7, 10–11, 170, 176n1 (chap. 6)

Coast Miwok, 30, 150, 151

Collaborative ethnography, 5–8, 15–16

Colombia, fieldwork and ethnography in, 6, 60

Co-theorizing, 12, 15

Cronon, William, 138

Davis, Mike, 140

Deppe, Ferdinand, 32

Dreamer Religion (Bole Maru), 3, 14, 39–41, 63, 64, 66–68, 69–73, 76, 82–82, 175n3

DuBois, Cora, 62, 67–71, 174n1, 175n3, 176n7

Ecosystem engineering, 145–46

Ecuador, fieldwork and ethnography in, 6

Esselen, 21, 150, 151

Ethnoaesthetics, 37–38

Fletcher, Alice, and Francis LaFlesche, 8

Flower dance, 95, 107, 109, 111, 112, 115–21, 133

Foraging: conservation and, 142–43, 145–47; theories about, 140–47, 177n2.4

Fox, Richard G., 6

"Fox project," 8

Gabrielino, 150

Galvan, Arnold, 23

George, Merv, Sr., 15, 39, 50, 111, 115–18, 130–34, 135, 157

Gifford, Edward W., 33, 36, 41

Goddard, Pliny, 116, 135

Gold, pre-Columbian, 59–60

Grace Hudson Museum (Ukiah, Calif.), 40

Grandpa Tom Smith, 150, 151, 152

Greengo, Robert, 149–50

Gwich'in, 144

Haaker, Pete, 149

Haida, 60, 152

Hailstone, Vivien, 15, 108, 111, 114–15, 153

Hale, Charles R., 6, 11

Harrington, John P., 29, 41, 95, 96, 137, 150, 177n3

Hoopa Valley Reservation, 15, 107, 109–11, 116, 122, 133, 134–36

Howe, Craig, 39

Hupa, 3, 5, 50, 84, 90, 92, 99, 100, 107–8, 109–36, 152, 163

Kakchikel (Guatemala), 38

Karuk, 3, 5, 14, 50, 51, 83, 84–87, 92–94, 99–102, 111, 112, 121, 127, 131, 132, 152, 163

Krech, Shepard, 144–45

Kroeber, Alfred, 20, 34, 64, 78, 163, 165; Robert Spott and, 164–65

Kroeber, Theodora, 164, 173n1

Kuna (Panama), 38

Lang, Julian, 14, 61, 84–103, 107, 109, 163, 168, 171

Lara, Callie, 15, 108, 112–14, 116, 118–21, 129, 153, 165

Lara, Walt, Sr., 129, 157

Lassiter, Luke Eric, 6, 7

Leventhal, Alan, 18, 23, 28, 173n3

Lewis, Vernon, 162
Loeb, Edwin, 81, 174n1
Lundy, A. L., 155–56

Makah, 1
Malinowski, Bronislaw, 70
Mannheim, Bruce, and Dennis
Tedlock, 12
Maori, 42
Marshall, Bradley, 15, 39, 76, 108, 111,
116, 121–29, 171
Marshall, Darlene, 15, 108, 111, 114–
15
Mattole, 94–97, 98, 99
McEvoy, Arthur, 146–47, 151
Meighan, C. W., and F. A. Riddell, 70,
72–73, 175n5
Miller, Joe, 40, 49, 174n7
Mt. Shasta (California), 134
Museum für Völkerkunde (Munich,
Germany), 30, 46
Museum of Anthropology and Eth-
nology (St. Petersburg, Russia), 30,
31, 33, 46
Museum of Archaeology and Anthro-
pology (Cambridge, England), 32,
48
Muwekma. See Ohlones

Nelson, Byron, 110
Nicaragua, 171; fieldwork and ethnography in, 6–7

Ohlones, 4, 5, 109, 150, 156, 168, 171,
178n2; Abalone Feast, 2–22, 157;
Alisal Rancheria, 28–29; Cho-
chenyo language, 44; "Costanoans,"
34–35; Cultural Patrimony, 19, 24;
Muwekma Tribe, 7, 12–13, 17, 19–
44; OFCS, 22–23; Verona Band, 29
Olivella shell beads, 31
Omaha Sacred Pole, 42
Ortner, Sherry, 38

Oswalt, Robert, 153
Owen, Buzz, 155–56

Patrick's Point (California), 117, 153,
157, 162, 166
Phoebe Hearst Museum of Anthropology (Berkeley, Calif.), 33, 48
Pomo, 5, 30, 36, 78–81, 150, 153, 156,
174–75n2; Boh-Cah-Ama, 77;
Kashaya, 3, 41, 93, 153, 175n5,
176n1 (chap. 6), 178n2; Point
Arena, 3, 14, 63, 64, 77, 78, 79, 109,
153, 154
Preston, William, 138

Rappaport, Joanne, 6, 11, 12
Repatriation and NAGPRA, 42
Riddell, F. A., and C. W. Meighan, 70,
72–73, 175n5
Ridington, Robin, and Dennis Has-
tings, 42
Rodriguez, Suzie, 23
Rosales, Rudy, 21, 156
Round Valley (Covelo), 80

Sand Creek Massacre, 107
San Jose, Calif., 22, 23; Mission, 26,
173n4
Santa Barbara Museum of Man (Cali-
fornia), 137
Sarris, Greg, 68–69, 78, 80, 150,
175n3, 175n4
Sartre, Jean Paul, 38
Saunders, Nicholas J., 59–60
Seidner, Cheryl, 13, 18, 51–52, 54–58,
85
Shaughnessy, Frank, 154
Shelter Cove (California), 153, 165,
167
Shoemaker, Drew, 81
Sierra Miwok, 33, 41
Silva, Florence, 14, 40, 61, 62–83, 102,
109, 153, 156, 159, 171, 175n3

Sloan, Norm, 152
Socktish, Rudolph, 116, 131, 135
Spott, Robert, and Alfred Kroeber, 164–65

Tartaglia, Louis, 148
Tciplitcu, 41–42
Teeter, Karl, 52
Theodoratus, Dorothea, 71, 174n1
Tohono O'odham, 127
Tolowa, 3, 50, 87, 90, 92, 99, 121, 152, 163, 165
Turner, Victor, 38

von Langsdorff, Georg Heinrich, 24, 25–27, 30–32, 40, 43, 44, 45
von Wrangell, Admiral Baron F. P., 32

Wampanoags, 36–37
Weighill, Tharon, 137, 156–57

Weitchpec/Weitspus, 93, 131, 132, 167
Wilkinson, Leona, 13, 51–52, 85
Williams, Chuck, 166
Williams, Tom, 166
Wiyot, 3, 5, 13, 50, 51, 85, 90, 96, 99, 109, 152, 156, 163, 168, 171; Indian Island/Tuluwat, 51, 56, 58, 90; Table Bluff rancheria, 51
Wolf, Eric, 138
World Renewal Religion, 3, 50, 58, 85–87, 90, 92, 93, 110, 121, 130–34, 163

Yuki, 150
Yurok, 3, 5, 16, 50, 84, 90, 92, 99, 100, 111, 121, 127, 131, 132, 152, 153, 156, 161–67, 177n1, 178n2

Zuni, 42

Les W. Field

is a professor of anthropology

at the University of New Mexico,

Albuquerque.

Made in the USA
Las Vegas, NV
16 August 2023

76159831R00122